W9-DBN-057

PE
1068
·J3
G84
1986

A GUIDE TO TEACHING ENGLISH IN JAPAN

Compiled and Edited by

CHARLES B. WORDELL

The **Japan Times**, Ltd.

GOSHEN COLLEGE LIBRARY
GOSHEN, INDIANA

To my parents
Charles F. Wordell, Jr.
Mary E. Wordell

"Teaching Oral English in Large Classes" and "Contest Conversation: A Shortcut to English Fluency in Japan" by Richard E. Freeman reprinted with permission from the *Chuo University Journal of English Language and Literature*.

"English Education in Japanese University and Its Social Context" by Hal E. Hansen appeared in a shorter version in the journal *Jinbun Ronshu* of the Kobe University of Commerce.

Exercise by Judy Winn-Bell Olsen reprinted with permission from Janus Book Publishers from *Communication Starters*, copyright © 1976 by Alemany Press, 2501 Industrial Parkway W., Hayward, CA 94545.

Exercise by Joan Morley reprinted with permission from University of Michigan Press from *Improving Aural Comprehension*, copyright © 1972 by University of Michigan Press, 839 Greene St., P.O. Box 1104, Ann Arbor, MI 48106.

ISBN4-7890-0283-7
Copyright © 1985 by The Japan Times, Ltd.
First edition: July 1985
Second printing: February 1986

Jacket design: Atelier Hirata
Layout and typography: Stephen Comee

Published by The Japan Times, Ltd.
5-4, Shibaura 4-chome, Minato-ku, Tokyo 108, Japan

Printed in Japan

Contents

CONTENTS

A Guide to Teaching English in Japan

要　約

教室のこどもたちからスタート

ロナルド・ザビスラク

　この章では，来日してこども英語教室で教えようとする人が，職探しのとき
に出会ういくつかの問題をとりあげている。現在ある外国語学校のタイプを例
にあげ，応募する際考慮に入れたい給料，交通費やその他の諸手当など，学校
により差があるものについて話をすすめる。前半は主に学校の選択と就職につ
いて。後半は，こどものEFL教室を指導，管理，発展させるために必要と思わ
れる考え方，ポイントについて。教室での初期目標，意思疎通，規律について
も述べられている。全くの素人を念頭に書かれているが，後半部はこの分野で
働くベテラン教師にも示唆を与えるだろう。

こどものための英語：こどもを中心に考えた言語習得

ウォルター・エンロー他

　この章は主として，これまでに少し英語を学んだことがある，あるいは全く
英語を知らない5歳から13歳までの日本人のこどもたちに英語を教える新米教
師のために書かれている。教師としての心構えと，授業をどんな方法でどのよ
うに進めるかに焦点をおいている。
　まず，一般的に教えることについて，また特に日本で教えることについて論
じ，幼児やこどもの心理的発達の概略を示す。次にことばを教えることに焦点
をおき，もっとも効果的と思われる取り組み方を説明する。最初の授業にどの
ように取り組むか，典型的な授業はどのように組み立てるかを論じたあと，英
語の語法や語い，聴く・話す・読む・書くの相互に関連するコミュニケーショ
ンの技術などを教えるときに役立つさまざまな方法をもりこんでいる。最後に，
教師が新米あるいはベテランにかかわらず，教室で不断に向上するためにはど
のようにしたらよいかを示し，締めくくりとする。

Abstracts

Getting Started with Children in the EFL Classroom
Ronald Zavislak

This essay discusses some of the problems a person coming to Japan would encounter in seeking employment teaching children. It gives examples of the types of language schools available and talks about variables such as pay, transportation, and other benefits to be considered when applying for a job teaching children. The first part of the article deals mainly with choosing and getting the job, while the latter half gives ideas and key points I consider necessary for developing, conducting, and controlling a children's ESL class. Initial goals, communication, and discipline in the class are presented. Though written with the complete novice in mind, the latter part of the article may provide ideas for experienced teachers in this field.

English for Children: Child-centered Language Acquisition
Walter Enloe, Philip Lewin, and Randy Morris

This chapter is primarily for the beginning teacher who is faced with the task of teaching Japanese children, aged 5–13, who have received little or no prior English instruction. We concentrate on the teacher's own attitude toward teaching, and on strategies and techniques for the classroom.

First, we discuss the problems of teaching in general, and of teaching in Japan in particular, and then provide an overview of psychological development in early and middle childhood. We next focus on teaching language, and describe the teaching approach we believe to be the most successful. After discussing how to approach a first class and how to structure a typical class, we include a variety of resources to use in teaching English syntax and vocabulary, and the interrelated communication skills of listening, speaking, writing, and reading. Finally, we conclude by suggesting how the teacher, whether a beginner or not, can continue to improve in the classroom.

日本の高校で教える

ローレンス・M・ウィーグ

　この章では，日本の高校で教える場合の概略に加え，高校での職を確保するにあたってのアドバイスを示す。次章，ジル・スチュワートの小論「中学校を考える——ひとつの返答」では，中学と高校の場合の違いを論じている。

　まず，日本の高校の種類と基本理念を述べたあと，高校，社会一般における英語学習の役割について論じ，最後に，英語を母国語とする教師の役割に焦点をあてる。教師は，出席や参加の規則を忠実に守らなければならないが，授業を計画し，おこなう面では，大きな裁量を持っている。生徒や父兄，規律の問題をどのように扱うかについて述べたあと，英語を母国語とする教師はその文化の代表者として貢献するには最適であろう，とまとめている。逆に言えば，そのような立場は，日本文化を広く理解するための，ひとつの素晴らしい方法でもある。

中学校について考える——ひとつの返答

ジル・スチュワート

　この稿は，先のウィーグ氏の日本の高校についての章に対するひとつの答えとして，日本の中学レベルの英語教育を特殊にしている問題のいくつかをみていく。外国人は日本の組織の中では本来余計者である点がまず考察される。教職のいろいろな側面での重要性が強調される。中学における暴力の問題は，外国人が日本で意思疎通をすることの難しさを考慮に入れて，個人的な観察から検討される。厳しい画一社会で少年時代を過ごす中学生の特異性を示し，それが生徒たちが教育を受けている，社会的，感情的環境に与える大きな影響をみていく。教師が得ることのできる見返りと理解についても言及する。

日本の中学校における英語教育

ミホ・タナカ・シュタインバーグ

　この章では，日本の学校制度の紹介を試みる。というのも，中学レベルの英語教育や，そこにたずさわろうとする英語を母国語とする人にとって，この学校制度はつきものだからだ。来日するほとんどの「外人教師」が気づく，非常にデリケートな彼らの立場を説明し，やりがいのある素晴らしい経験を目指して働けるような方法を提案する。著者は，教科書と関連づけたゲームや活動をつくり出すことによって，英語の教科書を生き生きさせる方法を見つけるよう，ネイティブ・スピーカーに勧める。三つの補記が章の後についている。補記Ⅰは，本文で示された五つの活動に必要な材料や資料を説明。補記Ⅱは，復習の例題。この大まかなガイドは，自分自身の授業計画を準備するときに役立つだろう。補記Ⅲは，より技術を要する，新しい授業を導入するための例題。

ABSTRACTS

Teaching in Japanese Senior High Schools
Laurence M. Wiig

This chapter gives an overview of the teaching situations at Japanese senior high schools in addition to suggestions for securing such employment. The essay following, Jill Stewart's "Thoughts on the Junior High School—A Response," comments on differences between senior and junior high-school situations.

First noting the variety and general philosophy of Japanese senior high schools, the chapter then discusses the role of English study in them and the society at large, finally focusing on the role of the native-speaking English instructor. While teachers are expected to adhere strictly to rules on attendance and participation, they have great latitude in designing and conducting classes. After describing students, their parents, and how to handle disciplinary problems, the chapter concludes that the native speaker of English may serve best as a representative of his or her culture. Conversely, such a position is an excellent way to gain a broad understanding of Japanese culture.

Thoughts on the Junior High School: A Response
Jill Stewart

This article, a response to Mr. Wiig's article on the Japanese high school, looks at some of the issues that make the teaching of English at the junior high level in Japan a special area. The unexpected nature of being a foreigner in the Japanese system is examined. The importance of the specifics of the job is stressed. The issue of junior high-school violence is examined in the light of a foreigner's difficulties in communicating in Japan, and from the viewpoint of personal observation. The special qualities of junior high-school students at this time of their lives in a rigidly conforming society are presented, showing the great influence of the atmosphere—both social and emotional—within which these students are educated. The rewards and understandings gained by the teacher are also alluded to.

English Instruction in Japanese Junior High Schools
Miho Tanaka Steinberg

This chapter attempts to introduce the Japanese school system, as it pertains to lower secondary-level (junior high-school) English education, to those native English speakers who are embarking on a career of teaching at this level. It describes the very delicate position in which most incoming "foreign teachers" usually find themselves, and suggests ways in which they can work toward a very rewarding and successful experience. The writer encourages the native speakers to find ways to make English textbooks come alive by creating games and activities around them. Following the chapter are three appendixes. Appendix I gives the necessary materials and information for five activities described in the text. Appendix II gives sample exercises for review lessons, rough guides that may assist teachers in preparing lesson plans. Appendix III gives sample exercises for the more demanding task of introducing a new lesson.

日本の高校で働く英語教師のための戦略と方法

トーマス・G・ギュンターマン

　この章は，高校に雇われた英語のネイティブ・スピーカーのために書かれている。この仕事の任務は，普通校の15歳から18歳までの生徒に教えることである。章は三つの部分に分かれている。最初に，普通の英語の授業をどのように進め，補足していくかを説明する。次に，独自の方法で教え，自分なりのカリキュラムを開発したいと思う教師が採用できる，いくつかの取り組み方を詳述する。最後に，前二節で説明された方法が，実際の授業でどのように用いられるかを示す授業計画を述べる。この記事の根底には，新しい先生はその学校内で活発な役割を果たすべきである，という考え方が流れている。

日本の大学における英語教育とその社会的背景

ハル・ユージーン・ハンセン

　この章は主に，日本の短大，単科大学，総合大学に専任，あるいは非常勤で雇われた英語のネイティブ・スピーカー，またそうした大学レベルの教職を求める有資格教師のために書かれている。まず，日本の大学（およびその英語教育プログラム）のより広い社会内での地位の検討から始める。批評家たちは，教え方のまずさが英語教育の弱点であるとよく評するが，英語教育の成功は，社会，教職，教師，学生の四者間の期待と実践の相互関係による。次に，神戸商科大学で行われたプログラムを詳しく述べる。これは，商科，国際貿易科の1，2年生が，毎年，関連する4つのコースを英語で学ぶもので，これによって，それぞれの英語のコースを全く別々のカリキュラムで学ぶとき学生が直面する共通の問題を回避できる。このプログラムは，最終的な結論に値するほどまだ長く行われていないが，実験としては問題を明らかにし，その解決に向かって動くのに役立っている。

人数の多いクラスで話す英語を教える

リチャード・E・フリーマン

　この章は，日本の大学で話す英語を教える，専任あるいは非常勤の教師のために書かれている。彼らは，50人またはそれ以上の学生に，「英会話」のコースを教えなければならない。学生は若く，知力はあるものの，しばしば学習動機に乏しく，単に必要単位を満たすために英会話の授業を受ける。

　まず，人数の多いクラスで会話を教える難しさに焦点をあてる。これは芸術と同じで，教室の授業だけで教えることはできない。教える上での大切な準備は，教育に対する適切な考えを持つこと，学習の動機づけを徐々に行うこと，そして，教えるときにはっきりとした目標を定めることである。いったんこうした準備ができれば，学習環境が定義づけられ，維持されなければならない。

ABSTRACTS

Strategies and Methods for English Teachers in Japanese High Schools
Thomas G. Gunterman

This chapter is designed to help the native speaker of English who has been employed to teach in a high school. The duties of this work entail teaching students who are between the ages of fifteen and eighteen in a formal school setting. The chapter is divided into three sections. The first explains how to work with and supplement the regular English classes. The second details some approaches the teacher may take who wishes to teach independently and develop a personalized curriculum. The final section presents a lesson plan that shows how the information given in the first two sections can be used in an actual lesson. The underlying philosophy of this article is that new teachers should take active roles within their schools.

English Education in Japanese Universities and Its Social Context
Hal Eugene Hansen

This chapter is directed primarily to native speakers of English who are employed as full- or part-time instructors at Japanese junior colleges, colleges, and universities, and to qualified instructors considering such employment. The chapter begins by examining the position of the Japanese college (and its English-education program) within the larger society. While critics often blame poor teaching for weaknesses in English education, success depends upon the interrelation of expectations and action among four groups: the community, the teaching profession, the teachers, and the students. The second part of the chapter details a program initiated at Kobe University of Commerce in which first- and second-year students of Marketing and International Trade study four related courses in English each year, thus avoiding the common problem students face of studying completely separate curriculums for each English course. While the program has not operated long enough to merit final conclusions, the experiment has helped to clarify problems and work toward their solution.

Teaching Oral English in Large Classes
Richard E. Freeman

This chapter is written for full- or part-time instructors of oral English at Japanese colleges who have to teach courses in ''English Conversation'' to groups that may contain fifty or more students. While the students are young and intelligent, their motivation is often low and they take the course in order to meet a requirement.

First, the chapter focuses on the difficulties of instructing large classes in spoken language, which, like an art, cannot be taught merely through classroom instruction. Important preliminaries to teaching are establishing a proper philosophy of education, instilling learning motivation, and setting clear teaching goals. Once these are determined, the learning environment must be

また，学生の興味を持続させるために，学生はその目標を理解し，受け入れなければならない。人数の多いクラスでは，学生が自分自身に，また二人一組あるいは小グループに別れたとき他の学生に教えることが要求される。章の後半部は，発音練習をするときや，歌，自己紹介，集中インタビュー，報告，即興のスピーチ，ディベート，教科書の課題，課外活動などのグループ活動を行うときの手順のあらましを述べる。

日本の教育制度の枠外で教える場合

リチャード・エバノフ

この章は，認可を必要としない学習環境で英語を教えたい英語のネイティブ・スピーカーのために書かれている。第一節「市場」では，いわゆる英語学校，塾などにおけるネイティブ・スピーカーの需要と，関係する生徒の範囲に焦点をあてる。第二節「制度上の待遇」では，外国人教師が獲得できる機会を詳細に説明する。三つの下位セクションにわかれており，それぞれ(1)外国語学校で教える機会，(2)日本の企業で教える機会，(3)独立して教える機会，となっている。労働環境，仕事量，時間割，給与の形態，福利厚生などに関する情報が，各セクションにかかげられている。最後の「個人教師」では，在日外国人教師に役立つ雇用の習慣，資格について論じる。

成人に英語を教える

リチャード・エバノフ

この章は，日本にいる英語を母国語とする教師で，外国語学校や企業内クラス，あるいは他の成人教育施設で日本人の大人に教える人のために主として書かれている。第一節「レベルの決定」では，成人学生の要求を特に考慮に入れる点から，従来の「初級」，「中級」，「上級」の段階区分を再定義する。学生がどのくらい上手に実際に英語での会話に参加できるか，を決定する要素が述べられ，学生をそれぞれの実際の会話能力に応じて組み合わせ，クラスわけする方法について指針を示す。第二節「さまざまなレベルでの教授法」では，第一節で定義された各レベルの日本人の成人学生に適した数多くの教授法のうち，いくつかを説明する。

企業で英語を教える

ロバート・スコット・ドーソン

この章では，本来語学教師でない人が，日本の企業で語学教師として専任で働くことに関する問題をとりあげる。生徒は会社のさまざまな部から来ており，

ABSTRACTS

defined and maintained, and, in order to keep student interest, the students must understand and accept the goals. Large classes require students to teach themselves and others in pairs or small groups. The latter portion of the chapter outlines procedures for giving pronunciation practice and carrying out such group activities as singing, self-introductions, intensive interviews, reporting, impromptu speeches, debates, textbook work, and outside activities.

Teaching Opportunities Outside of the Japanese Educational System
Richard Evanoff

This chapter is written for native-speakers of English who wish to teach English in non-accredited learning environments. The first section, "The Market," focuses on the current demand for extra-curricular English instruction by native-speakers and the range of students involved. The second section, "Institutional Arrangements," discusses in detail the opportunities available to the foreign teacher. Three sub-sections deal with teaching opportunities in language schools, opportunities in Japanese companies, and opportunities for teaching independently. Information concerning the work environment, teaching loads, schedules, modes of payment, fringe benefits, etc., is presented for each of these sub-sections. The final major section, "The Individual Teacher," discusses hiring practices and qualifications that are useful for foreign teachers in Japan.

Teaching English to Japanese Adults
Richard Evanoff

This chapter is written primarily for native-speaking English teachers in Japan who teach Japanese adult students in language schools, company classes, or other adult educational facilities. The first section of the article, "Determining Levels," redefines the traditional divisions between the levels "beginning," "intermediate," and "advanced" in a way that takes the specific needs of adult Japanese students into account. Factors that determine how well a student can actually participate in a conversation in English are discussed, and guidelines are offered as to how students might be grouped together into classes that are suited to their actual conversational abilities. The second section, "Teaching Methods for the Various Levels," describes a few of the many teaching methods appropriate for adult Japanese students at each of the levels defined in the first section of the article.

Teaching English in Companies
Robert Scott Dawson

The article describes various matters relating to working full-time as a language instructor in a Japanese company whose primary business is not language

ごくまれな例を除き，大卒の男子で工学，経営，経済，法律（日本では大学の学位）の学位を持っているか，他の専門的な訓練を受けている。三つのテーマで話題に取り組んでいく。まず，「典型的な１日」を描き，ある与えられた日に語学教師がするであろう仕事を説明する。次に，職探し，面談，契約の評価に的をしぼり，就職の過程を扱う。最後に，労働状況，従業員関係，そして雇い主と従業員双方からの期待について考えを述べる。

日本の企業で英語を教える：方法，教材を専門化させる
R・バーウィック，J・ハイネマン

　この章の主な目的は，企業内英語教育のプログラムがどのように組み立てられているか，またそこで教えるとはどのようなことかを示すことである。これから教師になりたい人，すでに教えている人で他企業のプログラムについて知りたい人，そして日本企業で働く外国人に一般的な関心がある人の興味を引くにちがいない。まず，これから企業内英語教師になろうとする人に要求される，ますます高まる専門レベル，特殊な学生のニーズを考慮する傾向，そして手づくりのコースや教材の計画について論じる。次に，五つの企業の外国語プログラムを，それぞれのコース，学生，目標，共通の問題等に関する情報とともに批評する。最後に典型的な仕事を説明し，役立つ教材のリストをかかげる。

個人教授
ウィリアム・アルバート・マクビーン

　この稿は，教えた経験がない人を含む，来日後まもない人を対象にしているが，ベテラン教師にとって有益な提言も入っている。時々こどもや青年に教えるよう依頼されることもあるが，英会話の個人教授を受けるのは，たいていは大学生ぐらいの年齢かそれ以上の人たちである。日本では個人教授が広くゆきわたり，収入も多い。しかし，個人教授は教室で教えるのとは大きく違う。世界的にみても個人教授は英語教育の重要な部分を占めているが，この分野の教師を導く，入手可能な情報は不足している。この稿では，研究と経験に基づき，個人教授が教室で教えることとどのように違うかを指摘し，問題点を論じ，ビジネス面について話し，また，個人教授の始め方など教師への提言をする。注釈つきの教材リストもかかげる。

teaching. The students to be taught come from different sections of the company and with rare exceptions will be adult male college graduates with degrees in engineering, business administration, economics, law (an undergraduate degree in Japan), or other professional disciplines. The topic is approached by means of three themes. First, a "typical" day is described to illustrate the work one might do on a given day. Second, the process of getting a job is dealt with by focusing on finding one, interviewing for it, and evaluating the contract. Third come some thoughts about work situations, employee relations, and expectations—both of the employer and employee.

Teaching English at Japanese Companies: Professionalizing Methods and Materials
Richard Berwick and Janet Heyneman

The primary aim of this chapter is to give an idea of how in-company programs are structured and what it is like to teach in one. It should interest prospective teachers, those already teaching who would like to know about programs in other companies, and those with a general interest in foreigners as Japanese company employees. The chapter begins with a discussion of the growing professional level looked for in prospective in-company teachers, the trend toward consideration of specific student needs, and the design of original courses and materials. The second major section reviews five company language programs, including information on their courses, students, goals, and common problems. The final section describes typical duties and gives a list of useful materials.

Private Lesson Teaching
William Albert McBean

This article is aimed at teachers new to Japan, including those with no previous teaching experience, though experienced instructors may find useful suggestions as well. Students for conversational English through private lessons are usually of college age or over, though teachers are sometimes called upon to instruct children and adolescents. Private lesson teaching in Japan is widespread and often lucrative, but it differs significantly from classroom teaching. While private tuition is an important part of English teaching worldwide, there is a lack of information available to guide such teachers in their work. This article, based on research and experience, points out how private lessons are different from classroom teaching, discusses problems, addresses the business aspect, and offers suggestions for teachers, including how to get started. Also given is an annotated list of teaching materials.

要　約

からだ全体で反応：簡単な動きからクラスのドラマづくりへ

デイル・T・グリフィー

　この章で紹介する技術は，高校や大学，あるいは外国語学校の教師が，青年から成人までの教育に用いることができる。学校の環境（教室，学生）を簡単に論じたあと，アクションの役割を特に強調しながら，言語習得における重要な活動として聴くことを奨励する。筋に一貫性をもたせ，動きに意味を与えるひとつの方法として，ミニ・ドラマを紹介する。ミニ・ドラマの書き方，提示のし方も論じる。役割練習について若干述べ，結びとする。

コンテスト会話：日本で英語に上達する近道

リチャード・E・フリーマン

　日本では英語のネイティブ・スピーカーの多くは，英会話を教えるよう依頼される。教える状況は，高校の教室から，近所の老人グループまでさまざまであろう。この小論は，こうした多様な学習者を教えるのに，ひとつの方法だけを用いることの難しさを認める。しかし，著者が開発したコンテスト会話の技術は，いろいろな場面で成功をおさめている。簡単に説明すると，生徒たちは，会話が一定の構成要素で成り立っており，そのあるものは英語そのものにかかわり，またあるものは会話自体の進行にかかわっていることを教えられる。次に生徒は 3～4 グループにわけられる。二人の生徒が話をしている間，グループの他の生徒は10項目の能力評価項目に従って，話し手の出来を評価する。（最初のうちは，ほとんど評価の対象にならないかもしれない）ゲームのような雰囲気が会話のできばえをよくし，判断に責任をもたせることにより聴き手の注意をも引き続ける。

リーダーズ・イン・カウンシル：日本の英語教育についての読者投稿

ジャパンタイムズ読者

　この本の他の章では特定の教育情況を扱ったり，ある年齢の人たちを教える方法を助言しているが，この章 "Readers in Council"（ジャパンタイムズ紙の読者投稿欄）は日本で英語を教えること，そして学ぶことについての意見を幅広くとりあげている。論争の発端は一日本人大学教授の手紙だった。教授は全国各地の英会話学校で働く外人教師の質が低いと批判した。何人かの外人教師は，現状を弁護するか，または外人教師が直面する不利な条件を説明するかのどちらかで反駁した。日本人投稿者は，完全な発音を学ぶことの難しさ，また極端に安い給料で教えなければならない，ある外国人たちの困難な状況について意見を寄せた。ほかにもたくさんの話題が紹介され，具体的な結論には至ってはいないものの，この稿は英語教育分野における問題点や論点の広範な，時としておもしろい概略を示している。

ABSTRACTS

Total Physical Response: From Simple Actions to Classroom Drama
Dale T. Griffee

The techniques in this article can be used by high school, college, or private language school teachers for the instruction of older adolescents through adults. After a brief discussion of the school environment (classroom and students), this article promotes listening as the primary activity in acquiring language, with a special emphasis on the role of actions. The mini-drama is introduced as a way to give extended coherence and meaning to actions. The writing and presenting of the mini-drama are also discussed. Concluding this article is a short discussion on role-playing.

Contest Conversation: A Shortcut to English Fluency in Japan
Richard E. Freeman

Many native English speakers in Japan are called upon to teach conversational English. The teaching situation may vary from a high-school classroom to a private group of retired people from the neighborhood. This essay acknowledges the difficulty of using a single method to teach such a diverse audience. However, contest conversation, a technique developed by the author, has proven itself successful in a variety of circumstances. In brief, students are taught that conversation consists of certain components, some pertaining to the English language, and some to the process of conversation itself. Then students are divided into groups of three or four. Two students converse while the other student(s) evaluate the speakers' success in ten areas of competence. (During the introductory period, fewer criteria may be evaluated.) The game-like atmosphere improves performance, and the responsibility of judging keeps the auditors attentive as well.

Readers in Council:
Letters to the Editor About English Teaching in Japan

While the other essays in this book deal with specific teaching contexts or advise methods for teaching certain age groups, "Readers in Council" (Japan Times) offers a wide range of opinions about the teaching—and learning—of English in Japan. The series was sparked by a letter in which a Japanese professor criticized the low quality of gaijin kyoshi (foreign instructors) in English conversation schools around Japan. Some foreign teachers wrote back either defending the status quo or explaining the handicaps that foreign instructors encounter. Japanese contributors commented both on the difficulty of learning perfect pronunciation and the difficult position of some foreigners who must teach for extremely low salaries. Many other topics were introduced, and no concrete conclusions were reached, but this article gives a broad and sometimes amusing overview of the issues and controversies encountered in the field.

About this Book

A GUIDE TO TEACHING ENGLISH IN JAPAN is written primarily for native speakers of English who teach or wish to teach English in Japan. A series of paired essays describes job situations (contexts) and teaching techniques (strategies) for language instruction to the Japanese. The number of contexts covered is large: children's classes; secondary schools; colleges; private language schools; private lessons; and teaching as an employee of a Japanese corporation. Such diversity is justified by the variety of positions most teachers will have opportunities to fill, particularly if they begin work as free-lance instructors or employees of private language schools. Even teachers at colleges may be asked from time to time to participate in other areas.

Japanese instructors of English and directors of language programs form a secondary audience for the book, and Japanese abstracts of each article have been included for their benefit. Japanese teachers can appreciate and make use of the methods presented here. Japanese teachers and administrators alike who read the essays on teaching contexts will better understand the concerns of the foreign instructors with whom they are in contact.

The next few pages contain brief biographies of the contributors to this volume. Then, in the opening essay, I describe the English learning situation in Japan, the general contents of this book, and the availability of scholarly or practical advice on teaching situations and employment in Japan. I give guidelines for job seekers, and also comment upon the outstanding differences between the expectations of Japanese employers and non-Japanese employees. Next comes a description and history of the

ABOUT THIS BOOK

Japan Association of Language Teachers (JALT), an organization with over 2,700 active members, both Japanese and foreign. My chapter concludes with a brief list of books useful in learning about Japan. The essay is quite diverse, but I think it serves my basic purpose of introducing the major issues associated with English teaching in Japan.

I wish to thank my contributors for their hard work and patience in writing and revising their essays. The following scholars allowed me to read valuable materials they had written relevant to the topics of this book: Professor Koji Wakamatsu of Mie University; Professor Luis Canales of Kyoto University of Foreign Studies; Dr. James Radomski, formerly of Kashiwa High School; and Mr. Roy Takumi of Honolulu. Richard Freeman, Richard Berwick, Richard Evanoff, and Dale Griffee gave me advice and encouragement during the course of planning and completing the text. President James White, Executive Secretary Thomas Robb, and the Executive Committee of JALT have generously supported the project in its final stages. Bert McBean has been a good friend to me, and my wife Miyoko has made this book and many other things possible. Finally, I thank Masayuki Ishida and the rest of the publications staff at the *Japan Times* for making this book a reality.

About the Authors

RICHARD BERWICK is currently a visiting lecturer at Kobe University of Commerce and a Doctoral Candidate (English and Adult Education) at the University of British Columbia. He also taught English for two and a half years at Kobe Steel, Ltd. He holds a master's degree in English Education (ESL) from UBC and has published articles on language needs assessment and group methods for Japanese learners of English.

ROBERT SCOTT DAWSON is Supervisor and Instructor for a major Japanese glass manufacturer near Kyoto. He first came to Japan in 1968 while serving in the Marine Corps. In 1976 he received his M.A. in History from Duke University and returned to Japan to study the Japanese language. Since then he has worked for language schools and in-house programs in both Tokyo and the Kansai area. He has been employed in his present position since 1982.

WALTER ENLOE holds a Ph.D. in developmental psychology and educational theory. For the past fourteen years he has taught children, from kindergarten through high-school students, and has served as a consultant for several child service agencies. Presently he is the Principal and an elementary teacher at the Hiroshima International School, where he is also engaged in research on global education and the problems facing Japanese returnee students. Dr. Enloe went to junior and senior high school in Japan.

RICHARD EVANOFF is presently instructor in English as a Foreign Language at Showa University in Tokyo. Besides, he is teaching at

ABOUT THE AUTHORS

Chuo University, the Rigaku Corporation, and the Asahi Culture Center, and has previously taught privately and at various other universities, language schools, and companies in Tokyo.

RICHARD E. FREEMAN is a professor at Chuo University in Tokyo where he has been teaching for the past twenty years. He also lectures at Rikkyo and Seijo Universities. He formerly wrote skits and appeared as a lecturer for NHK-TV's intermediate English program. He has co-authored numerous textbooks for high school and college students, the most recent being *College Students,* based on interviews he conducted at Georgetown University as a visiting researcher.

DALE T. GRIFFEE graduated from Baylor University with a degree in philosophy. He was a member of the Institute of Cultural Affairs (an educational think-tank based in Chicago) for eight years. He is chapter head of the Japan Association of Language Teachers in Sendai, where he teaches at James English School. He has served for two years as chairman of JALT's Long-Range Planning Committee. Mr. Griffee's interests in drama and Total Physical Response learning came together in his book *Listen and Act: Scenes for Language Learning.*

THOMAS G. GUNTERMAN was born and raised in northern California. He received his B.A. in Spanish from California State University at Chico in 1979. During the following year he taught English as a Second Language to Punjabi and Mexican children in Live Oak, California, as practicum for a teaching credential. Upon receiving the credential, he began working at Seirei High School, Hamamatsu, Shizuoka, becoming actively involved in the development of the English course and curriculum.

HAL EUGENE HANSEN received master's degrees in social ethics and human development from Harvard University. He has studied at the University of Saarland (W. Germany) and the Sorbonne, each for a year. His teaching experience includes one year with Berlitz in Paris, two years at the Boston School of Modern Languages, and three years at the Kobe University of Commerce. Presently he lives and writes in the Boston area.

JANET HEYNEMAN is presently a lecturer in the Division of Humanities at

Soai University in Osaka. She was previously curriculum coordinator and English teacher in Kobe Steel's International Communication Program in Kobe, and holds an M.A. in TESL from the University of Illinois at Urbana-Champaign.

PHILIP LEWIN contributed to his essay while on a leave of absence from Clarkson College in New York, conducting research with returnee children, and writing on issues in the philosophy and psychology of education. He was then Director of the Sun English School in Hiroshima. At Clarkson, Dr. Lewin is Assistant Professor of Humanities.

WILLIAM A. MCBEAN received his M.A. in Teaching English as a Second Language from the University of Hawaii. He has taught in the United States, Hawaii, Hong Kong, and, for nearly a decade, in Japan. He is presently lecturer in English Language at Oita University in Kyushu.

RANDY MORRIS taught children at the Hiroshima International School until 1985, serving as the head teacher in the school's English Language Program for children, as well as one of the directors of its program for returnee children. In addition to studying developmental psychology, Dr. Morris is a depth psychologist who researched nuclear dream imagery among the citizens of Hiroshima. He now teaches at Antioch College's satellite unit in Seattle.

MIHO TANAKA STEINBERG was born and attended elementary school in Vancouver, Canada. She received her secondary education in Japan and graduated from Kyoto Women's University. While studying for her M.A. in Linguistics at the University of Michigan, she taught at the English Language Institute there. As professor in the University of Hawaii's Department of English as a Second Language, she was director of their English Language Institute for a number of years. Having left Hawaii in 1982, she now lives in Japan, has taught at Kanazawa Institute of Technology, and teaches at Nagoya Gakuin University.

JILL STEWART has been a teacher in the Native Speaker Program of the Kobe City Board of Education for three years. She is a certified high-school and junior high-school English teacher in the U.S., as well as a registered nurse and sometime poet. She is presently finishing up her M.Ed. in TESOL at Temple University in Japan.

ABOUT THE AUTHORS

LAURENCE M. WIIG has taught Japanese, Spanish, and French at the secondary-school level in the U.S.A. He has been teaching English in Japan since 1979, first at Tokyo Foreign Language College and then at Hiroshima Daiichi Girl's Commercial High School. Wiig is currently working at Hiroshima Jogakuin Senior and Junior High Schools.

CHARLES B. WORDELL is visiting lecturer in English at the University of Tsukuba. He previously held the same position at the Kobe University of Commerce, and also taught as associate professor of English at Yasuda Women's University, in Hiroshima, from 1982 to 1984. He received his Ph.D. in English from the University of Chicago in 1982. Besides Teaching English as a foreign language in Hong Kong, Japan, Tanzania, and the United States, he has lectured extensively on English language, American literature, and American culture, including presentations at the 1983 and 1984 national conferences of the Japan Association of Language Teachers. He co-edited a book of sociolinguistic research, *Language of the Underworld*, and presently edits high-school English textbooks for a Japanese publisher in addition to his university teaching responsibilities.

RONALD ZAVISLAK has been teaching ESL to adults and children for more than ten years. After obtaining a B.A. in Political Science and Far Eastern History and getting his M.A. in International Relations from Sophia University's International Division, he recently received an M.A. in Comparative Culture from the Sophia University National Division's Department of Linguistics. He is presently Chief Instructor at Pacific Language School and teaches at Seijo University in Tokyo.

A Guide to Teaching English
in Japan

Diverse Perspectives
on English Teaching in Japan

Charles B. Wordell

JAPAN HAS A POPULATION of 120 million people. Nearly half of them have studied English in school for at least three years. Most Japanese, however, now receive six years of junior/senior high-school English instruction. Rigorous examinations in English and other subjects are prerequisites for admission to colleges. Of the 35% of high-school students who continue on to junior colleges or universities, most take at least another course in English language. At other schools, particularly women's colleges, up to a quarter of the student body may be enrolled in programs of English and American literature, taking sixteen additional year-long courses in English language or literature. Others prepare to be secondary or college teachers of English (though the market has been saturated in recent years); these prospective teachers submit to an even more demanding schedule of language courses and post-graduate English education.

In spite of the large numbers of Japanese who have studied the English language, few students, graduates, or even instructors are comfortable when called upon to converse in English. All the contributors to *A Guide to Teaching English in Japan* recognize this reticence. A few have attempted to explain it and most have suggested methods of dealing with the enormous gaps left by most forms of English-language education in Japan. Our book documents English learning environments as seen from the English-teaching foreigner's point of view. In this sense, it is an unusual perspective and one which I hope will assist both practicing and prospective teachers to do their work more effectively.

The teaching of English to junior high-school students reminds me greatly of my own introduction to Latin grammar and vocabulary at the age of twelve. I was taught to translate, and only one of my four teachers even intimated that Latin literature contained works of beauty. Quite naturally, we were never asked questions in Latin or encouraged to speak in the language, outside of oral reading of assigned texts. Second year classes, I recall, consisted of twenty minutes' study of grammar-translation rules followed by a half-hour's painful limp through the tale of Jason and his Argonauts.

Although pronunciation of English receives some emphasis in Japanese schools, and oral question/answer exercises are common, native Japanese teachers are most capable when teaching rules of grammar and guiding their students in the translation of English prose. This situation prevails even among teachers at the university level. The result is inarticulate literacy. A secondary result is a thriving market for native speakers of English who wish to teach in Japan.

Why do the Japanese study English? For one thing, the Japanese consider study to be an activity of great intrinsic merit, essential to the preparation of the young, and valuable in the continuing process of maturation that the Japanese see as a characteristic of growing older. Thus, Japan possesses a large pool of educable citizens. The facts that English speaking nations won the Pacific War and occupied Japan contribute to the historical importance of English study, but the increasing use of English as a language of international economic and scholarly communication bears more significantly on the current popularity of its study, particularly as Japan has achieved notable success in both fields. Japan's increasing wealth and gradually expanding leisure time have also brought English study within the reach of groups (such as housewives or retired professionals) who have no clearly pragmatic reason to improve their skills in the language.

English-Teaching Situations Described in this Book

Packaging is a fine art in Japan, and a well-wrapped gift from a prestigious shop is generally better appreciated—as a ''gift''— than an object of greater value stuffed into a paper sack. A desire to learn conversational English (which is not taught well in public schools) combines with the Japanese aesthetic of packaging to create a market for native speakers who wish to teach "conversation." Two articles by Richard Evanoff describing private language schools treat this theme in greater detail and give extensive advice on how to conduct classes in them. And though prejudice against, say, hiring Canadians of Oriental ancestry or English speakers from India will be encountered at many schools, this prejudice is not universal.

While private conversation schools are by far the largest employers of English-speaking teachers, any native speaker in Japan will probably be asked to give private lessons within the neighborhood. This sort of teaching and numerous practical techniques associated with private instruction are described in the article by William A. McBean. Recently-arrived native speakers of English are also asked, sometimes, to teach children informally. In this regard, many native speakers work as full-time employees in language schools that supply instructors, on a once-weekly basis, to grade schools. Ronald Zavislak describes the environment at the subcontracting schools, while methods for teaching children are outlined by the team of Enloe, Lewin, and Morris.

Although conversation schools have been known to hire merely on the basis of race and personality, for a good many years a bachelor's degree in some field has been a requirement for teachers who want a working visa. An increase in the number of instructors with credentials in teaching English as a foreign language, combined with weak job markets in some other countries, has led even conversation schools to occasionally require vocational preparation or experience of their job applicants. (A glance at the Monday "help wanted" section of the *Japan Times* will bear this out.)

"Professionalism," as some call it, is often a requirement for employment as a language-resource person in a Japanese industrial or commercial corporation. This relatively new job—becoming a full-time salaried employee in a Japanese firm—makes greater demands upon teachers, but the job offers particular benefits. An article by Robert Scott Dawson describes the working situation, while another by Richard Berwick and Janet Heyneman outlines professional issues and teaching techniques for this specialization. Industries may have hired only several hundred instructors on a full-time basis, but the articles document a growing segment of the field and should be of interest to most teachers at private language schools. Industries usually contract instructors from these schools in order to schedule the full number of courses they wish to offer.

Free-lance teachers and others seeking part-time work may find company teaching jobs as well.

Another employment opportunity that has grown recently is teaching English on a full- or part-time basis at private secondary schools. Although a foreign face may be placed on the staff mainly to add to the school's prestige, the responsibilities of teaching and maintaining order in the classroom are real and demanding. Laurence Wiig describes the teaching situation at a private senior high school, and his description is useful for understanding the structure of junior high schools as well. Jill Stewart, a junior high teacher, comments on similarities and differences between her experiences and Wiig's. Miho Steinberg and Thomas Gunterman describe teaching methods for junior and senior high schools, respectively. Some secondary school English teachers are called upon to teach conversation, while others are expected to supplement instruction that prepares students for demanding senior high-school or college entrance examinations. Steinberg and Gunterman are alert to both situations, and stress the importance of putting a human face on language instruction. These chapters will be of use to teachers of private lessons who are asked to instruct secondary-school students; teachers at private language schools who are called upon to participate in "juku," or examination-preparation classes, will also profit from reading them closely.

When I studied languages in American colleges, my classes met daily in the first year or two of training. Japanese college students, regardless of the extent to which they have mastered the basics of English, gather only once a week for any particular language class, spending up to a hundred minutes attempting to absorb information which would be much better communicated in shorter, more frequent meetings. (This situation does not hold at the handful of "universities of foreign studies" which offer certain language classes on a daily basis.) Hal E. Hansen explains the social background to this problem in teaching, and also describes how one Japanese school redesigned its English program to coordinate the curricula of four different classes taught to the same group of first- and second-year students. In a complementary article, Richard Freeman recommends varying both teaching methods and materials within a single 100-minute college class in oral English, the subject most often taught by foreign instructors. By maintaining variety, the teacher keeps students active and alert; and by dividing classes into groups of two, three, and four, the teacher can shift from the exhausting role of the sole instructor to the more fruitful and less demanding one of observer/advisor.

Though most sections in the book balance context with strategies, two articles describe methods that can be adapted to the teaching of oral English to students at most levels of language learning. Dale Griffee, in "Total Physical Response," discusses the relationship between action and language acquisition. He explains how classroom instructors can involve students in mini-dramas that foster a gradual progress from auditory recognition through comprehension, response to spoken commands, and finally production of speech integrated with action. Richard Freeman's "Contest Conversation" describes a technique, again based on dividing classes into groups of three or four speakers, for alerting students to the qualities that make good conversation and for giving them a stimulating situation in which to build their skills.

Language teaching supplies employment for many native speakers of English in Japan. It also generates controversy, among Japanese and foreign instructors alike. Some of these controversies—ranging from whether Japanese are physically capable of producing English sounds to whether Japanese students have the moral fiber to undertake the task—are aired in a series of letters drawn from the letter section of the *Japan Times*, "Readers in Council." The nineteen letters serve to alert newcomers to areas of contention and to furnish all readers with a variety of opinions on the state of English teaching in Japan.

Other Information about Teaching English in Japan

A great number of English-language publications take up the topic of teaching English in Japan. However, the bulk of the articles appear in Japanese university journals, which have a limited circulation, to say the least. The *TESOL Quarterly* and *Newsletter* carry an occasional article or note relevant to the topic, but books are hard to find. One excellent volume, *The Teaching of English in Japan*, published in 1978 (Tokyo: Eichosha), is a massive collection of essays by Japanese and native English-speaking teachers. The essays focus on particular aspects of the teaching task, however, and neither describe work contexts nor give general information about making lesson or course plans.

Teaching English in Japan, printed privately in 1975 by Ken Damon

May, is basically a typewritten list of schools in Japan that hire native speakers to teach English. He gives two pages of practical hints that are still relevant, but this booklet may be impossible to locate now. A 1983 book which presents an overly optimistic view of employment opportunities and life in Japan is John Wharton's *Jobs in Japan, the Complete Guide to Living and Working in the Land of Rising Opportunity*. The book is sometimes stocked by Kinokuniya in Shinjuku, Tokyo, and it can be ordered directly from Global Press, 2239 E. Colfax 202, Denver, CO 80206, U.S.A. The price has been $8.95 sea mail, $12.95 air to Japan. A note of inquiry should reveal whether these prices still stand. Like May's booklet, *Jobs in Japan* contains a lengthy appendix listing schools that hire foreigners. Other publications of interest are the Japan Association of Language Teachers' monthly magazine, *The Language Teacher*, their *JALT Journal*, and *Cross Currents*, another language teaching journal printed in Japan. Their articles, while well written, address specific teaching situations or theoretical questions.

In *A Guide to Teaching English in Japan*, we attempt to offer the reader original material aimed at creating a unified picture of English-teaching jobs and methods in Japan. All but three of the essays in the book have been written specifically to fit this pattern, and those three essays, by Richard Freeman and Hal Hansen, served in the formulation of the guidelines that I set for contributors. I began the project not only to fill an empty spot on my bookshelf, but also to help new teachers in Japan avoid painful and unnecessary mistakes, because they often neither understand the structure of the institutions that employ them nor the expectations and capabilities of their students. In the first case, novice teachers may experience frustration, rage, or even depression; in the second case, teachers may fail to teach.

Finding, Keeping, and Changing Positions

A major contradiction exists in the English-teaching job market in Japan: in order to work in Japan, you must have a working visa issued outside of Japan, but in order to get a job, you must be in Japan. Although this is generally the case, I want to examine the situation in which work is obtained outside the country.

Using a guide such as Wharton's *Jobs in Japan*, you can write directly to schools in areas where you would like to live. I tried this with eight colleges, and was sent discouraging notes by all of them, in spite of two year's teaching experience in Japan and another two year's college teaching in the U.S. On the other hand, letters and personal histories sent to schools *may* yield results, and postage is cheaper than air fare. Such an application should include a typed cover letter and an educational/teaching experience summary, perhaps on both sides of a single sheet of paper to save postage expenses. Almost no schools expect foreigners to stay for many years, so besides showing interest in the school in your cover letter, you might explain the areas of Japanese society or culture that interest you. On the other hand, neither in the letter nor in any communication with a school that employs you should you indicate that you have intentions of moving to another school. The chief virtue demanded of Japanese workers is cooperation, and the "polite fiction" that prevails in all workplaces is that "We are working together in continuing harmony." If schools are interested in you as a teacher, they will write, asking for more information or perhaps offering you a position.

Naturally, there are many sorts of schools. The schools that hire with the least scrutiny are likely to be ones with the least pleasant working conditions. In this regard, commercial language schools are to be more carefully screened than colleges, although a college run by a patriarchal despot can be quite an unpleasant working environment, particularly for women. The advantage of applying to language schools from abroad is that if a contract is offered, you will be able to examine it at leisure. Richard Evanoff's chapters should give you some idea of which schools are to be avoided.

Once a contract *has* been offered, you must obtain a series of documents to be submitted to a Japanese consulate in order to obtain a visa. These details are intricate and many. For a college position (which, by the way, is exempt from taxes for two years—though British subjects lose the exemption more easily than Americans), a letter offering employment, a document from the Ministry of Justice in Tokyo, and a letter from a Japanese guaranteeing your support are all necessary, as well as your passport and forms you must fill out. In other words, start early. Employment at private language schools requires you to furnish the consulate or embassy with evidence of completion of a bachelor's degree in any field, proof of employment, and a letter of guarantee from your school. The Japanese consulate can tell you what other information is necessary. In such cases, however, the application must be sent for processing in Tokyo—a four- to eight-week delay before your visa can be issued.

Those who come to Japan to study, either as college students, as skilled artists, or as disciples in such fields as flower arranging, pottery, or martial arts are allowed to work within certain limits. Once in Japan on a student or cultural visa, however, you should inquire at the local immigration office, perhaps indirectly, to see whether a planned job will violate the terms of your visa. Several friends have pointed out that working with a cultural visa violates the spirit in which the visa was granted; also, each renewal will be scrutinized by the immigration office, and your cultural sponsor will probably be asked to evaluate the progress of your studies.

Much hiring in Japan is done on the basis of personal introductions. If you are outside of Japan, you may find that by making friends with Japanese, you will be helping them in your country, and they may help you in theirs. Besides the importance of personal recommendations in the hiring procedure, the fact is that if a language company needs an employee, it will not generally have the two or three months necessary to recruit a teacher from abroad and complete the paper work. In such circumstances, students and sometimes even tourists find that they have skills that are in demand. Richard Evanoff has supplied me with the following information on this subject.

If such a person does not have a visa that allows teaching, that person will first have to be accepted for employment by a school or company, obtain the necessary sponsorship papers, and then temporarily leave Japan in order to obtain the new visa outside the country. Seoul (the closest and most popular spot), Hong Kong, and Guam all have consulates that can deal with such applications. After the visa has been processed and approved—a procedure usually requiring about a month—prospective teachers will need to return to the point of application to have the new visa stamped in their passports.

Only after the new visa has been obtained is a teacher legally permitted to commence employment. However, many teachers will return to Japan while their visa applications are being processed and begin work immediately. Such a procedure is illegal and cannot be endorsed, though in actual practice it is done quite often. The expense of traveling abroad twice for one's visa and the burdensome expense of getting set up in Japan (persons are sometimes charged six months rent as deposit when they occupy a rented house or apartment) mean that you should make sure of adequate resources before coming to Japan.

Recently, I learned from Ronald Zavislak that the visa statuses have been revised. Those holding a 4-1-16-3 visa—a catchall visa for "cultural studies"—can usually stay for six months (though it can be given for up to three years). Teaching can be done with this visa if that was the stated intention when the visa was applied for. Otherwise special permission from immigration authorities is necessary and usually obtainable. If you have a student visa for one year, then permission to teach (labeled "for conducting other activities") is necessary. If you have a Japanese spouse, a 4-1-16-1 visa can be obtained initially for a year, but later upgraded to three years after you have been confirmed to be a non-menace to Japanese society. This last visa gives you the advantage of being able to change jobs or employers without notifying Immigration. The other visas require notification if you change jobs or employers.

Some positions are unbearable, but, as Scott Dawson pointed out to me, the proper procedures must be followed when terminating a position. First of all, if you find yourself in an intolerable situation, you would be well advised not to complain. Poor administrators may be vindictive, and when you find another position you will need your employer's cooperation. Most contracts may be terminated by either party if written notification is given thirty days in advance (be wary of a contract that does not permit termination). According to immigration guidelines, you should secure permission from the local immigration office prior to leaving a job. This is usually facilitated if you secure 1) a letter from your employer stating that you have met the terms of your contract and the separation is amicable, and 2) a copy of your *gensenchoshu,* verification that you are paying your taxes. One can usually notify the authorities of the change and file the required documents for the new job on the same day, but it is best to clarify the procedure at the nearest immigration office. Do not forget to notify your local city office of any changes in your status. If you are leaving the country, you must be able to show that you have paid all taxes that are due.

One book that supplies information about visas and forms necessary for obtaining them is the Ministry of Justice's booklet *A Guide to Residence and Registration Procedures in Japan for Foreign Nationals* (Tokyo, 1983). Those in Japan may inquire at immigration offices about where to find a copy, or can look for one at Kinokuniya and Maruzen bookstores.

The book is distributed by Nippon Kajo, P.O. Box 67, Toshima Post Office, Tokyo 170-91, Japan. They will send a book-order form to people in Japan—the book costs ¥500.

In order to get a rough idea of general opportunities in Japan, I recommend the classified section of the Monday edition of the *Japan Times*. Monday classifieds usually contain about twenty job offerings for language teachers, information on inexpensive accomodations in the Tokyo area (¥1500 a day), and numerous offers from Japanese language schools to enroll you in a study program which will qualify you for "cultural" visas. Some of the schools can arrange accomodations, and though the schools only give phone numbers, a call requesting information might be worth the long-distance charges. The Tokyo School of the Japanese Language (16-26 Nampeidai-machi, Shibuya-ku, Tokyo) is one respected center. Their curriculum aims at reading proficiency. Enrolling would limit you to the Tokyo area for at least three months, however.

Authors of chapters dealing with teaching contexts have generally supplied detailed information about how to apply and interview for positions in their areas.

Expectations and Disappointments

This section is the one I least enjoy writing, partly because it reminds me of my own mistakes and partly because it must examine critically some areas of Japanese behavior that tend to mystify and disturb foreigners. Kazuo Yoshida, writing in the summer 1983 number of the American *Journal of Popular Culture,* states succinctly differences in cultural traits of Americans and Japanese: "One would attribute to American culture, for example, freedom, equality, effort-optimism, democracy, individualism, abstract rationalism, technology, virtuous materialism, fast food and so on. One would assume that Japanese culture would include group consciousness, close identification between man and reality, seniority, institutionalism, harmony, etc." (p. 121).

Americans, and to some degree other Westerners living in Japan, will recognize the accuracy of the psycho-social distinctions drawn above. What disturbs some visitors is not the existence of differences, but the Japanese reaction to violators of accepted norms. In an article from the same number of the *Journal of Popular Culture,* Seiji Shibata tries to analyze the unexpectedly harsh treatment meted out to Japanese children who return to Japan after living abroad and absorbing both language and behavior patterns from their host countries: "What the society at large frowns upon is not the bilingual aspect of those returning children, but those social distractors of bilingualism that seem to upset the norms of Japanese society, such characteristics as independence rather than dependence; self-reliance rather than group-cooperativeness; innovativeness rather than conformity; rational-legal authority rather than accepting personal authority" (p. 113).

Still, these are reactions of the society at large, and we would expect administrators and educators dealing with foreign teachers to be sympathetic to differences between Japanese and non-Japanese social behavior. Such is not the case, however. After five years of living in Japan and interacting with Japanese employers, I would generalize that few of them understand the goals of young Western teachers, and even fewer sympathize with—let alone approve of—those goals. This is no place to present a full-blown cross-cultural study. However, I will state a few of the areas or situations in which deep misunderstandings may occur, and I will try to explain the sources.

Young Americans, particularly those with recently-completed professional educations, expect to prove themselves as soon as they are hired. Thus, a young assistant professor may propose a new program and offer to guide it. In Japanese faculty meetings, however, the most recently hired members are not expected to speak unless spoken to, and new members are never expected to put forward suggestions about changing departmental procedures. Young teachers working in Japan, unless their programs are headed by Westerners, would be best advised to remain silent.

Young people from the West, unfortunately, often feel they have to prove their worth and demonstrate their value systems through what they consider appropriate behavior. Young Japanese realize that in Japanese organizations their first duties are to learn who holds power, how things are done, and how to avoid offending anyone. Seniors naturally expect this behavior from their subordinates. Therefore, those who behave differently will create confusion, if not open hostility.

Those who challenge such a system may win a minor victory—only to find that the results did not merit the effort. Other reactions are depression or a cynical retreat into the classroom, or into one's private life if, as in some language schools, the classrooms have microphones for monitoring teacher behavior. Tales of mistreatment are many, and one dissatisfied teacher even started a journal to deal with "both the positive and negative aspects of conversation teaching in Japan." In the first issue, he wrote criticisms of several language schools, claiming that even American managers can be indifferent to the goals of their employees.

Two areas that I have found rife with misunderstandings are goals and truth. In a general sense, Japanese do not care to state goals. The purpose of most language programs, as a result, seems to be survival. Change is entertained only if the existence of the program is threatened. If a foreign-language teacher suggests that two fifty-minute lessons a week would be more productive than a single 100-minute class, presenting the plan at a meeting and asking for a decision would make no sense from a Japanese point of view. Properly, such a proposal would require months and years of informal contacts with colleagues. And, even when such a proposal is raised informally, a Japanese must weigh the consequences of assisting a foreigner in achieving a goal that may never have been considered in the past. Thus, novel requests for assistance and information may result in misleading information or silence. Incidentally, you can usually get exactly one special favor from a Japanese chief executive, so I advise non-Japanese teachers in Japan to think very carefully before making their one request.

Misleading information and silence are but two of the strategies employed by the Japanese in dealing with "the truth." Because of Aristotelian prejudices (things are either A or non-A, etc.), some Westerners tend to believe that what they hear is what they may expect to experience. When in a wicked mood, I sometimes say that truth in Japan, like other contract variables, is negotiable. When in a more expansive mood, I state it this way: When Japanese discuss a proposition, they always try to be as agreeable as possible.

Accepting the request of another person, a Japanese may well be thinking, "Certainly such a case would be pleasant for this fellow. However, he must realize that we are only discussing the best possible case, and what we intend to achieve must always be subject to future circumstances"—such as if the negotiator should change his mind later. Somehow, this line of reasoning makes sense in Japan, people accept it, and society continues to function. I realize that I have neither the knowledge nor subtlety to explain this dilemma accurately. However, I would suggest that Westerners who receive glowing promises from Japanese should consider the Spanish phrase, *"Mi casa es su casa."* Obviously, your host does not expect you to take possession of his home. Promises, I have found, are often best-case scenarios that are subject to change. My recommendation is that you never leave yourself only one option. Always keep two channels open. In particular, do not make it known that you have accepted or are contemplating a new position until that new position is a reality.

A big difference between Japan and the West is the absence of collegiality—you are not a "fellow" anything. Chie Nakane explains that teachers do not exist on a plane with those of similar interests and achievements. They line up behind a central power figure who guards his own position by promoting the interests of his subordinates. Each new relationship entered upon is evaluated in terms of this long-range scheme.

Moreover, Japanese employers load responsibilities upon new employees. This ultimately benefits native Japanese, who assume positions of power as they grow older. Young non-natives are expected to work as hard, but they will never experience the rewards. Similarly, employers have no concern for your *personal* career—the concept is alien to them: one advances with a group. Therefore, you are outside the system and are treated alternatively as an honored guest and possibly as a showpiece. Ultimately, however, you are likely to be treated as an expendable human resource—very much in line with historical treatment of *Gästarbeiter* in Japan.

What, then, are the points at which a foreigner can contact Japanese society, or more importantly, how can he or she survive? Here are several suggestions, some only half facetious:

1. Throw yourself upon the mercy of a Japanese superior and pledge absolute support.
2. Get your own office and stay there.
3. Teach on a free-lance basis after arranging a legal but non-demanding justification for being in Japan.
4. Marry a wealthy Japanese and have the family buy you a language school.
5. Put your emotions in suspended animation during your working hours, and depend upon [Western] friends for emotional support.

15

6. Study Japanese, make friends with your fellow workers, and hang in there.

I've chosen the last one, simply because the Westerners whom I know who are happiest in Japan have taken that path.

The Japan Association of Language Teachers—JALT

One of the easiest ways to get an idea of current English teaching activities in Japan is to become a member of the Japan Association of Language Teachers—JALT. Membership entitles you to the monthly magazine *The Language Teacher,* and the twice-yearly *JALT Journal.* Each *Language Teacher* contains over fifty pages of useful information: articles that give advice on teaching techniques for Japan; reviews of local meetings and announcements of future meetings (JALT had twenty-one chapters as of January 1986); interviews with noted language teachers, both in Japan and abroad; opinion columns; letters; language text advertisements; book reviews; and even a few notices of teaching positions. The *JALT Journal* contains theoretical essays on language learning and intercultural communication, drawing contributions from scholars throughout the world, but also includes extended practical essays on methods for teaching specific information or dealing with particular classroom settings in Japan. (Send membership requests to JALT, Kyoto English Center, Sumitomo Seimei Bldg., Shijo-Karasuma Nishi-hairu, Shimogyo-ku, Kyoto 600, Japan. Telephone: 075-221-2376. Foreign membership is $30; local membership is ¥6,000.)

Local chapters are found in Sapporo, Sendai, Tokyo, Yokohama, Hamamatsu, Nagoya, Osaka, Kyoto, Kobe, Okayama, Hiroshima, Takamatsu, Matsuyama, Fukuoka, Nagasaki, and Naha. Membership entitles you to attend any chapter meeting for free or at a reduced member's charge. Most chapters hold monthly meetings at which an experienced teacher describes classroom techniques or the theory behind an instructional approach. Such meetings are valuable for making contacts and learning about job openings.

The high point of the JALT year is the annual conference, held for three days every autumn at a different location. The conference for 1984, held in Tokyo, featured experts from Japan and overseas giving over 200 workshops, demonstrations, and lectures. Among the featured speakers were Stephen Krashen, Peter Strevens, Michael Swan, and James Alatis, executive secretary of TESOL (Teachers of English to Speakers of Other Languages). A random selection of the presentations included "Technology English for Anybody," "English Teaching Contexts in Japan," "Principles in Teacher Refresher Courses," "ESP for Nurses," "A Reading Workshop," "Introducing Japanese Children to English," and even "Origami for Language Teaching."

Nearly all colleges, many high schools, and some commercial language-instruction programs pay transportation and expenses so their teachers can attend conferences such as JALT's. Besides the opportunities to learn, attendees can meet or make friends, search for jobs, and have a good time in a new city. Before my first JALT conference in 1982, I had had six months of frustrating and rather unproductive experiences in the classroom. At JALT '82 I heard speakers who had not only shared my experiences but had discovered methods of dealing with the problems. I returned to my school with a broader understanding of my responsibilities and a number of techniques for dealing with them.

The first Japan-wide conference of language teachers, in 1975, was sponsored by the Language Institute of Japan (LIOJ) in Odawara. It was not until the following year, however, that the forerunner of JALT, the Kansai Association of Language Teachers (KALT), was established in Osaka. KALT sponsored a weekend conference at the Kyoto YMCA in August of 1976, continuing the tradition begun by LIOJ. The following year, organizations of language teachers in the Tokyo and Nagoya areas were formed, and these joined with KALT to form the Japan Association of Language Teachers the same year. Also in 1977, JALT was recognized by TESOL as their Asian affiliate, a connection which has continued and strengthened to the present day. With more than 300 members nationwide, JALT became an established organization in November 1977, when the third conference was held in Nagoya as "TEFL Japan '77."

Since then, JALT has grown to more than 2,700 members, slightly more than half of whom are Japanese, with approximately 100 members living outside Japan. JALT is the largest affiliate of TESOL in Asia, and has recently become a branch of the British-based IATEFL (International Association of Teachers of English as a Foreign Language). Admirable as JALT's size and affilations may be, I respect the organization for simpler reasons. I have found that the leadership responds personally and directly to requests for assistance and advice. At meetings and conferences, everyone is on a first-name basis, and anyone willing to help is welcome. Although local and national officers receive certain privileges such as free admission to conferences and reduced membership fees, in the year I served as program director of the Hiroshima chapter I saw that many JALT expenses were met by officers out of their own pockets—they seemed to put in more than they took out.

JALT gives language teachers in Japan a chance to speak as well as listen. Local chapter meetings and national conferences provide a forum at which to present research findings or share instructional techniques. *The Language Teacher* accepts well-written reviews and articles, and encourages teachers to share useful methods in the "My Share" column. The *JALT Journal* offers a chance for scholars and teachers to present their research results. I most appreciate JALT, though, because it brings together teachers, both non-native and Japanese, who desire to improve their skills and are willing to help one another.

Japan: An Introductory Reading List

First-time visitors to Japan should certainly learn something about the country before traveling and should carry several reference works as well. These should include a history, a description of the country today, an evaluation of the society and the psychology of the Japanese, a Japanese-English phrasebook, a guide, and a map in Roman letters. Many books are published in English about Japan, so there should be no difficulty locating materials. The two major Japanese bookstores, Kinokuniya and Maruzen, can supply literally hundreds of books related to Japan. The following titles have been useful to me. Some are controversial, but I recommend them in order to open a dialogue rather than make a final statement.

History

Edwin O. Reischauer. *Japan: The Story of a Nation.* New York: Knopf, 1970, etc. Also Rutland, VT, and Tokyo: Tuttle.

DIVERSE PERSPECTIVES

The Country

Don Maloney. *It's Not All Raw Fish* and *Son of Raw Fish*. Tokyo: The Japan Times, Ltd.
Jack Seward. *The Japanese* and *More About the Japanese*. Tokyo: Lotus Press.
Momoo Yamaguchi and Setsuko Kojima. *A Cultural Dictionary of Japan*. Tokyo: The Japan Times, Ltd.
Research Committee for Bi-Cultural Life in Japan. *Now You Live in Japan*. Tokyo: The Japan Times, Ltd., 1985.
Janet Ashby. *Gaijin's Guide*. Tokyo: The Japan Times, Ltd., 1985.

The Society

Chie Nakane. *Japanese Society*. London and New York: Penguin, 1973.
Ian Buruma. *A Japanese Mirror*. Middlesex and New York: Penguin, 1985.

Psychology

Takeo Doi. *The Anatomy of Dependence*. Tokyo: Kodansha, 1973.

Language

Osamu and Nobuko Mizutani. *Travelers' Japanese*. Tokyo: The Japan Times, Ltd.
Say It in Japanese. New York: Dover Publications, Inc.

Guides and Maps

For these publications, contact the Japan National Tourist Organization, which supplies them with no charge. JNTO has six branches in the U.S., and one each in Canada, England, and Australia. [JNTO, 45 Rockefeller Plaza, New York, NY 10020. Embassies and consulates will be able to supply other addresses.]

19

Getting Started with Children in the EFL Classroom

Ronald Zavislak

NATIVE SPEAKERS OF ENGLISH who come to Japan often become involved with English education. Some are hired by schools solely on the basis of their ability to communicate in English. These jobs involve classes of adult businessmen or local housewives who pursue English as a hobby rather than a means of communication.

However, one of the most rewarding experiences for the language instructor is the day when his or her student or students are able to communicate some basic idea in the target language. Instructors working with children can achieve rapid progress toward this goal depending on their teaching skills, their environment, their goals, and especially their innate sense of fun when dealing with children. The speed with which children learn and their unhindered curiosity toward new things makes them the most interesting, enjoyable, and yet challenging of students. In this essay, aspects of environment and getting started with children will be considered.

Who Are the Students?

Scanning the English newspapers and local bank or university bulletin boards, a person can easily find openings for teaching English. In recent years the market for teaching children has been expanding considerably for a number of reasons. Many Japanese families are being sent abroad as Japan's international trade expands and Japanese companies increasingly locate branches overseas. The parents would like their children to have some familiarity with the language, often English, before going abroad. Upon returning to Japan, they feel it would be a waste if the child lost what language skills he obtained in the country he had visited.

Secondly, there is an increased awareness that children's learning and language habits are easily formed at a younger age, and that waiting till junior high school to acquire a second language is too late. Other reasons include simply allowing the child to enjoy English in order to form a favorable attitude toward using English and meeting foreigners. Last are those parents, particularly education-oriented mothers, who feel that English ability is one of the most important factors in obtaining entry to a good university or company.

In dealing with children in a class or individually, these various reasons must be considered at some point in order to direct the goals of the class to satisfy both the school and parents.

Prospective Teachers and Types of Jobs

The wide variety of people in search of a teaching job is too broad a field to cover completely. However, there are some general categories. There is the student whose basic goals in Japan are not to teach English but to advance his or her cultural background in Japanese, Japan, or any other area (martial arts, cooking, tea ceremony, flower arrangement, or pottery). This person is usually looking for a short term, financially beneficial position. Another type would be someone who already has a permanent job or occupation and turns to teaching children for extra income or for variety. These people usually seek or make a semi-permanent commitment. The third type is the person educated in EFL or sufficiently interested in it to make a vocation of it. Some of these teachers, wanting to remain here semi-permanently, or because they have found their calling so to speak, elect to teach children. These people I would classify as long-range prospects.

Turning now from the types of job seekers, let us look at the types of jobs available. Here again the variety is overwhelming, but from my experience the types of jobs available can be categorized generally. The private home or language exchange program (English for Japanese) is probably one of the first types of jobs a person in Japan would come into contact with. It usually involves several hours of teaching per week with remuneration in the form of meals, room, and perhaps a small fee for one's trouble. A strictly "time for pay" system is preferable here as payment in kind and the other types of remuneration usually involve obligations that later become burdens. For example, in a room and board situation, one might end up being on call day and night to provide proofreading, translation, or English outings with the kids and their friends more often than was originally bargained for.

The reverse of this would be classes held and taught at one's home and convenience. This type of situation is created by offering to teach the landlord's or adjoining apartments' kids for a small fee per kid/per hour, or one may advertise locally with a sign on the door, in the window, or on telephone poles in the area. These jobs are particularly well suited for the person studying here who wants to teach part-time for extra income. There are advantages and disadvantages with this system. The main advantage is that you teach what you want at your convenience—with no travel, rent, or other expenses. The disadvantages are that during vacations or in the case of long absences your income is rather unstable. Also you have children and parents coming into your apartment, leaving you little privacy. Your teaching materials will also have to be individually created.

The third type is a franchising operation whereby a company provides materials, students, and advertising, and you work on an hourly basis. Here you are limited to the texts, materials, and programs they've set up, as it is their outlet for their materials. This type of school usually accepts both part-time and full-time teachers.

A fourth type is a language school that contracts out to kindergartens or elementary schools. The language school provides teachers for elementary schools or kindergartens and is allowed to use the facilities for its own English classes. The language school also acts as a very important go-between: it provides the teacher with an hourly wage, and the school or kindergarten with a fixed commission or one based on student number. This is usually beneficial to all parties. Schools and kindergartens often want to add English to their curriculum and are willing to provide classroom space and students, but are unwilling to barter and argue with a foreigner or go through the trouble of recruitment and selection (though a few do). Some of these language schools leave the curriculum up to the teacher, or provide a little help. Others provide complete training and a teaching program. It would be wise to check these points before signing on. In some kindergartens or schools, a Japanese teacher or helper is provided. As the students usually turn to that teacher when they don't understand you, they don't pay as much attention to you as they would in a class without an assistant. However, depending on how the teacher incorporates the assistant into the class and lesson, this person can be a valuable demonstrator of the language. In this type of teaching situation, you would probably be sent to a different location every day. This type of language school would probably require a full-time commitment.

There is also the language school whose classrooms or schools are permanently located, which gathers the children from the surrounding areas by advertising and word of mouth. The school I'm involved with is a combination of the permanent-location and kindergarten-classroom type of school. Depending on the language school's size and on the responsibility it feels toward the children, part-time or full-time jobs are available.

Finally, if one is lucky enough to have connections, some of the private elementary through university schools have English programs available in their elementary schools. Usually these positions involve teaching two or three days per week, and as previously mentioned are acquired through introductions. Your pay would be on an hourly part-time scale, but the long hours required for this type of job would tie up much of your week.

Applying for the Job

At some schools you would be hired on sight for fitting the qualification of being a foreigner. It may be more difficult at language schools if you are second generation Asian—part of your job is the role of a foreigner, and you may not look foreign enough. If you get involved with this type of school, you can be sure they're not interested in the children's education, but only in a short-term money-making project. Most schools whose purpose is educational as well as financial will require a personal history, particularly focusing on one's educational background (very important here), probable length of stay, and visa status. At some schools recommendations or introductions can be influential.

Each school or institution has its own criteria for determining prospective teachers, but let me discuss what may be considered. Appearance is important. Though it would seem self-evident that a person applying for a job should be clean and well-groomed, modern trends tend toward the "dress-as-I-like" style. In Japan, the teacher must look and act the role to command the respect the title of teacher has entitled him to. With children, a shirt and tie may not be required, but generally blue jeans and no socks would be regarded unfavorably and probably deemed disrespectful by children and parents alike.

A college degree (preferably in language or education) is necessary, as well as experience in dealing with children. Language ability in Japanese would usually be regarded highly, though some schools would debate this point. My own feeling is that when dealing with children Japanese language ability is valuable. Communication and rapport, as well as clear understanding by both teacher and student of what is happening, can be achieved more quickly and successfully.

A prime concern at our school is longevity. Most schools require a one-year contract (though immigration may only give you six months). We like most of our teachers to make a two-year commitment. Children usually take a few months to adapt to the teacher's rules and style. It also takes the teacher this much time or longer to understand his students, depending upon his level of rapport and language ability. Actual forward progress and development can usually be seen after about six months, leaving the teacher and students only six months of progressive learning under a one-year contract. Some will argue with this, but in a new environment both teacher and student will be in a state of semi-confusion initially—whether or not the class be new or old, or the teacher experienced or not. At first, the children will be checking to see how far they can go with the new teacher, and the teacher will be trying new things, learning new materials, and seeking out the levels of the children in his class. There is a tendency for students in classes that change teachers often to have a looser commitment to each other and to their studies: the class eventually breaks up. This results because the teacher must continually backtrack and cannot create a progressive learning environment. At most schools, however, one year is the common length of contract.

Remuneration

In Japan, any occupation paying hourly or daily wages is considered and taxed as part-time work. A salaried job fares a little better but one must be careful to figure out whether the salary is reasonable on an hourly basis. I will not mention pay scales because the cost of living changes rapidly, and differing expenses in city and country create too many variables to permit even an average pay scale. If you get paid by the hour, you should inquire if you get paid when you're sick, or when your teaching days fall on national holidays. Some schools do and some don't. There are twelve national holidays in Japan, with those falling on Sunday taken on the following Monday, so your Monday teaching jobs will bring in considerably less over a number of years if you are not paid for holidays. There are also spring, summer, and winter vacations to be considered. Even if the school operates, attendance will be so small that many schools take time off during these vacations. As a result of holidays and vacations, the actual number of classes ranges from about 38 to 42 classes per year at a once-a-week school. A full week of teaching is considered twenty hours here, but again you should inquire whether you will be paid for the 5 or 10 minutes between classes, or only for actual "in-class" time. If a salary is chosen, this usually eliminates holiday and break-time problems, but you should total the hours put in per week or month to see if you would be getting a comparable amount if working hourly.

If traveling time is long, this can be a loss in earning time. Some schools pay for transportation to and from work and others only partially for transportation. If you work at a fixed location two or three times per week, a commuter's pass might be a reasonable investment, with the school paying part or all of the cost, if some agreement can be worked out. Travel time also depends on where you locate in relation to the classroom. For example, rent might be relatively cheaper outside of town, but the time and money for train fares might make it more practical to get an apartment nearer the job's location.

If employees are paid hourly, the tax law requires the employer to withhold 10%, like it or not. If you are on salary, withholding tax usually ranges from 4% to 7%. Some of this can be recovered when you file your Japanese tax return at the beginning of the following year. It is usually through the company's tax records that visa violators are caught. Another minor point should be considered. In writing the sponsor letter for your visa, the company will state that it will guarantee your return fee to the U.S. or your home country. However, this is only a matter of form, and you will be paid only if such payment was agreed upon when the contract was signed.

Finally, after deciding upon full-time or part-time, large classes or small classes, and the type of school you'd like to work for, you should evaluate the local market to decide what pay is reasonable for that area and type of class.

Classes

You've got your visa, pay, holidays, transportation, and length of commitment worked out, and you feel satisfied until you enter the classroom. Some schools will allow you to watch classes to give you an idea of what you're getting into. Others keep it a trade secret till you've joined. At our school, it's a requirement to observe classes before deciding. You should check out various methods and schools to find the type that suits you. But let's face it, if you want to work with children that means lots of action and energy on your part.

Class size can range from 25 to 40 students at elementary schools or kindergartens, to four to twelve students at small language schools, or even one or two students at the homes of the children. The approach and energy used will be considerably different, and teaching time will also vary. Some schools have a two-time-per-week program, while most offer from 45 minutes to one hour per week. Classes may be mixed or combined, according to either English level or what grade they are in. Personally I find that students of the same age or only one year apart in school are the easiest to teach, as the children's interests and dislikes change with age and grade.

As for class size, six to ten students is an ideal number: teams can be made, and the shyer students can initially hide in the group. As Japan is a group-conscious society, the children find it easier to react in that kind of atmosphere. Some schools will take you into a class, give you their texts, and say teach. Others will provide materials and ideas. These two types of schools are common. Full-fledged teacher-training programs for teaching children are few and far between in Japan. Even the major language-teaching conferences have few lectures on teaching children. At our school the teacher will observe classes, be given written as well as oral explanations and demonstrations, or be asked to do some substitute teaching before being assigned classes. Also one or two meetings for idea exchange per year are held.

Finally, though I have taught many types and sizes of classes, my main experience is with children in classes of four to twelve students ranging from upper level kindergarten through elementary school. In most cases, you'll probably be dealing with younger children, so I would like to turn my attention to some "getting started" ideas.

Getting Started: Goals

In the English conversation class many times the teacher is apt to lose sight of what he or she would like to achieve. This leads to an over-enthusiasm, in which the students are overburdened with homework as the teacher attempts to get them to a higher level. A lack of direction in the class is the other side of the coin, leading to the same material being taught for two or three years with little substantial student progress. The term "English conversation" itself expresses such a wide goal; and what has taken us a lifetime to accomplish, we expect our students to master in one or two hours per week! Adding up one hour a week including vacations for holidays, summer, and winter, we see that the student gets 35 to 40 hours of language per year—a mere three or four days of exposure to English. It is not surprising that many people will say, "Taro has been studying for 5 years and still can't discuss politics in English." What has taken us a lifetime to accomplish is expected of Taro in a mere one month of exposure to English.

Obviously, a child studying swimming, piano, or crafts has something tangible to show for his efforts and his parents' money, for these are easily measured (though not easily attained) skills. English, on the other hand, is not so easily measured or performed. If the child, when forced to say "good morning" to every foreigner he meets, doesn't perform, the English lessons come under suspicion. Language, we must not forget, is a habit or a skill and the child's only use and practice of this skill is in your class. It must be obtained through practice over a long period of time. It is like swimming or any other sport in that one can understand how to swim without being able to swim: furthermore, one can achieve a level of competency in swimming but not be able to swim the butterfly or breaststroke. English conversation must be given as much or more time and practice as any other skill for the results to become visible. Does that mean teaching English on a one or two hour per week basis is a losing proposition? In some ways I would say yes; but in others I would give an emphatic no. So take heart, and let's go on!

One of the first things necessary for teaching is to gain a rapport and establish communication with the students. This is one area where the use of the native language can be as important as the target language. I believe some skill in the children's native language is necessary. Others may disagree, but using their own language when establishing trust, rules, and understanding goes a long way. It helps the teacher have an EFL class for children that moves along at a pace fast enough to prevent attention loss and smooth enough to accomplish a good many things in the limited time available. With university students, I never use the native language. With children, however, at times I feel it is necessary to clarify the meanings, verify the child's understanding, or just to find out why Ichiro was jumping up and down (not out of joy at the new game but because he needed to visit the toilet).

Some ways of improving or developing this rapport on the first day are determined by age group and class size. With children from kindergarten age up to second graders, I would pick up everyone over my head. The teacher teaches up and down by physically lifting the child and gently putting him or her down. This serves many purposes. One is that after everyone in the class has gone up and down, a bond of unity has been formed. We all experienced something thrilling together! Another is a sense of trust that has been developed. The child helpessly lifted into the air has visions of being dashed to the ground like he has seen the professional wrestlers do, only to be brought down to a safe landing (whew!). He can trust this big guy. As a supplementary advantage it also shows that the teacher has the physical power to enforce, if the need arises, the rules of the class.

Other techniques for younger children are physical touching: shaking hands, with a "Hello"; tickling with "Tickle me, please" demonstrations; and touching the teacher's nose, hair, mouth, and ears (watch out for ruffians), accompanied by "brown hair," "soft hair," "big nose," and so forth.

Using the children's names as much as possible helps to hurry the pace of a good teacher-student relationship, particularly if the teacher has some way to make his name memorable and fun. As my name, Ron, is easy, the children somethimes call me "Ran Ran the Panda" or "Zavislak" becomes "Zabuton," a cushion in Japanese. A word of caution here might be that the name the teacher is called should at no time be disrespectful, so the choice of good clean fun names is necessary. Also feigned disappointment with laughter when children misuse the teacher's name should be followed by a challenge as to whether the teacher's correct name can be produced. As a name is very personal, teasing using the children's names should be done only with extreme caution, and with everyone equally, as when in the second year I ask the children what would happen if the first letter of their name were changed.

Finally, proximity is important for communication and rapport. Sitting on the floor in a circle promotes a warmer and closer atmosphere than having two or three tables between the children and teacher. Also, overactive children can be kept within arm's length for a tap on the knee or shoulder in times of crisis. This does not mean that tables and chairs are never used. A table may be necessary for writing and board games. The point is that close proximity usually means a warmer, more informal, and more controlled class situation.

What about the older children? As children get older, the teacher can work more with explanations of things and a wider range of vocabulary—rather than just pantomime and persuasion—to develop rapport and communication.

Discipline

In Japan, generally speaking, discipline has not been a large problem in children's classes. Recently, however, the number of homes where both parents are working is increasing. This has had, in many ways, an effect on how well-mannered the children are. The area one teaches in, the level of the school, and the parents' occupations also have a strong bearing on the type of demeanor the child and class will have.

Respect for the "teacher" has been on a steady decline, as is evidenced by an increase in school violence in Japan. Children teasing and bullying any child weaker (physically or educationally) has become common. The impression of television on the children's use of their own language, and a flippant if not disrespectful attitude toward Japanese and English as languages, have been the result. How does this affect the EFL class? In many cases I have seen classes where 85% of the teacher's time and energy go into controlling one or two rowdy children and only 15% goes into actual teaching. Should a child be able to show disrespect, or not respond to the teacher's appeal for discipline, the general atmosphere of the class will be destroyed. Here I would like to discuss a few of the problems and make some suggestions for dealing with them. Of course the child, class, parents, and teacher's attitude must be considered before taking any drastic measures.

The first day you arrive in class the children will, of course, be fairly well-behaved. The unknown reaction of the teacher to any lack of discipline is still to be seen. Some teachers take an overly strict attitude the first day, and the children are scared to death—not only to do anything wrong but to do anything at all. Initially I was this type. My method now is to have a huddle to discuss discipline problems and how they will be handled. This requires using the native language (and could be done with a Japanese-speaking person on the first day). In the huddle I tell the kids that we're going to have fun at times, be serious at times, and just fool around at times, all with fairly clear signals designating the transitions. These can be commands like "By the count of three be back in your seat" or just "Let's get serious now." My rule is patience until the third time. I tell the kids if I feel something is out of line. I'll warn them once, tell them I'm angry the second time, and use punishment the third time. Punishment can be a number of penalties, from saying "I'm sorry" in English, losing points in a game, extra homework, to a physical slap on the knee. Physical punishment is not regarded as bad here, but it isn't thought of as very good either. You won't be hit with a lawsuit if you do it for good reason and as a last resort. In eight years of teaching I've only needed it on two or three occasions. I don't advocate its use, and how the reaction to it is handled is just as important as its use.

Rules decided on in advance, an interesting class, and fast pace usually prevent the occurrence of any act needing such methods. Use of disrespectful language at any time in the class toward the teacher or fellow students is prohibited. Usually an "I'm sorry" elicited on first violation and losing points in a game for his team brings enough peer pressure to bear that the student will reconsider his language. If a child has been censured, bringing him or her back into the group and showing that all has been forgiven by you the teacher is an important aspect of discipline. If a child has continuing problems, these can be discussed with the child alone first, then with the parents. If conferences have no effect on the child, the class is more important than that child and his monthly fee; but in some situations, like at a kindergarten, the problem of discipline will have to be faced in every class.

The type of rule infraction should also be considered. In the heat of a game emotions run high, and slips of behavior occur. After all, they are children. It is easy to excite children, but returning the class to a controllable learning situation is not always easy. However, voice variation, counting to three, or starting a song or new activity work well in regaining control.

Inevitably, the teacher will face the hyperactive student. He blurts out everything, can't sit still, and has an attention span of five to ten seconds. He should be kept near the teacher and made to feel a responsible part of the class (teacher helper), while being penalized through losing a game or point or apologizing when the teacher is striving for serious class concentration. The bully is another type. Usually giving him some class responsibility, such as teaching other students if he is a bright boy, or helping if not, will give him the attention he wants through constructive means. If this doesn't work, a final resort is to tell him the next time he wants to pick on someone, you'll be available to give him a go at it.

Whatever the situation, discipline not only is your responsibility as an educator, but is also important for class rapport and for any learning situation. Defining your rules for the class or any game clearly and strictly will prevent many problems from occurring. Handling the problem quickly, firmly, and fairly is necessary. Finally, giving the child a chance to rejoin the group, to feel that he still can be your friend, and the option, through some activity, to make amends, will benefit both you and him in the eyes of the class.

In conclusion, much depends on the commitment you are willing to make (part-time or full-time), the level you are going to teach, the size of the school, and its materials and training program. All of these determine the level of enjoyment you will get from teaching children. It should be stressed that any material taught with enthusiasm and creativity will be successful. Any game or activity done for the first time will probably end in confusion or only partial success: give it another chance! Pacing is important, long explanations or large amounts of time spent on any activity will have a tendency to destroy its interest factor. Speed and variety not only maintain interest but allow students weak in one game or area to become heroes or successful in others. Keeping the children close to you and active will help eliminate discipline problems or prevent them from arising as the children's energy will be focused on learning rather than plotting against the teacher. Children are much more sensitive than older students to the true feelings the teacher has toward them and toward teaching. This will be reflected in their progress and in the enjoyment you and they experience in the EFL class.

English for Children: Child-centered Language Acquisition

Walter Enloe, Philip Lewin, and Randy Morris

TWO PRINCIPLES underlie all of the suggestions that we will make concerning how to be a successful teacher of English to Japanese children. First, a child, as part of his nature, wants to learn. A successful teacher will build upon the child's desire to participate actively in the learning process. Second, a child will learn the most from a teacher who is open and compassionate, from a teacher who first creates a classroom ambience of trust and support, and only secondarily is concerned with activities and lessons.

A teacher must be aware that children think differently than adults do, and that the cognitive abilities required to think like an adult are the result of a long process of biological maturation that is not complete until the age of 15 or 16. As a result, children between the ages of 5 and 13, whether they are Japanese or American, possess ways of thinking and learning that are radically different from those of adults. And these patterns of thinking, learning, and interacting also differ among age groups. For this reason, good teachers must be aware of the particular cognitive, emotional, and social capacities of their students, and devise methods of instruction that are age-appropriate.

You should also be aware that children between the ages of 5 to 13, whether Japanese or not, are playful and enjoy cooperative activities. Moreover, they are oriented toward concrete objects and activities, and not toward abstractions. Above all, they are easily bored or distracted if the learning environment is not responsive to their natural tendencies for

35

trust and friendship, for playfulness and cooperation, and for challenging and concrete tasks.

Perhaps the most frustrating problem confronting the teacher of children is that of maintaining order in the classroom, particularly with the youngest ages. Our experience has been that Japanese children between the ages of 5 and 8 are considerably less disciplined than their American or British peers, while Japanese children between the ages of 8 and 13 are more disciplined. The problem of discipline is exacerbated by the fact that the teacher often does not speak Japanese well enough to make his demands understood to his students. Of course, many of these dynamics depend on class size, the ratio of boys to girls, and age. But clearly, teaching English to a class of 20 six-year olds is an extremely demanding task. However, while teaching English to Japanese children between the ages of 5 and 13 presents unique problems to the teacher, it can also be extremely gratifying, offering the opportunity for personal ties of trust and affection to develop between student and teacher.

This article will present a theoretical context through which to understand children, and will then provide some concrete suggestions for teaching a child-oriented, age-appropriate English curriculum. But there is no single *best* method of teaching English to children. What is required is a balanced approach that uses a variety of techniques and materials, and that takes into account how human beings learn and develop. Above all, teachers need to be active learners, ever experimenting and revising techniques, learning from their mistakes, and trying to keep up with progress in their field.

On Teaching In General

Every teacher makes certain assumptions, often implicit, about learning and teaching. These assumptions act as a lens through which learning and the learner are viewed. It is important that a teacher make these assumptions as explicit as possible, especially since many of them may need to be modified in the course of a teacher's career. Many young teachers have preconceived notions of what constitutes good teaching, based on the methods with which they themselves were taught rather than on experience of how children actually think, feel, and act. Our approach to teaching and learning is based on the assumption that children are born with the ability to build or construct knowledge as they interact with their environment. This "active" approach contrasts sharply with the so-called "passive" approach frequently taught in university education departments, which assumes that children are empty receptacles into which the teacher pours information through repetition, stimulus-response exercises, and techniques of rote learning.

Let there be no misunderstanding, however. The receptive modes of memory, passive obedience, and imitation of the adult are as natural to the child as spontaneous activity. But they alone are not enough. Education, like medicine, is both art and science. To be an effective teacher, you must develop your own gifts of empathy and creativity, and refine your understanding of the child as you acquire more experience in the classroom. The passive view sees education as simple instruction, in which the child receives already perfected information produced by adults. The active perspective sees the child as builder, experimenter, and collaborator, who follows his interests to actively create and reinvent what he learns. You as a teacher must learn how to facilitate active, as well as passive, learning.

On Teaching Children in Japan

Four social contingencies should be noted when considering English-language instruction in Japanese culture. First, Japan is the most literate society in the world, and by the age of 12 children have learned three different phonetic alphabets (including Roman letters, beginning in grade four) and have mastered at least 960 Chinese characters. All students study English for several hours a week, starting in grade seven. Second, the emphasis in English classes at Japanese schools is on grammar and reading comprehension, and not on speech. Most high-school graduates can read and write what they want to communicate, but cannot say it. From our experience, most educated Japanese adults understand English grammar as well as most American high-school teachers of English, though they are not proficent at, or even capable of, simple conversation. A recent international survey showed that while the Japanese are in the top 5% of English-language comprehension among the peoples of the world, they are in the lower 20% in conversational ability.

Third, Japan, though having a rich and unique language base of its own, has borrowed heavily from those countries which have influenced its trade and culture, including the Chinese, the Koreans, and even the Portuguese. But we can think of no better example of second-language assimilation than the introduction, particularly after World War I, of English into Japan. According to authoritative sources, there are some 2,000 loanwords from English in the Japanese language, and though most are highly scientific or technical, there are some 200-400 words known by the typical 12 year old taken directly from English (though most never recognize that they are English derivatives). Finally, a cursory tour through the supermarket or several hours of watching TV will convince you that "English is everywhere," from labels to advertisements, from commercials to T-shirts. Ask your students to open their *bags* and take out *pencil box, notebook, pencil,* and *pen* (all English loan words). What is surprising is that the English phrases written on these products (or the T-shirt, or spoken in the commercial) are rarely understood even by those who have studied English for six or more years in school.

Psychology and Teaching Children

Our ideas on psychology and education have been influenced by Jean Piaget. Piaget's work is important because his insights provide tools for encouraging the learning process. Specifically, Piaget's work has provided an empirical basis for the idea that children develop through a series of "stages" of understanding. Each of these stages provides a unique perspective on the world. In Piaget's view, the child literally constructs his knowledge about the world as he interacts with his physical and social environments. Children create what they know through actively making, inventing, and experimenting with the concrete objects that they encounter. What are the implications of this work for language instruction? We will divide our discussion of activity-based pedagogy into three parts—the cognitive, the social, and the emotional.

Cognitive. The mind is constantly assimilating new information. This assimilation slowly increases the mind's ability to acquire new information, in turn making new insights into the world possible. As a result, the child is always unlearning and re-learning what he has already mastered as well as acquiring entirely new knowledge. The driving force of the knowing process is activity, first with physical objects, then with ideas. The child must be free to construct and alter his own understanding. He should not be forced to learn only from a single perspective, or with the sense that there is only one right way.

Two implications emerge from this view. First, the child should be understood as an intelligent, knowledge-seeking learner who has already mastered a huge quantity of information prior to his or her first English lesson.

A second implication of this view is that learning grows from the concrete to the abstract. Children first learn by manipulating objects; then they gradually abstract from these physical objects until they are performing actions abstractly, purely in thought. For the teacher of English, two very important ideas follow. First, especially for younger children, no English word or phrase should be introduced without a concrete object or action to represent it. For instance, when teaching introductions, two people should always be facing each other with an appropriate backdrop to indicate the context (e.g., a night sky drawn on the blackboard to indicate that it's nighttime when you teach "good night"). Likewise, each vocabulary word should be introduced with at least a picture of the object to accompany it, or better yet, the real object itself (e.g. have plates, forks, spoons, and napkins in hand when teaching these words and the contexts in which they are used). This is especially important when teaching the alphabet. We have found such devices as blocks or "alphabet worms," which have a separate block for each letter and which fit next to each other only in the correct order, to be very useful. Or you can purchase cards with sandpaper letters, blindfold the children, and see if they can recognize the letters by tracing their shapes. The challenge of teaching children comes in making up a variety of games and activities, a "bag of tricks" using concrete materials.

Second, because knowledge begins with the concrete, children should be given a variety of contexts in which to use their knowledge. Parroting or repeating a stock phrase in a single stiuation does not mean the child really understands. The child should be able to use the phrase and act appropriately in various situations, even, in more advanced classes, to rephrase its meaning in his own words. Short skits and role playing are effective means to accomplish this end.

Emotional. The key word to consider when thinking about the emotional life of children is empathy. The teacher must be able to see the world, both physically and emotionally, from the perspective of the child. A major obstacle to empathizing with children is "adultcentrism," or the tendency to view things only from an adult's standpoint. Good teachers must be willing to get down on their knees, both literally and figuratively, in an attempt to see the world from their students' perspective. Only this way, for example, can you understand why children at the ages of 5 and 6 frequently draw human faces with two circles to represent the nose, for this is how the nose appears when looked up at from below. We suggest, therefore, that before each new class, the teacher should enter the classroom from a child's point of view. Spend a few moments sitting in a child's seat and imagine what it must be like to be on the receiving end of the day's lesson.

Further, it is not enough for an adult teacher to marvel at the fact that many five year olds believe the moon follows them wherever they go, or that monsters lurk under their beds. For the sensitive teacher, the question should be how do these and other equally "inaccurate" beliefs (from an adult's perspective) fit into the child's total view of reality, and how can these notions be extended and manipulated to further his understanding. The point here is not to "correct" the five year old's belief system, but rather to co-exist within it and to share its wonders. From this standpoint, the teacher is better able to help build, rather than "correct," the child's understanding.

Another major obstacle to empathizing with your Japanese children will be your own ethnocentrism, the tendency to view things from your own cultural viewpoint. But class atmosphere, teacher expectations, teacher-student relations, and student-student interactions for your Japanese students are all very different than they were for you. Only by becoming active students of Japanese culture can good teachers begin to understand the subtle but critical differences between class dynamics and expectations in Japan, as opposed to in their own countries. We especially encourage prospective teachers to visit as many Japanese schools as possible, and as many grades as possible, perhaps with a Japanese friend to act as an interpreter. Just walking the halls of Japanese school (don't miss break time) can greatly enhance your understanding of what your students are accustomed to. Such a visit also provides a common experience you can share in class discussion. Children prefer to talk about familiar things, and they will be greatly impressed that you took the time to visit one of their schools.

There are several crucial points to keep in mind when empathizing with a Japanese child in an English class. First, remember that most of these children, especially the younger ones, are only present because their parents want them to be. For many children, this is counter-productive to the learning process, and it takes patience from you to sustain their interest. On the other hand, wanting to learn is natural for the child, so the problem is not so much to win their interest initially (they will come to you with curiosity, at the very least), as it is to refrain from dulling it. Avoid an overly rigid curriculum that disrupts the children's own rhythm and pace of learning.

You can expect to encounter a certain number of behavior problems from your students, but you can be certain that behind every overt problem there is a reason. The younger the child, the greater the likelihood that the main factor behind a behavior problem is a parent, usually the mother. In Japan, anxious mothers so frequently prod their children to overachieve that they have earned a special name for themselves, the *Mama-gon,* or "Mother monster." In fact, stress on schooling, and particularly the severe competition to matriculate at a prestigious university, leads to a great deal of anxiety on the part of Japanese students. Remember, too, that your older students may be involved in a great number of extra-curricular activities, including *jukus,* or special "cram schools," aimed at giving the child an academic advantage.

Another point to remember is that you are a foreigner, perhaps the first one these children have known, and as such you are serving the very important function of role model. From their interaction with you, your Japanese students will form the first (and probably the most lasting) impression of what *all* foreigners are like. Good teachers should try to be conscious of how their personality is being projected through their actions in the classroom. Messages of international friendship and cooperation are best expressed, not through the formal teaching curriculum, but through non-verbal qualities of warmth and understanding. In other words, a well-timed smile can be worth more than a whole essay on international cooperation.

Since the teacher is serving as a role model, whether he likes it or not, he is advised to become a learner again. Many people who teach English to Japanese students have had no formal English-teaching experience.

But beginning teachers can be just as effective as more experienced teachers if they are willing to maintain a friendly and open attitude toward their students, try to keep informed of current knowledge about teaching, and are aware of the biases of their students against learning English. Most important, the teacher should learn from classroom feedback, from the questions the students ask and the verbal and non-verbal messages they make concerning class activities, homework, etc. A good non-verbal message to look for is the inevitable ''restless squirming'' that signals it is time to end one activity and to begin another.

Social. Finally, we would like to mention the social context in which your students are learning. Recent research in child psychology has returned again and again to the importance of peers in the middle years of childhood. The period between 7 to 13 is the period when close friendships first form, and when the child enters a larger social universe than the one provided by his family. Peers serve as teachers, guides, and role models during this time. There is no doubt that children learn a great deal of factual information from their peers, but the most important thing they learn is a general conception of how they ought to behave: for instance, whether learning is important or not, or whether the teacher deserves respect. In Japan, although the infant and pre-schooler are restricted in social interaction to the immediate family, and are completely indulged within that context, this initial socialization to a group norm is even more pronounced than in the West. It is through the society of the classroom and playground that the Japanese child internalizes the patterns of deference to authority and group consensus that will characterize his adult life.

What does this mean for you? A classroom's atmosphere is shaped in large part by the response of the students to the teacher's message rather than by the teacher's message itself. It is important, therefore, for the formal expectations of the classroom to be kept within reason, and for the teacher to realize that a spontaneous group game or song is not simply a waste of time or a challenge to his authority, but serves the vital function of promoting class unity through shared activity.

A good barometer that will indicate the patterns of social interaction in your class is the seating arrangement the children assume upon entering the room. Usually, boys sit on one side, girls on the other. Rowdy boys usually sit together, near the rear. Since these spontaneous seating arrangements are a source of information to the teacher, we suggest that you allow them to take place naturally before making a minimum number of judicious choices in separating the troublemakers. Usually, the removal of one person will serve to make your point clear. It is unfair, though, and will interfere with the learning process, if you do not at least give a chance for the rowdy element to work together. Be aware also that boy/girl relations (or the lack thereof) are crucial elements in your students' worldviews, and should not be treated lightly. It is important when separating students that a boy not be forced to sit right next to a girl, or vice-versa. A face-saving alternative should be found. Boys and girls work well together in competitive situations and in group efforts like singing.

Since much negative behavior arises from students goading one another to be "bad," we usually put the perpetrator in a chair in the corner of the room where he or she (usually he) can still hear and see the lesson, but is separated from the group. It is an example of the group's power that being separated from it is usually sufficient punishment to resolve behavioral problems. Misbehavior in the corner chair can be dealt with by expelling the student from the room. Consistent behavior problems by the same student are symptomatic of deeper issues, and must be dealt with by communicating directly with the parents. In general, remember that your teaching influences and is influenced by the group dynamics of the classroom, and that the teacher is responsible, primarily through the force of his personality, for maintaining a cooperative class atmosphere.

Linguistics and Teaching Children

One of the most important questions in the education of the child, and particularly in the teaching of language, is whether language, provided from without by the adult, stimulates the development of thought solely through imitation or whether it is the child's cognitive capacities that reconstruct language according to his own understanding. The answer to this question has far-reaching consequences for teaching.

At present, there are three general trends in linguistic theory which give different answers to this question: the structural, the transformational-generative, and the developmental.

The structural approach holds that the mind absorbs language through imitation. The classroom method that follows from this view relies greatly on repetition, and a typical textbook based upon the structural approach combines dialogues for memorization with substitution pattern drills. Transformational-generative theory, pioneered by Noam Chomsky, argues that language acquisition results from an inborn ability to generate sentences, which unfolds as the infant matures. The ability to absorb a first language, then, develops automatically as the mind develops. But Chomsky himself has warned that his theories may hold little value for the acquisition of second languages, and attempts to apply his theories directly (e.g., adding transformation drills to substitution drills) have met with limited success.

We believe that the developmental approach holds the most promise. The developmental approach incorporates the perspective of the transformational-generative apporach, but goes beyond it. Developmentalists argue that what seems to be innate in terms of thought and language capabilities is acquired through the child's active experience of building knowledge. Language is not ready-made, but must be constructed through the general cognitive actions of classifying, ordering, and corresponding, and moving from the concrete to the abstract. Thinking is the basis of language acquistion, and activity is the basis of thinking.

In this developmental view, verbal language is but one of several important semiotic, or sign, functions. These also include symbol formation, dreams, mental images, deferred imitation, drawing, dramatic play, and object play. All of these forms of thought co-develop in the child with verbal language, and all have their origins in the child's activity.

A child's language is often a misleading indicator of what he knows and thinks. If a child really understands what is said, for example, he should be able to act appropriately, rephrase the meaning in his own words, and most importantly, be able to modify the basic sentence construction to express different but related thoughts. Mere parroting or repeating is not the same as true understanding. The developmental perspective, which stresses pedagogy based on concrete activity, will best facilitate and support children's acqusition of linguistic competence.

Pedagogy and Teaching Suggestions

The developmental perspective demands a child-centered rather than a teacher-centered classroom. Typically, teaching is a rigid, unidirectional affair in which the teacher guides or "runs" the child through a pre-arranged curriculum of "lessons." The successful learner in this situation is the child who does exactly what he is told, and precisely regurgitates what is heard. The poor learner is the one who does not pay attention or listen well. In contrast, the developmental perspective recognizes that children have different rates and styles of learning as well as different degrees of interest. This perspective maintains that learning results from an interaction of child, materials, and teacher, in which the experience of the child is as important as the prepared material in promoting learning. A child-appropriate curriculum recognizes the existence of a variety of developmental levels, and attempts to match learning materials to the capacity of the individual learner.

Generally, it is suggested that children learn to hear before they speak, and speak before they read and write. We believe that if this approach is taken too seriously, the integrated features of communication are fragmented. We suggest that this sequence only serve as a general orientation for you in your teaching, for we have been very successful in helping children as young as six years of age develop these four communicative functions simultaneously. Our success is based on (1) patience, (2) clear goals, and (3) the utilization of a variety of activities that "stretch" the learner in active and thought-provoking ways.

But the question immediately arises: individualized learning sounds great, but how do you do it when you have only one hour a week to teach 12 children of different ages, abilities, and interests? The standard solution seems easy: teach to the typical child, or to the majority. However, this approach requires that the teacher not only neglect some students but teach using rigid lesson plans. When teaching includes appropriate strategies that increase flexibility, however, the class becomes more rewarding for teacher and student alike. Though child-centered teaching is more demanding and requires more thoughtfulness than the standard approach, it is also more successful. The child becomes an active learner, not a passive recipient. You may recall experiences from your own schooling that indicate that a person learns not what is taught but what he or

GOSHEN COLLEGE LIBRARY
GOSHEN, INDIANA

she decides to learn, and that the most important learning is not so much content (what) as process (how and why).

Our first suggestion, then, is for you to define the goals you have for a particular class. Sometimes your employer, through a curriculum syllabus or particular text, will provide you with specific goals for the particular class, but more often than not, you are the professional ''native English speaker'' and teacher. It is up to you to determine the goals for your teaching based on the ages of your students, their familiarity with English acquired informally or through previous classes, and the actual class time per week. We suggest that you try not to lean too heavily on your textbook. Current textbooks are attractive and colorful, with plenty of pictures and sequential exercises. But English study involves a set of interrelated skills that are all part of the single act of communicating: speaking, listening, reading, writing, acting, and observing. These skills cannot be taught from a textbook alone.

Usually students will study with you an hour per week, and it is this time factor, more than aything else, which will determine what you will and will not accomplish. If you can, divide the time available into several periods per week. Two or three 30-40-minute periods will facilitate retention and maintain interest better than one 60-90-minute period.

Realize that your students will not learn to speak English with conversational fluency. But do not let this deter you from making your best effort, and do not let it lower your expectations of what children can accomplish. Bear in mind that your beginning students will receive English-language instruction in the public schools for at least six years, and most will continue to take English classes in university. It is not necessary for you to achieve miracles with them. However, you should lay strong foundations upon which further study of English can be built.

The single most important task to accomplish is to build an atmosphere of trust within which the child will not be afraid to make mistakes. Having created this atmosphere, realistic goals which you can help children achieve include:

1. Overcoming hesitation in interacting with foreigners;
2. Acquiring proper English phonetics;
3. Recognizing English loan words, words they already know;
4. Learning letters, numbers, and a basic sight vocabulary;
5. Acquiring basic patterns of English syntax.

Within these overall goals, we suggest you keep the following teaching principles in mind:

1. Emphasize practice and activity in the classroom. Don't explain too much, and don't talk too much. Let your students do the work.
2. In any lesson, try to incorporate speaking, hearing, reading, and writing, usually in that order.
3. Emphasize learning the alphabet, both the names of the letters, and their phonetic equivalents. Students should know the alphabet and phonetics well enough to recognize them, even when they are presented in random order.
4. Use number and color words.
5. Use a basic sight-word vocabulary to supplement phonetics for irregular forms, e.g. "was," "saw." (We have included a basic list of the most common English words at the end of this article.)
6. Use only the present tense of "to be" and "to have."
7. Teach a basic sight-word vocabulary for common English sentence patterns, e.g. "what is. . ." "that is. . . ."
8. Practice writing by pointing with fingers in the air, letting your students practice the muscular movements involved in writing. Then do it on paper.

The First Class

In a first class, remember that you are far more threatening to your students than they will be to you. You do not need to "impress" them. Instead, just relax and enjoy yourself. The most important thing you can establish at the outset is a sense of rapport with your students, which of course will grow as you come to know one another better. Japanese students are very shy, so be patient and kind. With beginning students, have a simple game ready—say a color recognition game—that you can use to involve them from the outset in a non-threatening way. With more advanced or older students, you might begin by volunteering information about yourself, and asking students in turn a series of easy, neutral questions such as "Have you been outside Japan?" "Where do you go to school?" "Do you have any brothers or sisters?" Try to discover some of their specific interests—cars, sports, life abroad, etc.—which can be used to prepare classes that will be of natural interest to them. When you ask questions, do not ask general questions of the whole class, but instead, ask particular individuals. If a student is reluctant to respond, respect his silence. Let the students learn they can trust you, that you will not humiliate or embarrass them.

Try to get a sense of the overall competence of your students. The sooner you ascertain this, the sooner you will be able to prepare lessons of the appropriate ease or difficulty for them.

A Typical Class

In a typical, one-hour class, try to include a series of activities that both keep the class stimulated and offer the students an opportunity to practice all the skills of communicating. An ideal class might include a short, ice-breaking introductory period, followed by drillwork involving hearing and speaking; then come pair work and concrete activities. Have enough variety to engage the children's interest in a limited amount of material. Don't overwhelm your students with new vocabulary or sentence patterns; instead, introduce new words in familiar sentence patterns, or new patterns using familiar vocabulary. Most of all, lessons should be planned that present the same materials in a variety of ways. Teaching that allows a student to creatively master the lesson enhances his sense of achievement and self-esteem. This not only fosters effective learning and retention, but also helps keep the child interested and motivated.

For instance, you might begin a class with a letter or word-recognition game (reading, listening) like "concentration," then have the students tell each other through question-and-answer what or how many letters/words they have (pair work, involving speaking/reading/listening/counting). You might introduce new material, such as animal names, by having a set of toy animals on hand. Students could work alone or in teams to try to "win" animals by remembering/writing the animal name. Again, this is an opportunity for question-and-answer based on concrete objects: "Who has the dog?" "How many cows are there?" "What color is the cat?" and so on. Finally, children could draw and label animal pictures, or invent stories in English about the animals, again, either alone or in small groups. In short, use concrete materials and the child's spirit of play to reinforce English-language skills.

Some Specific Strategies

Japanese children live in a world that includes an unusually large amount of English. The essential problem for Japanese students is that they are reticent or unable to speak English in conversation. So in teaching, try to build upon the concrete, using as a basis for language instruction what children have already experienced as part of their culture. Here are some specific suggestions:

1. Since most Japanese children by age six have learned from kindergarten and television the names of the English letters and their order in the alphabet, as well as color names and the numbers from 1 to 10, we may build upon this familiarity by teaching the short sounds that are difficult, especially the short vowels. To do this, we use letter cards and short words.

2. There are hundreds of words in Japanese borrowed directly from English. In teaching vocabulary, these words should be used whenever possible, especially at the beginning. (Dictionaries of English loanwords are available at bookstores, and we have included a basic list of them at the end of this article.)

3. Try to use concrete words, and nothing is more concrete than food names that are borrowed from English. So we have, from A to Z, apple, banana, cake, doughnut, egg, fruit, grapes, ham, Indian curry, jam, kiwi, lettuce, milk, nuts, pineapple, quiche, raisin, salad, toast, umbrella chocolate, violin gum, x-ray gum, yellow gum, and (inedible) zebra. (Ask, "Do you eat a zebra?") The point is to make your teaching familiar and funny. Try to provide a base you can build on.

4. The next step is to substitute words for sounds (for example, for "b," try bus, ball, baseball, base, ballet, balloon, baby—all loanwords).

5. Alternative approaches might include learning to sing the "ABC" melody using short letter sounds rather than letter names (i.e., ah, buh, cuh, duh, eh, fuh, etc).

6. We suggest further that children, using flash cards (both group and individual sets), learn the letter names and short sounds in varying orders so that they are known with flexibility and facility.

7. A child really knows the names of the letters of the alphabet when he can sing the ABC melody with the letters in random order—for example, B D G K I J M, etc.—and still know their phonetics.

8. Furthermore, if the teacher introduces concrete materials, for example, real apples, bananas, and oranges, kids can eat what they can speak.

9. Acting out their speech patterns reinforces what they are taught by you. By actually holding a slice of apple or orange while talking about it, the learning of additional grammatical patterns is facilitated, based on inquiry such as "What is this?" "What is that?" "What is his?" "Who has an apple?" "How many apples does she have?" "What color is the banana?" and so on.

To teach reading, we incorporate the necessary skills into our instruction in other basic aspects of English. Typically, reading is taught by memorizing the alphabet and then acquiring a sight vocabulary that is sometimes supplemented by phonics and word-attack skills. We emphasize the opposite aporoach. First, by emphasizing phonics, we are able to meet our goals of hearing accurately and producing the correct pronunciation, and only later recognizing (reading). Second, children learn the alphabet sounds and names by writing them following basic manuscript exercises.

For instance, within a thirty minute period, we can:
1. introduce food names;
2. write letters based upon the sounds heard by tracing manuscript patterns with our fingers in the air;
3. then produce them on paper;
4. respond verbally to letters and sounds; and
5. play various sound- and letter-recognition games.
6. One clear favorite is to have two sets of letters on small cards (3x3 cm) for groups of four of five children. The cards are turned over one by one, and then matched (much as in the game "Concentration"). The game may be modified to practice sounds, letter names, words beginning with a certain letter or sound, and words themselves.

We have found that the use of cards and card games is of such tremendous educational and social benefit to children that it is indispensable in our classes. First, from the child's point of view, cards are interesting and fun. Second, they are concrete and they provide activities in which children can help make the materials. Third, they bring the teacher and the children playfully together on terms of equality. Most importantly, card activities are an excellent way to introduce, reinforce, and extend vocabulary and grammatical patterning in the active and cooperative context of gaming. A successful game with numerous variations for children as young as five builds on the card game, "Go Fish." You may remember that in "Go Fish" each player receives five to seven cards from the deck and each player in turn asks another player for a "red six" or "black Queen." If the other player has the card it is given to him and the pair is placed in front of him; he continues by asking another player for another card. However, if he asks for a card (e.g., "black Queen") and the other player does not have it, he takes a card from the deck ("goes fishing") and his turn ends. By creating card decks of pairs of numbers, letters, words, pictures, etc., children learn to ask and respond to questions such as: "Do you have a red six?" "No, I don't have a red six" and other appropriate questions and responses (e.g., "Pass 2 cards to the left," "Who gave you 2 cards?" etc.).

Another example of this kind of play with purpose is to have children raise their hands to identify letters, letter sounds, words, colors, numbers, objects, or pictures of objects. For instance, first hold up a card with the letter B. A student responds with the name or sound of the letter. Second, review by asking, "What is this?" "That is a B." Third, give a word that begins with the sound of that letter (e.g., *banana*), or use objects or pictures. Make sure you have several cards beginning with the same letter or sound (e.g., *ball, boy, bicycle,* etc.) to both reinforce the sound and to give the less proficient child a chance to answer. Then, when the cards are exhausted, ask how many cards each child has and ask the children to return the cards by saying, for example, "Who has B?" "Where is B?" "Give me B" "How many B's do you have?" etc. By the end of the year, the children should be able to lead these exercises themselves. We extend this card play in the following ways to reinforce alphabet names and sounds and to build up a sight- and family-vocabulary as discussed below. As children master the alphabet you can offer a sequence game played individually or in groups. You say (and hopefully later a child will lead), "C," "A," "T," and the children place the cards in front of them or a team holds them up in order. Points may or may not be kept, but keeping them does build on the natural inclination of children to compete. Gradually as you ask children to repeat the letter sequences you can facilitate their recognition that the letter order of "C," "A," "T" spells cat, which can then be written on paper or cards. Conversely, the teacher can say the word "cat" and the children can make it with the cards.

Concurrently, we provide children with word rings and word boxes (such as file-card boxes) for word families (e.g., words ending in -an, -at, -ap, -en, -et, etc.) and cards with short words that children can read on sight. Initially, the sight words are words used in basic conversation. The word ring (sold in every Japanese stationary store) begins with the alphabet. At first, we present the alphabet in order, upper case and then lower case; next, we randomly shuffle it on the ring as the child masters the letters. We have found that children most often memorize and remember the letters in the order of "A, B, C. . ." But to know a letter is to recognize it no matter where it appears.

Using the word ring and word boxes as our "universe," we can combine these letter and word cards to construct sentences that can be heard, spoken, read, and written. For example, if we are working with the basic grammatical forms of "This is a . . ." "What is this?" "Is this a . . .?" and words to match concrete objects, such as *a pen, an orange, a bag, a pencil, a cup,* etc., then each of these words can be written on separate cards and placed in front of each student. As the teacher asks questions ("What is this?"), the students can take their cards and order them into the question ("WHAT" "IS" "THIS" "?") and then form the appropriate response ("THIS" "IS" "A" "RED" "PENCIL" ".").

What we are suggesting here is that learning not only must be based upon real objects and concrete activities (including role playing, puppets, drawing, and arts and crafts, including those traditional to Japan, such as origami), but that the activities need to build upon the child's pleasure in inquiry and enjoyment of creative dissonance. Too often the primary learning mode in the classroom consists of responding directly to the teacher rather than asking a peer, who responds in turn to you. One of the most successful teachers we have known was a woman who taught her students not simply to answer a question, but to respond and then ask another question in a sequence repeated several times. For instance, child A would say, "What is that?"; child B would respond, "This is an orange. What is that?"; and so on. This kind of teaching not only reinforces basic sentence patterns and vocabulary but also actively involves the child in what is in reality a simple English conversation.

By creative dissonance, we mean the child's natural tendency to take pleasure in being challenged. Children gain a vital sense of mastery and self-respect from solving problems that are within their range of competence, yet that stretch their ability to perform. This tendency can be a very powerful tool for a teacher. If exploited properly, it will keep the class alert and involved, and promote authentic learning. Many word games—such as anagrams and simple crossword puzzles—or communicative pair work and problem solving can be used with creative dissonance in mind.

Becoming a Better Teacher

Finally, no matter what teaching situation you find yourself in, we recommend that you learn to evaluate your teaching seriously by seeking feedback from other teachers, by continuing to read and discuss with other teachers your ideas and strategies, and above all, by asking yourself each time you plan a class:

1. What am I going to have my class do today?
2. Why is it important? What is it good for?
3. How do I know?

These questions will help you reconsider what you do. At the least, they may make you uneasy about simply following the prescribed curriculum or passively repeating what you were taught or have read is the best thing to do or the best way to accomplish it. If you evaluate what occurs in your class with a two-way mirror, both from your perspective and from that of your least interested students, you will pick up valuable clues on how to improve your classes. Then try to answer honestly the following questions:

1. Does my experience and background keep me from understanding the behavior of this student?
2. What kind of efforts have I made to modify my teaching strategies and style in order to make what I am teaching more accessible to him?
3. To what extent do I reward a student simply for saying what I want to hear, whether or not he understands what he is saying?

You may find your answers to these questions to be disturbing; at the very least, they will be informative. As a native speaker of English, you already have the skills necessary to teach Japanese children successfully. You are in a privileged position where your competence will not be challenged, but where your compassion will. Through paying attention to your students' responsiveness and your own feelings, you will have the opportunity not only to become a better teacher, but to understand better your overall experience in Japan.

Resource Books

We have found the following books to be helpful in understanding children or in providing specific activity-oriented strategies for the classroom:

Games for Second Language Learning, Gertrude Nye Dorry, McGraw Hill, New York, 1966.
Language Teaching Games and Contests, W.R. Lee, Oxford University Press, Oxford, 1979 (includes an excellent bibliography).
Pinch and Ouch: Acting Games, Yoko Nomura, Lingual House, Tokyo and Tucson, 1982.
Pinch and Ouch: English Through Drama, Yoko Nomura, Lingual House, Tokyo and Tucson, 1982.
Piaget, Education and Teaching, D.W. McNally, New Educational Press, Sydney, 1973.
Contemporary Influences in Early Childhood Education, Ellis Evans, Holt, Rinehart, Winston, New York, 1981.

Supplementary Materials

In order to help you in your teaching, we have provided the following supplementary materials:

1. A basic sight-word vocabulary.
2. A list of common English loanwords.

Basic Sight-Word Vocabulary

a	believe	chair	door	flower	half	island
able	belong	child	doll	fly	hand	it
about	below	children	double	foot	handle	its
above	best	chimney	down	for	happen	it's
after	better	circus	draw	forward	happy	
afternoon	between	city	drink	found	hard	juice
again	big	class		four	has	jump
all	bird	clean	each	friend	hat	just
almost	biscuit	climb	ear	frog	have	
already	black	close	early	from	he	keep
also	blouse	clothes	earn	front	he's	kept
always	blue	cold	eat	fruit	head	key
am	boat	color	egg	full	hear	kind
an	book	comb	eight	fun	heard	knew
and	both	come	either	funny	heavy	knife
angry	bottle	could	elevator		help	knock
another	bought	cousin	end	game	her	know
answer	box	country	engine	garage	here	
any	boy	cover	enough	garden	herself	lady
anything	break	cow	escalator	gave	high	large
apple	breakfast	crayon	even	get	hill	last
are	bridge	cried	ever	giant	him	late
around	bring	cry	every	girl	himself	laugh
as	brother	cup	except	give	his	leave
ask	brought	cupboard	eye	glad	hold	left
at	brown	cut		glass	home	leg
ate	build	dad	face	glove	horse	let
aunt	bus	dance	fall	go	hot	life
baby	busy	danger	far	goes	hour	light
back	but	dare	farm	going	house	like
bag	buy	dark	fast	gone	how	lion
ball	by	day	father	good	hurt	listen
be		dead	favorite	got		little
beautiful	cake	desk	fell	grandfather	I	live
because	call	did	few	grandmother	I'd	long
bed	came	didn't	fierce	great	if	look
been	can	different	find	green	I'll	lose
before	can't	do	finish	grow	I'm	lost
began	car	does	fire	guess	in	love
begin	carry	dog	first		Indian	lovely
behind	cat	done	fish	had	into	
being	caught	don't	five	hair	is	machine

made	not	please	see	take	try	while
make	nothing	police	seem	talk	turn	white
man	notice	pretty	seven	tea	twelve	who
many	now	pull	shall	teacher		whole
marry		push	she	tell	uncle	whose
may	of	put	shirt	ten	under	why
me	off		shoe	than	until	will
mean	often	queen	shop	thank	up	window
meet	oh	quick	short	that	upon	wish
men	old	quiet	should	that's	us	with
might	on	quilt	shovel	the	use	without
milk	once	quite	show	their	used	wolf
mind	one	quiz	sing	them	usual	won't
minute	only		sister	then		word
miss	open	ran	sit	there	very	work
Miss	or	read	six	these	voice	world
money	orange	ready	skirt	they		would
month	other	real	sleep	they're	wait	write
more	our	really	small	thing	walk	wrong
most	out	red	so	think	want	
mother	oven	rice	some	this	warm	year
mouse	over	ride	something	those	was	yellow
mouth	own	right	soon	though	wash	yes
Mr.		river	sought	thought	wasn't	yet
Mrs.	package	road	spell	three	watch	you
much	page	roll	square	through	water	you'll
must	pants	rough	start	time	way	young
my	parcel	round	station	to	we	your
myself	part	run	still	today	wear	you're
name	party		stood	together	weather	
naughty	path	said	stop	told	weigh	zipper
near	peace	salt	street	tomorrow	well	zone
nearly	pencil	same	such	too	went	zoo
need	people	sauce	sugar	took	were	
neither	pick	saucer	sun	top	what	
never	piece	saw	sure	touch	when	
new	pig	say	sweater	toy	where	
next	place	school		train	whether	
no	play	scissors	table	tree	which	

English Loanwords in Japanese

apron
American
autograph book

baby car
baby shoes
baby wear
beach ball
beach towel
beach wear
bed cover
bedroom
bed jacket
beef
bell
biscuit
black coffee
boat - speedboat
boat - sailboat
bonus
bookcover
bookend
boots
boss
bowling
boy friend
bucket
bulldog
bus
butter
buzzer
bye-bye

cake
camp
candy
captain (team)
card (index)
case (pencil)
cash register
catch ball
cement
chain
chalk

chance
change
check
chicken
chocolate
Christmas
cider
class (school)
classic
club
coffee
cola
collar (shirt)
collection (stamp)
collie
color - film
color - hair
color - school
commercial (TV)
communication
computer
concert
concrete
control tower
corduroy
corned beef
corner (field, ring)
cost - down
cost - up
count (baseball, boxing)
court (tennis)
cream
crew (rowing)
cup (paper)
curry
cushion (not *zabuton*)
cut
cutlet

dark blue
dark green
dark grey
date
decoration cake

denim
department store
dessert
dining kitchen
dock
door
double
doughnut
dry cleaning
dry ice
dump truck
dynamite

egg
error
eve (Christmas)
evening dress
excite (athletics, concert)
extra (film)

fan
fan (sports)
fight
film
first base
flannel
fly (baseball)
fork
foul ball
fresh
fruit cake
fruit juice
fruit parlor
fruit salad
fry (food)
frying pan

game
gang
gas
gasoline stand
gift card
gift shop
glass

57

glove
goal
Golden Week
gossip
gray
green
ground (baseball)
group
guest (TV show)
gum

hair brush
hair pin
hair style
half - size
half - time
ham
hamburger
handbag
handkerchief
handle (door)
happy end
heavy smoker
heavyweight
hello
highway
hit (ball, song)
home drama
home plate
home run
home wear
hose
hostess
hot coffee
hot drink
hot sandwich
hurray

ice cream
image - down
image - up
ink
instant - coffee
instant - ramen

jam

jean pants
jet
juice

kick (ball)
king - size
kiss
kitchen

laboratory
lamp
league
lemonade
life mask
life work
lighter
loose fit
loose leaf
love (tennis)
love letter
love scene

maker (manufacturer)
mama
manners (court, table)
mansion
mass communication
mass production
medal
meter - barometer
meter - cab
meter - measurement
milk
modern dance
modern jazz
mood (music)
motor boat
motor oil

napkin
net (sports)
new face
new fashion
new town
no iron
noodle

note
now feeling
number (one)
number (license)

oil (auto)
overcoat
pajama
pants (underwear)
papa
parking (auto)
parts (auto)
part-time
party (formal)
party (mountain climbing)
peanut
pen
permanent wave
picnic
pink
pool (swimming)
pork
post box
present
print (mimeo)
pro
plastic
pudding
puncture

radio
radio speaker
    (loud speaker)
raincoat
rain hat
rain shoes
range (cooking)
record
remote control
request (radio)
rice
rink (ice)
romance
room cooler
running (sport)

safe (baseball)
sailing
salary man
sale (store)
sandwich
service (customer)
set
sharp pencil (mechanical)
sheet (bedding)
shepherd (dog)
shoot
shirt (under)
shirt (white)
shop
shopping center
short (baseball)
short hair
short skirt
shot (soccer, hockey)
slipper
snack
snow tire
snowmobile
socks
soda

sofa
soft cream
song - commercial
song - folk
sports
sports car
sports shirt
stand (sports)
star (film)
steak
speed
spelling
stocking
stove
strike
style
summer coat
summer wear
supermarket
supertanker
sweater
sweet corn
sweet potato

toast

tomato sauce
T - shirt

ukulele
unique

violin
volleyball

waitress
water ice
water polo
wedding cake
wedding dress
wedding march
weekday
weekend
window (shop)
winter sports
wool (clothes)

yacht

zipper

Teaching in Japanese Senior High Schools

Laurence M. Wiig

JAPANESE SENIOR HIGH SCHOOLS follow various models that serve different purposes. Virtually all require prospective students to pass competitive entrance examinations. There seems to be no policy, such as prevails in some other countries, that guarantees a youngster's right to a high-school education. However, nearly all Japanese students do attend high school.

There are a number of conventional categories of senior high schools in Japan, and a prospective foreign teacher would do well to understand them before signing a contract to teach in a senior high school: private college preparatory, public college preparatory, semi-rural multi-track, public commercial, private commercial, public technical, public agricultural, private technical, and others. On the whole, Japanese teenagers seem, increasingly, to be attending all-girl or all-boy senior high schools, and a foreign teacher is quite likely to be placed in a single-sex school.

To a teacher from a liberal tradition, Japanese senior high schools will probably appear to be rigid institutions. Almost all senior high schools require their students to wear uniforms that have undergone few changes in design over the past 100 years. Much emphasis is put on rote memorization—of Chinese characters, of mathematical formulas, of English vocabulary items. Tests, whatever the subject matter, are generally made up of easily-graded little boxes or spaces which must be filled with a correct answer. Seldom are there essay-type questions on examinations, rarely are students required to give speeches in class, and never are questions encouraged. Schools do not hold "senior proms," and dating is not formally recognized by school officials. In general, students are required to wear their uniforms whenever they go out into the community, even on Sundays and other holidays and during vacations.

Almost beyond a doubt, Japanese senior high schools have played a major role in the modern "Japanese economic miracle." The schools have produced large numbers of compliant, unquestioning, capable employees for Japanese corporations, and the same sort of mothers and housewives necessary to carry on the society. This writer is hard-pressed to think of a more intense introduction to the inner workings of Japanese society for a Western foreigner than to be immersed in the day-to-day functioning of a Japanese senior high school.

The Purpose of English Education in Japanese High Schools

The Japanese are in many respects a huge, nearly-homogenous tribe living on easily-isolated islands. Few Japanese people, including most of those who make their income from teaching the English language in secondary schools, are ever called on to converse in any language other than Japanese. In the realm of foreign-language education in Japanese senior high schools, with extremely few exceptions, there is only one language which is considered worthy of study: English! French, Chinese, German, Spanish, Russian—although they might be studied diligently as foreign languages by high-school students in other countries, and are taught excellently on NHK, Japan's public television company—are virtually nonexistent at the secondary level in Japan.

English study serves a number of societal purposes, seldom verbalized, at the pre-college level in Japan:

1. It is part of an elaborate, intense rite of passage in which the more ambitious of the young people in this country demonstrate their capacity for drudgery and self-denial to the powers-that-be, and, in so doing, hope that they will be granted admission to the institutions of higher learning, which will lead to the best jobs the society has to offer.

2. For policymakers in education, it is a way of simplifying an overly complex world; there are only two languages on the planet that really matter: Japanese and English.

3. A marginal ability in reading English on the part of masses of Japanese people serves a commercial purpose in a business world that relies heavily on foreign trade for its prosperity. A fair number of employees in Japan are occasionally called upon to dissect a letter from abroad, or a pamphlet or advertisement in English. Even persons involved in the creation of advertising copy for internal consumption in Japan need to use a smattering of English words and phrases in their work.

The Purpose of Instruction in English by Native Speakers in Senior High Schools in Japan

Native speakers serve as English teachers at a limited number of secondary schools throughout Japan. One of their functions is to be an actual living, breathing, sometimes unpredictable representative of the some five billion non-Japanese people in the world. Foreigners about to start work in a Japanese high school, especially in one without a tradition of employing teachers from abroad, should be prepared for a surprising amount of naivete and ignorance concerning the feelings of non-Japanese people, the nature of language, and facts about other countries, on the part of administrators and fellow teachers as well as students.

A foreigner is likely to be hired to teach English at a senior high school in order to enhance the school's prestige, especially in its competition with other schools for qualified students. For this purpose, a foreign teacher who looks racially different from most Japanese people is likely to be given preference over other applicants. A foreigner on the faculty makes life interesting for all concerned, and a number of students are probably made more aware of their "Japaneseness."

Only a small fraction of Japanese high-school students learn to speak English, and any teacher who sets out to have a majority of his/her pupils start to converse in English is likely to have a frustrating and short career in this field. Classes are frequently large, many having forty or more students, and even if a foreign teacher is asked to teach classes with twenty to twenty-five students, the teacher is not likely to meet any given class of students often enough to develop significant conversational ability in the new language. Better students in any given school are generally interested in learning the kind of English that will help them in their academic careers, and although a foreign teacher is likely to meet many charming and pleasant students, the students will probably think of "real English" as that which they need for entrance into good universities.

At best, the majority of students exposed to a native speaker teacher of English at the secondary level will:

1. develop a slightly better ear for spoken English;
2. have some memorable experiences;
3. overcome some fears about foreigners.

Finding Employment at a Japanese Senior High School as a "Native Speaker English Teacher"

Is this the kind of work for you? Would you like to try a year or two of English teaching at a Japanese senior high school? Here are some suggestions about securing such a job.

1. Graduate from a four-year college. It does not matter which major you have a bachelor's degree in; it may simply be said that it is quite difficult to be hired legally to teach English in Japan, at any level, if you lack at least a B.A. or B.S. There are exceptions from time to time, but they are probably rare at the secondary level.

2. Read the excellent study by Thomas P. Rohlen, *Japan's High Schools*. To fail to do this simple task would be as foolish as a freighter captain trying to enter a new port without the assistance of detailed charts or a local pilot.

3. Start to learn spoken Japanese, if you have not already done so. (Imagine for a moment the frustrations of a non-English-speaking person attempting to function as a teacher of a foreign language in Scotland or Arakansas.) This writer is hard put to imagine a Japanese high school where a foreigner with no interest whatsoever in learning even a little bit of the Japanese language would be able to fit in.

4. If at all possible, visit Japan and get to know the country a bit. The Japan Rail Pass, available at Japan Air Lines offices outside of Japan, offers people coming from abroad the opportunity to see distant parts of the country at bargain rates. Wherever you go, make it known that you would like to visit high schools in order to meet students and English teachers.

5. Acquaint yourself with the Immigration Bureau and the laws, regulations, and policies it enforces. Japanese authorities can, on occasion, be particularly strict.

6. The best way for both the high school and the foreign teacher to make a contract which will provide maximum satisfaction to both parties is for at least one on-the-spot interview to take place. You might arrange such an interview while, say, living in Japan and teaching at an English conversation school or studying aikido. Many teachers have had interviews for English-teaching positions while in Japan as tourists. You are, however, responsible for observing immigration regulations.

7. Employment in Japan often depends upon personal recommendations and word-of-mouth information. You would do well to meet many people in the field of education, and to follow up on even far-fetched suggestions. Once you start to make your availability known, Japanese educators who have met you and who like you, but who are not in a position to offer you a high-school teaching job, can easily put in a good word for you with other employers. Of course, some lucky job-hunters find what they want by reading or placing a want-ad in the *Japan Times,* but I would guess that more foreigners find jobs in Japanese high schools by visiting schools, getting to know English teachers, and making friends.

8. Use your imagination. There are a lot of high school administrators in Japan who might be interested in hiring a native speaker English teacher. Have Japanese friends make phone calls and write letters. If you are outside of Japan, get to know Japanese people and let your desires be known. At any rate, sooner or later, it is quite likely that you will show up at a Japanese high school for an interview.

The Interview

Generally, you will not be invited for an interview unless you are considered as a very promising candidate. Put simply, there are not many foreign applicants around for most Japanese high schools to interview. There will probably *not* be a waiting room full of eager faces, so it is best to think of the interview as "your interview." You should take the opportunity to ask serious questions about the school, just as you will be asked serious questions about your background.

Before you sit down with the principal, or chairperson of the board, to discuss the fine points of a contract, get to know the school. For instance, you might ask to have the job interview in the afternoon, and to spend the morning visiting English classes, meeting teachers in the faculty room(s), eating in the lunch room, and the like. It probably would not hurt if you dressed conservatively, a jacket and tie for a man, a dress or suit for a woman.

Bring all the important documents you can think of, your diplomas, passport, alien registration certificate, transcripts of your college work, teaching licenses, past contracts. It will be appreciated if you have a resume, however simple, in Japanese. Be friendly with all the people you meet, and ask to be shown around. Be aware that most senior high schools are more interested in having a new teacher fit in with the faculty than in having innovative teaching taking place in their English classes.

To avoid embarrassment to your future colleagues in the English department, it is best to assume that any given native Japanese who is teaching English in a Japanese high school does *not* speak English. Use whatever little Japanese you might know in your initial meetings with the English faculty, and give them the opportunity to surprise you with their ability in English. Many are the foreigners with experience in Japan who have stories to tell about the inability of Japanese secondary school teachers of English to make their thoughts intelligible in English. To understand the reasons for this seemingly paradoxical situation, the high-school job applicant is strongly recommended to read *Japan's Modern Myth: The Language and Beyond* before going for an interview. Roy Andrew Miller, in this book, explains how the Japanese education establishment long ago decided to "de-conversationalize" the English language. One of the curious side effects of this policy is that there are, throughout the land, countless secondary schools that employ English teachers who are practically non-functioning in spoken English.

Be ready for a group interview. It is quite likely that you will meet at the same time with the principal, the vice principal, the business manager, and one of the English teachers. Some of the important questions you might wish to ask are:

1. Can you grade your students? If not, why not?
2. How many students will you have per class?
3. Will you receive the traditional Japanese bonus, paid annually or

biannually to Japanese employees? (Bonuses usually total more than four times one month's salary.)

4. Are the other teachers on contract? (The answer will probably be no.) Will you be on contract? How will the other teachers feel about your contract? Will you be free to talk to the other teachers about your pay and conditions of employment?
5. Will you be responsible for club and team supervision?
6. Will you work on Saturdays? If you want to be treated "just like one of the gang," then you should consider working six days a week as the Japanese teachers do. If you want time to be on your own, to travel, to recuperate, or what have you, it is possible to negotiate a full-time contract which includes only five workdays a week, but there might be some envy and resentment within the rest of the faculty. (Be advised that even five workdays per week, especially in a difficult high school, can be fatiguing.)
7. Finally, it is good to avoid complaining to a potential employer about your previous jobs, employers, or Japanese ways of doing things.

Administrative Structure of a Senior High School

Japan's High Schools by Thomas P. Rohlen will be extremely useful if you desire an overview of the structure of Japanese secondary schools. Dr. Rohlen spent fourteen months doing an in-depth study of five Japanese high schools in Kobe, which he blends very effectively with statistics and generalizations about most high schools in Japan.

What he explains in depth can only be touched on briefly in an article of this length. I was surprised to discover how similar the first high school I taught at in Japan, Hiroshima Daiichi Girls' Commercial High School, was to some of the high schools Rohlen describes. With that in mind, I will explain how Daiichi functioned administratively during my tenure, and hope that the description will help my readers to understand the operation of other high schools.

At the top of the structure, and quite out of touch with the daily functioning of the school, was the Chairman of the Board of Directors. This man visited Daiichi approximately once every month or two, primarily to consult with the principal and business manager, and occasionally to give a speech at an entrance, graduation, or other ceremony. The Board of Directors, or sometimes the Chairman alone, makes long-term, large-scale financial decisions, usually at the recommendation of the principal.

The principal at Daiichi was involved in the day-to-day workings of the school. He was a former teacher who had risen through the ranks to the school's highest paid job. The principal's office is spacious, calm, and impressive. There is a metallic bust of an old Shinto educator that keeps an eye on visitors to the office. Whenever I paid a visit to the principal, he would stand up from his desk and usher me over to the soft, upholstered chairs to have a chat. The principal would generally spend a number of hours every day reading publications about education and education administration.

Immediately adjacent to the principal's office at Daiichi is the business office. When I was talking with the principal, the business manager would frequently step into the principal's office to clarify a point or discuss some matter. Working under the business manager and seated near him at a typically Japanese cluster of desks were two female secretaries and a couple of male office workers.

From the perspective of the teachers and the students, the administrative center of the school is the faculty room. The so-called "vice principal" (the Chinese characters for the position actually mean "chief of instruction") dominates the faculty room like some kind of benevolent plantation overseer. It was my observation at Daiichi that the vice principal was to the faculty much what a homeroom teacher is to his/her 45 charges.

The vice principal arrives around 8:05 a.m. and sits at his desk at the far end of the faculty room, which contains some forty desks. The whole of the regular faculty arrives, or calls in late or absent, by 8:29 a.m. At Daiichi there are approximately 33 regular teachers. Substitutes are hired only when a regular teacher will be out for, say, two months or more. At Daiichi, the year I was there, the school had 22 homerooms, and 22 of the regular teachers served as homeroom teachers.

Homeroom teachers at Daiichi have many responsibilities. They meet their fifty homeroom students for approximately ten minutes at the start and again at the end of the school day. Students at Daiichi were seldom late or absent during my year there, and it was the duty of the homeroom teachers to make sure the students did not miss a minute of school. Homeroom teachers had to read notices, maintain accurate records for all the members of their homeroom, and oversee the cleaning of their homeroom after the last period of instruction. It should be mentioned that, except for receiving instruction in fields that require special equipment such as cooking, sewing, singing, sports, or tea ceremony, all members of a homeroom stayed at their desks in their homerooms hour after hour.

On Wednesday mornings during the first period, homeroom teachers would meet their homerooms for an hour, during which time they would play a parent role, guiding their charges into desired behavior. For instance, if the principal decided that throughout the school too many girls had been tinting their hair or having permanents, the task of reversing the trend would fall upon the homeroom teachers. (Incidentally, I heard reports that some students with naturally brown or slightly reddish hair would feel pressure to dye their hair darker in order to avoid the wrath of the homeroom teacher or principal for looking different from the vast majority of people at Daiichi.) Whenever a girl experienced serious legal, family, or academic problems, it was the homeroom teacher who had to counsel her, visit her home, or attend a parent's funeral.

A teacher who has a freshman homeroom one year will have a junior homeroom the next, though only a few of the students will continue with the same teacher. The composition of the junior homeroom remains the same when those juniors go on to become seniors, and this homeroom teacher stays with them through their senior year and quite likely will begin the cycle again with a new freshman homeroom the following year.

Overseeing the homeroom teachers for a particular grade level is a faculty member who serves as the grade-level supervisor. These three people, the freshman, junior, and senior grade-level supervisors, are some of the most powerful people in the school. They call frequent meetings of the seven or eight homeroom teachers under them, and I can recall only a few instances when a particular homeroom teacher failed to attend a meeting of his/her grade-level homeroom teachers. The remaining full-time teachers who are not homeroom teachers serve as student guidance supervisor, graduate placement supervisor, and assistants to these supervisors.

At 8:30 a.m. sharp, the recorded chimes sound, announcing the start of the faculty day. The principal enters the faculty room and walks to his special desk next to the vice principal, and the business manager goes to his special faculty-room desk on the other side of the vice principal's desk. The rotating "teacher-in-charge" for the day rises and says in a loud voice, "Well, it is now time. Let us perform the morning bow." The assembled faculty, administrators, the school nurse, and the librarian all rise and bow together. They quickly sit down again and the teacher-in-charge asks if anyone has an announcement; the vice principal usually has lots of them and asks permission, which is never denied, to give his announcements first. The vice principal first informs everyone which faculty members are late or absent. He will say something like, "Mr. Yamada is still sick, and Miss Tayama just called to say that she will be 25 minutes late because she had a flat tire." If any faculty member is tardy and has not called in, the vice principal will say some thing like, "Mr. Yagi seems to be late, but I haven't heard from him." This kind of pressure to be on time is so effective that it is a rare teacher who walks into the faculty room after the morning bow.

After the vice principal finishes, other teachers make their announcements. One teacher who often speaks is the teacher in charge of schedule changes for the day. Inside the faculty room is a blackboard with spaces to list class changes. For instance, Mr. Toyama might have to go to a meeting of the Hiroshima Prefectural Conference of English Speaking Society Supervisors starting at 1:30. Because a full-time teacher usually teaches only three 50-minute classes per day, it is fairly easy for Mr. Toyama to exchange classes with another teacher who teaches the same group of students during one of the morning periods.

I have gone through the trouble of explaining the practice of changing classes because there is no end to the surprises in the life of a foreign English teacher at Daiichi, and a fair number of them are concerned with being aware, or unaware, of last minute changes that have arisen. The foreign teacher must keep aware of these announcements by asking for a daily translation.

The working day is divided into six 50-minute periods with thirty minutes for lunch. At 8:40 a.m., all of the homeroom teachers move out of the faculty room to meet their homerooms. They take attendance, make announcements, and then return to the faculty room. At 8:50 the chimes sound once more, and all the teachers with classes pick up their chalk and other instructional materials and go to their first 50-minute class. Except for the physical education, science, and home economics teachers, who have their own classrooms to which their students come, the other teachers all return to their desks in the faculty room when the chimes sound at 9:40. By the start of Period 2, at 9:50, a number of part-time teachers have arrived. Part-timers are responsible for teaching roughly a fifth of the classes at Daiichi. Lunch is from 12:40 to 1:10, and most of the students eat in their homerooms. Teachers generally have lunch in the student lunch room the period before the students' lunch break, or they eat at their desks in the faculty room.

Daiichi Parents and Their Expectations

To attempt to speak of all Japanese parents of high-school students, and perhaps to include the parents of youngsters who will be high-school students in the near future, or of young adults who were high-school students in the recent past, is to speak of a significant portion of the mainstream of the Japanese adult population. I generally like to avoid statements about nations as a whole such as "Icelanders are good dancers" or "People from Bermuda collect stamps."

I will here tell the reader about my knowledge of, and my experiences with, parents at Daiichi during my year at that school. At the same time, I wish to remind the reader that Daiichi, a girls' commercial high school drawing on the middle class and laboring class, might be noticeably different from a high school that includes the children of doctors, lawyers, successful businessmen, educators, and the like.

By "parents" at Daiichi, one generally means mothers. From time to time a father of a student can be seen on the campus, but such moments are a bit unusual. It is Mom who accompanies her daughter to submit an application to attend Daiichi; it is Mom who shows up at PTA meetings, Mom who accompanies a daughter who has been suspended from the school for a misdeed and is in need of a parent's conference. It is Mom who attends her daughter's solemn graduation ceremony on a chilly morning in early March.

Daiichi mothers interfere with the functioning of the school amazingly little. It is, to the best of my knowledge, rare for a parent to telephone the school to express outrage to a teacher or administrator. Even when students are given corporal punishment—a favorite physical punishment in extreme cases is for a teacher to hit a student over the head, sometimes

71

with a briefcase full of books—a teacher would probably not have to worry about parental reactions. (Lest any reader think that head-hitting is common at Daiichi, I should point out that for every student who gets hit, probably ten or fifteen are punished by being made to sit alone on the floor and ponder their misdoings, or by being bullied into tears, or by being threatened with the school asking their parents to punish them.)

Virtually none of the parents of Daiichi students seemed to be directly interested in English instruction at the school. By this statement, I mean that only the rarest of parents would make an inquiry to any English teacher, Japanese or foreign, as to how the parent might help her daughter study English better. Students would occasionally relate stories to me about a discussion they had had with their parents concerning my classes.

English can be seen as a screening device, a means of letting relatively uneducated people know their place in Japanese society. It seldom is viewed as an important means of communication, and by looking carefully at how a cross section of high-school students and their parents view instruction in English one can get a fairly good idea about how foreign languages and foreigners are regarded in various sections of Japanese society. As I have indicated before, the core of English learning in Japan is the memorizing of the meanings of individual words and phrases to enable the student to fill in the correct word in a particular box, or draw a circle around the correct answer, on crucial examinations. I was encouraged to attend PTA meetings, held perhaps three times a year. At those meetings English was low priority, and I came to realize further that I was just a kind of "international" decoration on the Daiichi cake. Incidentally, most of the parents were interested primarily in how to control their children.

The Students

Foreigners interested in teaching in Japanese high schools should familiarize themselves with the spectrum of high-school students in Japan before jumping into a particular type of high school. A commercial high school furnishes, in general, a terminal course of study. A lot of the Daiichi students behaved accordingly. While the great majority were pleasant, some of the students were incredibly disruptive. It was usually hard to get a class of 45 students to be quiet. Even to get a half-class of, say, 23 to calm down was often difficult.

Commercial high-school students do little homework, except at examination time. Most of the students at Daiichi would not ask questions during class. Passivity was generally encouraged, both through peer pressure and through other means such as tradition and faculty pressure. Daiichi students are expected to become competent with the abacus, the Chinese-character typewriter, and the Japanese-syllabic typewriter, all of which they manipulate with remarkable ability, and all of which are passive activities. The usual sources of conflict between students and teachers involved the students altering their natural hair style and hair color, wearing cosmetics, or having something incomplete or improper about their uniform or bookbag.

Beneath the surface was a pronounced interest on the part of the Daiichi girls in the opposite sex; administrators and teachers generally did not make comments about this area. Daiichi students are not allowed to ride in cars while travelling to and from school. A good number of times, I would see a Daiichi student get into, or out of, a young man's car two or three hundred meters from the school's entrance. Technically speaking, I was supposed to report such misdemeanors to the proper authorities at the school, but I would recall my own ribald high-school days, and file such infractions away in my memory. Other teachers, especially some of the younger ones, would insist that the majority of Daiichi girls were sexually active, and my suspicions and observations would tend to confirm those assertions. There were occasional exceptions, such as a formal report on sex education in Hiroshima Prefecture being issued to each teacher; however, on the whole, most teachers preferred to avoid bringing up the subjects of sex and sex education.

As for my being a foreigner, I would like to mention that a number of the Daiichi students wanted to touch a non-Asiatic person. Occasionally, a student would approach me from the back as I was speaking after class with some of her classmates and would pull a hair from my arm. Sometimes students would inform me that they detested English and occasionally would notify me that they did not like foreigners.

There is no end to what I could say about the students I met during my year at Daiichi. I will summarize my experience of them as follows: Most of them were not interested in English, most were intelligent, and most are still willing to chat with me when we happen to meet in downtown Hiroshima.

Mental Attitude of the Native Speaker of English at a Japanese High School

The mental attitude that will best prepare a teacher from abroad to teach successfully at a Japanese high school is a desire to stay on good terms, from beginning to end, with the majority of the faculty. The center of your existence at a high school such as Daiichi, and many other educational institutions, is the faculty room. Make a habit of greeting the other teachers and of chatting, even for just a moment, with them. You have no idea when you will be eagerly requesting their assistance with a difficult problem. Ask the other teachers "What-would-you-do-if. . ." questions from time to time.

During your first year or two at the high school, do your best to accept all invitations to socialize with other faculty members. For female foreign teachers, it would probably be best to ask that at least one other female teacher join the festivities. Many Japanese adults, at least in my experience, feel they do not know someone until they have done some serious drinking and singing with that person. This would be especially true in the case of a foreigner. Even if you do not care for the smell of tobacco smoke or the taste of saké, consider it part of your job to go drinking from time to time. (Incidentally, plan to come in contact with a good deal of tobacco smoke during your days at a Japanese high school, and if you are a female, realize that the men who are paying you would prefer that you *not* smoke.)

Study something—anything—about Japan. Decide to learn ikebana (flower arrangement), karate, judo, calligraphy, karaoke (barroom) singing, koto, or tea ceremony. Ask the faculty for assistance in getting started, if you have not already started. Do whatever you can so as not to appear threatening to any native Japanese teacher of English; you should especially avoid criticizing the English-speaking ability of any such teacher.

Until you have completed your first two or three years at the high school, avoid comments such as, "Well, in New York, we do it this way." Smile a lot, and do not be too devastating in your criticisms of Japan.

Realize that during the lifetime of some of the older faculty members, the study of English was forbidden by the Japanese government. You do not have to search far in Japan to find people who are unable to say the ABCs. Learn about the manner in which the American presence was reestablished in Japan during the final year of World War II through bombings, both nuclear and conventional, and the military invasion of surrounding islands. Realize that it was only after this massive, uncontrollable assault on their homeland that the Japanese government reinstituted the teaching of English throughout the country.

It would help to appreciate that life for both high-school students and teachers contains much drudgery and unpleasantness, especially if you find yourself, as I did, in a non-academic high school. Realize that at Daiichi, except for Sundays and national holidays, teachers are either expected to show up at school, or to have a stamp that reads "AT HOME STUDYING AND PREPARING" placed in their attendance record. A teacher at Daiichi, and I suspect at many other Japanese high schools, does not have the right to vacations. At Daiichi, the only officially recognized time to relax is the overnight (males only) faculty drinking trip in August. Realize that right in the middle of the students' six-week summer vacation at Daiichi, a day is set aside for all the students to put on their uniforms and, along with the entire faculty, to spend a good part of the day at school. Teachers use the occasion to check hair styles and to make sure that students are behaving themselves during their leave. An understanding of this curious custom, known as *tokobi*, will go a long way toward helping create a desirable mental attitude in a foreigner who hopes to have a pleasant teaching career at a Japanese high school.

My advice to new foreign teachers is to:

1. Make friends with the other teachers.
2. Be pleasant and firm with the students.
3. Learn Japanese as soon as possible.
4. Smile.
5. Have a good time.

The Responsibilities of a Foreign Teacher of English in a Japanese High School

The teaching responsibilities of your job may be amazingly simple. If you find yourself in a school with another foreign teacher of English, as often happens, then just do things the way that teacher has been doing them, and you are likely to fit in well. If, like myself, you find yourself in a teaching situation where a "foreign presence" is not firmly established, your job can still be fairly simple. (If you decide to have the majority of your students actually start to speak English, you might end up in a psychiatrist's office back in Pasadena before your visa expires.)

The following are the basic responsibilities I set down for the foreign teacher who followed me at Daiichi:

1. Show up, sober, before 8:29 a.m. each workday.
2. Stamp your name into the Daily Faculty Attendance Record (Shuk-kinbo) next to the vice principal's desk.
3. Stay on the school grounds at least until 4:30 p.m. on weekdays and until 1:30 p.m. on Saturdays.
4. Be in the correct classroom within two minutes after the start of a period assigned to you, and remain there until the end of the period. (What you do in the classroom is not particularly important as long as the students and the other English teachers don't complain about your classes.)
5. Notify the vice principal *immediately* of any inability on your part to fulfill any of the above requirements.
6. Within reason, do what the principal, the vice principal, the teacher in charge of school curriculum, the English Department chairperson, and the other regular English teachers request you to do—which might amount to much less than you expect. (If you let the administration and the faculty connected with English teaching know that you want to handle your classes in your usual way, and that you would prefer not to be bothered, not many requests will come your way.)

So, concentrate your energies on fulfilling the above responsibilities for the duration of your contract, and few problems will befall you. (From time to time, you might want to return to this page and reread the above six recommendations and remove from your mind any obligations that *you* yourself have created and that the people who run the school are not particularly concerned with—such as expecting your students to start to speak in English.)

Foreign teachers in Japanese high schools would do well to realize that, in the eyes of the officials of the Japanese Ministry of Education, they (the foreign teachers) hardly exist. Although I have heard of exceptions, it is my impression that only native Japanese teachers are supposed to issue term grades to students in Japanese high schools. This means that a foreigner is expected to teach as an adjunct to the Japanese faculty at all times.

When a high-school teacher is not in a position to issue permanent grades to students, his/her powers are severely limited; this is the way the Japanese Ministry of Education seems to prefer, and it is the way you might find things working in the high school you choose. Therefore, I would suggest that a foreign teacher of English in a Japanese high school quickly establish a modus vivendi with all the native Japanese teachers of English he/she will be working under, and especially with the department chairperson. If you do not have the cooperation of the teachers who are actually issuing the grades that go into the students' records, you might have serious problems with some unruly students who choose to cause trouble for you while behaving adequately for their regular English teacher.

It can be somewhat difficult if your department chairperson, or some of the other English teachers, are unable to speak English. A so-called teacher of English who is a native Japanese and who is functionally monolingual might easily feel embarrassed by the presence of a foreigner at the school, and might have a significantly different perception of the foreigner's role than the foreigner does. In other words, help the other English teachers feel comfortable about your presence. Ask permission to visit at least ten or fifteen different English classes at the school during your first month or two in your new job. Observe how your superiors go about ''teaching English.'' After a number of weeks of such observation and limited participation, you will probably come to understand how both the teachers *and* students of English at that particular school view English instruction.

Such a task might be maddening, but it is the feeling of this writer that the longer you can endure it, and the more so-called "English classes" that you can observe, the more likely you will be to have a pleasant teaching experience in the long run. It goes almost without saying that if you are the first foreigner employed by your school, for your first couple of weeks you will be viewed as an extreme curiosity, and on the initial occasion that you visit any given class, a mood of excitement will take over the clasroom. This might be a heady experience for the foreigner, and at the same time, unless the foreigner is careful, might be somewhat ego-damaging for the English teacher in charge.

Let the teacher introduce you, and, if possible, have the students ask you "Yes/No" questions. "Yes/No" questions are those that are worded in such a way to create maximum language production on the part of the students, and minimal production on the part of the teacher: "Do you come from *Canada?*" "Do you live in *Nagoya?*" You simply answer each question with a "yes" or a "no." Such questions generally give a great sense of accomplishment to the students, are easy for the Japanese teacher in charge to handle, help prevent you from babbling on and on when you have no idea how much of what you say is being understood, and also are safe. Difficult subjects that you might accidentally have brought up do not even get mentioned.

After a few weeks of visiting clases, the Japanese teachers of English will probably have a fairly good idea of how they would like to use you during the hours you are expected to be teaching. Hopefully, you will have a number of ideas about what you would feel most comfortable doing with the students and which will be acceptable to the teacher(s) in charge. At Daiichi, I was allowed to use a spare classroom for my instruction to the juniors and seniors. Although there were an amazing number of disruptions to our planned cycle—assemblies, national holidays, culture festival preparations, special long homeroom periods, physical exams, job interview orientation, students being allowed to return home early because of PTA meetings, school cleaning—the general idea was that I would take half the students from a regular English class of some fifty students on one week and the other half of the class the following week. Some of the Daiichi students looked forward to my instruction and would greet me in the halls with sentences such as, "Oh, we'll be seeing you this coming Thursday." They frequently knew my schedule better than I did, especially during the first term I was at Daiichi.

At no point was I asked to memorize students' names, and, yet, I feel that my days at Daiichi would have been more pleasant if I had devoted more effort to memorizing the names and faces of my 1,020 students. Files were easily available with photos of the students, but I must confess I relied entirely on class seating charts until some of the more troublesome students in the school started to switch name tags and seats before the start of my classes. In my entire year at that high school, hardly anything made my teaching more unpleasant, nor unnerved me more, than being made to appear the fool by assuming that, say, Miss Tanaka was Miss Yamada just because she was wearing a name tag which read "Yamada" or was sitting in Miss Yamada's seat. Whether you are in an academically-oriented setting or not, the more names, and nicknames, you remember, the easier you career at that school will be. (Volunteering to help with club and sports activities, incidentally, is a good way to become familiar with the students and their names; even if you are not required to participate in the activities of the school's English Speaking Society or other English club, you would probably find it advantageous for many reasons to assist the students in this way.)

Come the end of a term, you might be asked to help prepare parts of the English examinations, and you might be asked to submit grades for your students to be calculated in the overall grades being issued by the Japanese teachers in charge. (Japanese students are graded on a scale of 1 to 10, with a 3 being about the lowest grade you give to a student who is "trying," and a 9 being generally the highest grade you give in many of your classes.) My experience was that everyone was happiest when my grades had an average close to that used by the teacher in charge.

You should attend all meetings you are asked to attend, even if you understand little of what is taking place. A faculty is considered a "group," and it is important to help maintain that feeling, even if it includes the slightly absurd situation of a teacher who does not understand the language being required to attend faculty meetings.

Your contract is likely to require 20 teaching hours per week. Not taking into account the summer, winter, and spring vacations, your actual teaching time is likely to come to an average of 17 or 18 hours per week rather than the contracted total. In brief, your job will be to add a conversational flavor to English. You may do this in a number of ways: by creating your own materials, by using a supplementary conversational English textbook, and/or by improvising upon the students' assigned textbook in grammar-translation English.

Starting Off Right—How to Teach Your First Classes

Suggestions for your first class:
— Before the start of the class, even days ahead, start to memorize the students' names, either by visiting their class with the regular English teacher, or by acquiring their photos from their homeroom teacher or from the previous year's school annual. Ask the teachers who know the students well to identify likely troublemakers and give special attention to memorizing those names.
— Ask the regular English teacher to step into the classroom and to spend perhaps just one minute informing the students that "Ms. Jones" will be teaching them, asking the students to study hard and to cooperate with the new teacher,
— Create an up-to-date seating chart with the students' names written in a writing system that you understand. Make sure that the seating chart is portable and is not inconveniently taped to the lectern. (In some clasrooms at Daiichi, the students had filled in their names on a seating chart in such a way that when a teacher looked at the chart and tried to match it to the class, he/she would discover that all the students' names were, in effect, upside-down.)
— If you are starting to teach in a school that does not require the students to wear name tags, ask the students to make name cards, in Romanized writing, to place in front of them.
The following guidelines will prove useful:
— Assume that any given student, until proven otherwise, does not understand spoken English.
— Before the class starts, have the regular English teacher introduce you to the class monitor and/or a student who is likely to understand your English and can help interpret your wishes to the rest of the class. Pay these leaders a bit of respect, and they can help make your first day go well.
— Create a lesson plan that includes a written assignment to be turned in to you. A carefully-controlled, written self-introduction, such as follows, is useful even months later.
  1. My name is *Yuko Tahara.*
  2. I live in *Hondori.*
  3. I *walk* to school. It takes about *15 minutes.*

4. My favorite subjects are *Art* and *Japanese*.
5. I am in the *Badminton* Club.
6. I like to *draw pictures* and *go scuba diving*.

My experience with Japanese students is that they usually appreciate a straightforward written assignment such as a crossword puzzle for their level or a fill-in-the-blanks-with-the-right-answers game.

— If the class goes well for the first 30 minutes or so, then you might wish to employ one of my time-tested conversational activities. Inform the students that they may now ask you some questions about yourself, and that there are two conditions: first, the whole class must stand up and, second, no student may sit down until he or she has asked you one question. I have never discovered a better way to have the hands of Japanese students pop up demanding a chance to ask questions. As I wrote earlier, you might want to have the students ask Yes/No questions.

— If you, or the regular English teacher, would prefer that the students not ask you questions, then you might have them stand and make sentences such as, "I can see some *clouds*," or "I like to eat *fruit sandwiches*." Each student must insert a noun that has not been used by any other student up to that point in the exercise. Again, inform the students that they may not sit down until they have said their sentence. (Incidentally, when using the "You-may-not-sit-down-until-you-say-your-sentence" technique, you might decide to take pity on the last two or three students and let them sit down before speaking, to prevent anyone from being the last.)

Preparing for Your Classes

Most likely, you will have at least a number of days, and possibly a number of weeks, to prepare for your teaching after the start of the school year. As I mentioned earlier, do your best to spend many hours observing the classes of the regular English teachers. Be sure to consult thoughtfully and warmly with the English Department chairperson, and with the other English teachers you will be working with, to choose the materials for use in your instruction. At Daiichi, I was given freedom to choose and make my own materials, and you should be ready for such an opportunity.

Before choosing a set of published materials, I would suggest that you meet each class two or three times in order to get an idea of their interests and abilities. In my experience, more important than a textbook is a workbook—one for each student. You should go to an English-language bookstore, choose appropriate workbooks, and perhaps some texts. (You might order one workbook for each of your students and one set of 45 textbooks for each different level you are teaching, which you can then use with many different classes.) Two fairly satisfactory series, which I would suggest that you consider carefully *after* getting to know your students, are the *Streamline* and the *New Horizons* series.

Ten Horrible Things That Can Happen
(and How to Avoid, or Cope with, Them)

1. The students in a particular class start to make so much noise that you are sure not much learning is taking place and/or suspect that teachers and students in nearby classrooms are being disturbed.

    — What not to do: Even though teachers at your school believe in practicing corporal punishment, and might urge you to follow their example, I feel that you, as a foreigner, will be creating a bad international environment if you hit a noisy student. Do not hit the students no matter how angry you become.

    — Threaten to inform the class's homeroom teacher. (Be absolutely sure of the homeroom teacher's name, and have copies of the schedules of the homeroom teachers for all your classes with you. If the homeroom teacher has a free period while you are suffering with his/her class, then notify the unruly class that you will go to call the homeroom teacher for help. If the homeroom teacher is not available, locate another teacher who actually knows the class. If both of these alternatives are not possible to carry out, ask the vice principal for help.)

    — Prior to your next meeting with the class, memorize every student's name and face. Practice the names you have memorized by calling students one by one to answer simple questions. In other words, let the students know that you have memorized their names.

— For the next class, prepare a written assignment to be turned in to you that takes at least 25-30 minutes to complete.

— During the next class, offer to play a game such as Bingo in English if the students behave.

2. The homeroom teachers and other teachers you request assistance from in dealing with unruly students decide to take the students' side rather than yours. (This actually happened to the foreign teacher of English who succeeded me at Daiichi.)

— Learn the Japanese language more diligently.

— Go drinking with the faculty more often.

— Submit your resignation effective at the end of the academic year.

— Cultivate friendships with faculty members who have been cooperative, and ask them to find out what is going wrong.

— Ask to visit classes in other subjects in order to learn how teachers of subjects other than English handle problems with students.

3. The students switch name tags and/or seats.

— Take the homeroom teacher's homeroom register with photos to class with you.

— Memorize the names and photos of the students in that particular class diligently.

— Reread my explanation of this problem in the section, "The Responsibilities of a Foreign Teacher of English in a Japanese High School."

4. An individual student hits or kicks you.

— Ask the homeroom teacher of the student to meet with you and the particular student for a three-party conference.

— Don't hit or kick back.

— Take up the study of Japanese martial arts during your after-work hours.

5. You are walking through the red-light district of the city where you live and you encounter some of your high-school students.

— Avoid talking to them; a nod or glance will suffice.

— This is a complicated matter with no easy solution. Don't be surprised if the story of your encounter is brought up during class, especially if you are working at a school which is not academically oriented.

— Realize that nighttime entertainment districts are an integral part of life in Japan and that the principal cannot expect you to stay completely away from such parts of town.

6. The majority of students in a particular class inform you that they dislike English.

— Inform the class that you will take their feelings into consideration.

— Reread the basic responsibilities for foreign teachers at Daiichi at the start of the section "The Responsibilities of a Foreign Teacher of English in a Japanese High School." Get a clear idea of the *bare minimum* you are expected to do with any given class.

— Acquire a copy of *English Without Anguish,* a handbook for amateur English teachers in Japan published by the College Women's Association of Japan, and put their suggestions for games and other interesting classroom activities to use. This valuable publication might be difficult to obtain, but it is the aid my wife and I have most consistently referred to since we started teaching English in this country.

— Set aside a certain number of minutes each time you meet a class that detests English for the students to "teach" you Japanese.

— Start attending the meetings of the JALT (Japan Association of Language Teachers) chapter nearest you. Ask other teachers you meet through JALT how they would handle such students.

7. You find that you are taking too much time correcting assignments.

— Draw little circles around errors; let the students figure out *what* their mistakes are. Don't assume that a teacher must write out corrections.

— Watch how social studies, bookkeeping, or math teachers correct large numbers of students' notebooks. At Daiichi I saw many teachers open notebooks just long enough to place a red stamp on the last page completed.

— Be aware that what counts at most high schools are the midterm and final examinations. For these, especially if you must grade many hundreds of them during the course of a trimester, it will be worth your time to construct tests with answers that are easy to grade.

8. You decide that you cannot stand teaching six days a week.
— Don't sign more than a one-year contract.
— Consult with the principal and tell him/her something along these lines: You came to Japan because you wanted to get to know the country and to visit various places. Say that you would like to visit five or six specific historic, beautiful locations within 300 kilometers of your school. Ask if you might rearrange your schedule at the end of the current term so that you will have no classes on Saturday (or Monday) in order that you might experience more of Japan's beauty before returning to your own country.

9. The other teachers become envious of the salary you are being paid as a starting teacher.
— Before you ever discuss your salary with the other teachers, make sure you have the principal's permission to discuss it. The principal might prefer that you keep quiet about this matter.
— Tell the other teachers how much you would be paid for comparable work in your homeland.
— Point out that Japanese teachers receive bonuses and retirement pay, and that you receive neither.
— If such is the case, let them know that you must pay both Japanese taxes and taxes overseas.
— Explain how much it cost for you to come to Japan and to rent and furnish accomodations here. As most Japanese people feel a strong desire to visit their parents at least once a year, point out how much it costs you to visit your parents.

10. You can't stand Japanese sexism and/or racism at your school any longer.
— Get together, even if you are a male, with some of the female teachers, and let them air compaints about Japanese sexism. They may not see any solutions forthcoming, but you might be surprised at how clearly they perceive the problems.

— Delicately ask questions about the roles of men and women in Japan. Say something like, ''Gee, I just don't understand why you men smoke at all. Can someone explain what's happening?''

— Racism is harder to deal with because most Japanese are not aware that they live in a society that practices racism. One fairly inoffensive way to open discussion on the issue is to bring up the problem of racism in your own country, and see if any teacher or student is willing to start talking about Koreans, Chinese, or other foreigners in Japan.

— Another conversation starter in this area is to pull out your Certificate of Alien Registration, open to the page with your photo and fingerprint, and ask your colleagues and students to explain why the fingerprinting of foreigners, in particular of Koreans and Chinese born and bred in Japan (and virtually indistinguishable from Japanese), is necessary.

Conclusion

I think I have touched on all the major areas connected with becoming a foreign teacher of English at a Japanese high school, and with having a pleasant and productive experience at such an institution. I still have another 200 or 300 suggestions on how to make your life easier, but what you want is probably a constitution and not a complete set of laws. If just two or three of your students become excited about foreign-language study while you are their teacher, please consider your teaching at least somewhat successful. Keep in mind that one day you will be sitting on a beach or walking down a street in the land you come from, and the high school you worked at in Japan will be just so many memories. Hopefully, most of them will be favorable.

Recommended Reading

Berglund, Jeffrey L. *A Japanese High School*. Kyoto: Chuo Tosho, 1984. (Published as a reading text for Japanese students, this small book contains practical and useful information.)

College Women's Association of Japan, Publication Committee. *English Without Anguish.* Tokyo: College Women's Association of Japan, 1975.

Miller, Roy Andrew. *Japan's Modern Myth: The Language and Beyond.* Tokyo: John Weatherhill, Inc., 1982.

Rohlen, Thomas P. *Japan's High Schools.* Berkeley: University of California Press, 1983.

Thoughts on the Junior High School: A Response

Jill Stewart

I'VE WRITTEN IN RESPONSE to Mr. Wiig's article, since his experience did not include the junior high school, and because the junior high school seems to be such a special level in Japan. First of all, I'm glad Mr. Wiig disclaimed the ability to speak about the junior high school, not only because it *is* a very special level, but because it is the right thing to do. It is an especially difficult thing to do for any foreigner in Japan where one's foreign status (appearance) automatically puts one in a special class (discrimination even when the special treatment is to put one on a pedestal), and of course makes one falsely "omniscient" about one's own country, if not the entire Western world. This is an acute problem for the teacher in Japan where students are accustomed to having the teacher hand down "the answers" and where the foreign teacher is often the only foreigner that the students or teachers have ever met. With all those expectant faces staring at one and not another foreigner in sight, one often gives in to temptation. It's not that one—especially a teacher—would deliberately lead anyone astray, but after numerous experiences when one finally realizes that *their* language level will not allow for one's *own* nuance, and their "We Japanese" attitude finds one's "I'm-only-one-opinion" attitude somewhat suspicious, one finds oneself walking around saying such ignominious things as, "My people like *chocolate* ice cream best." This is an especially virulent disease and can often be an accurate assessor of how long a foreigner has been in Japan—yearly trips home are required for remissions.

This being said, I want to state that the following opinions in this article *are* opinions, they are mine, and like Mr. Wiig's article, based on specific experiences.

There were a great many similarities between what Mr. Wiig describes and what I have seen and felt, particularly his descriptions of the facilities and procedures, as well as his sardonic expression of the very real frustrations that meet the isolated culture-shocked foreign teacher who walks into such an environment.

Our differences, I think, were conditioned as much by the terms of our contracts or job descriptions and our personalities as by grade level or immediate external environment of where we taught. I work in a special "native speaker" program for the public school system in Kobe. The teachers in this program at the junior high level are expected to go to three to five schools per year, the length of time at each being determined by the size of the school. We do team teaching with the Japanese English teachers. Hence, for the good and the bad of it, our job is one of seeing and dealing with a great variety of experiences, trying to find ways to make maximum impact in minimum time. To a large extent our successes and failures in a school depend on how courageous and cooperative our team teachers are. I have been at this job for three years, have worked with about thirty-five teachers, and have taught approximately 1,500 students with an average class size of about forty-five. This is the bias from which I speak.

School violence at the junior high level is a much discussed topic. I haven't seen much of it. I'm not disputing that it is a major problem. I read about it in the papers, and there is no doubt that some kids at this age have done terrible things—to their classmates and to their teachers. But I haven't seen it. I have never felt fear for my person in any school I have walked into in my three years. I think there are two major reasons for this.

One reason is the nature of my job. I am not at the school all day, day-in, day-out, not even on Saturdays—I have a westernized schedule. I am also protected from knowing: it is often difficult to find things out. Generally speaking, the Japanese do not often talk about difficult topics, and if they do, certainly not directly, as an American would. They have elaborate codes in their language to enable them to let a listener understand a "no" without ever having to say it. It is all very intuitive and quite baffling to the uninitiated. At first, one misses all the signals. Then it gets worse. I can now recognize a cut-off or danger "vibration" from several rooms away—it can get quite "noisy" with these unspoken messages. The trouble is, I haven't been able to learn how to understand intuitively *why* the signal is being sent, and, therefore, whether or not I agree to it.

It is the American way in times of confusion or trouble to suggest talking things over. This almost led to an international incident, when one day in class some boys started laughing and causing a slight disturbance. While I was questioning some students on the other side of the room, my young male team teacher scolded them severely. I thought perhaps the students had been making fun of me or I had broken some cultural taboo without being aware of it, since he had been so hard on them. I tried to look stern in support of his disciplinary action and went on with my lesson when he was finished. After the lesson was over, and we were on our way back to the teacher's room, I asked him what had happened. I got no response—silence, as if I hadn't said anything. This was not a new behavior, as this gentleman had often done this when I asked him whether or not he was willing to go along with some suggestion I had for a lesson plan. I was new to the school, and I was trying to figure out what this cut-off signal meant. Did he hate the idea, was he afraid to try it, did he think it wouldn't work, did he hate foreigners, did he hate women, did he hate women foreigners with ideas, did he understand my English, did he recognize that it was a question form, was he deaf, had I actually asked the question, did I really exist? From my cultural background I recognized his behavior as passive-aggressive manipulation. He was silent, and I ran the gamut of questioning everything from my grammar to my existence, and of course decided that everything I am had failed. Most days I can go from this step to immediately putting the whole incident into the cultural difference slot in my brain and "try not to take it personally." But this was one of my paranoid days, and I wasn't in the mood to rationalize coolly and accept this behavior. I ignored his silent cut-off and asked him again. He got very nervous, crossed his arms, and said, "It is not your concern." Red flag to the bull. I told him that I was a teacher just like he was, that we were team teachers, that anything that went on in *our* classroom was of concern to *me,* and that we needed to talk about a few things back in the teacher's room.

I walked away to calm down before we tried to understand each other. I had to explain to him what was going on in terms of my culture, to find out what part of all this was cultural, what part language difficulties, and what part actual disagreements or "real" problems rather than misunderstandings. Luckily, we had a good talk where I found that the problem was a little of each. We ended up having a somewhat grudging admiration for each other and were quite successful with the students. The actual cause of all this had been an ordinary case of a rowdy boy talking out of turn. However, one can see that when one runs into blocks against discussing problems, out of whatever motivations, it is difficult to understand the complete picture of what goes on. Still, I have developed an intuitive sense for the general tenor, and I have been in many classrooms, and I have never felt hatred or violence directed toward me.

This leads me to what I believe is the second reason I haven't seen junior high school violence. As real and as serious as the problem is, the vast majority of the students do not cause that kind of trouble. The subject of what constitutes news, and the subject of violence perpetrated by students that are of an age that we adults like to think of as innocent, needs to be considered when thinking of junior high-school violence. And, of course, it must be added that violence in the junior high schools needs study and action.

But I think the junior high-school level is special because it encompasses a special age range. As in the U.S., as in many cultures, these students are at the age where they are beginning to change from children to adults. They are trying to figure out how they fit into the world. It is a hard, wonderful time when their bodies and minds are humming, and they can't decide from minute to minute whether they want to be grown-ups or children.

It is this exact time that the Japanese educational system chooses (by design or default) to decide the child's future. The system is gearing them for "examination hell." The students must pass the examination to get into the right high school in order to get into the right college— and what university they graduate from will determine their job opportunities in a lifetime employment system. The student may not know whether he is successful at this age, but many of the ones who aren't going to "make it" in society are beginning to realize it. And, just at this time a hierarachical society is trying to put them in harness and break them to the system. It is easy to understand that frustration and anxiety from the pressure could lead to violence, especially if coupled with a military or corporal punishment style of discipline and a basic intolerance for things different. Most Japanese have been brought up to think that there are certain things that all Japanese like and dislike, certain thoughts and feelings that all Japanese have—and anyone who differs from that pattern (including themselves) is not really Japanese. Since most people can't guard against random thoughts, most Japanese secretly believe that they are different, that they have thought un-Japanese thoughts—and that because of that their Japanese-ness is in jeopardy. This fear in the less intelligent or less secure is often acted out on others who show signs of difference. Of course, at the junior high-school level, before the students have had a chance to sort out their own minds, everyone is insecure. The ones who start to perceive that the game is all over before they have even had a chance to figure out what they would have wanted or the smart ones who are different in some way—it is they who are prone to bullying or getting bullied, depending on their strength and nature and how many others they can win to their side.

This is the kind of violence that I have seen—the emotional manipulation or ostracism of group pressure. It is the special age of the junior high students that makes them so vulnerable to this. I have also seen "playful" scuffles among the boy students, but it is hard to judge some of these acts when both I and the students have also seen other students slapped in the face or hit on the head with paperback books, as well as receiving other corporal punishments at the hands of teachers.

And so, it is true that I, like Mr. Wiig, have seen many things that I am in disagreement with. But after three years, I find that these things do not take predominance in my thoughts or feelings. The first two years were difficult, more difficult than I realized at the time, as I tried to deal with culture shock, homesickness (for the first time in my life), and studying Japanese, while at the same time taking on a job that required constant readjustments and an isolation from other foreigners in my workplace.

I can't remember when the enjoyment started taking precedence over the frustrations, for, of course, the frustrations never go away—the system does not change. Little by little, things shifted and fell into a different pattern—facts, understandings, feelings—about Japan, about teaching, most of all about myself, about changes like growing. One morning I walked down my hill toward the train station and I glanced out across the tile roofs of the city to the bay, where I could see the sunrise reflecting off the water, and the ships, shadows against a pink brilliance. I breathed in a gust of cool autumn wind, smiled at my neighbor who, white-aproned and efficient, was sweeping up the first fallen leaves from the street and the rain gutters in front of her house. The season was changing again, and this time the change was familiar. I realized that on this day I could feel no tightening of the stomach muscles, no clenching of the jaw, no gird against the day. I thought of Otani-kun, precocious "Paul," who would come into the office and speak English fluently while he patted me on the shoulder like an uncle giving advice, and then would clam up and pretend not to understand anything when I called on him in class. Today, when we acted out *Tom Sawyer,* a new startled star would be born, an actor who didn't know she could speak English and act at the same time. She would be the shy one that I didn't expect; why am I always surprised? During my lunch break I would have a chat with "Arthur," a slow learner always brought in by his classmate "John" who would coach him through an English conversation with the foreign teacher. "Sandy," whose home life has been a series of sorrows and disappointments, would she speak today? Yesterday she gave me a hand-knitted scarf warm with perfume because I always speak to her and smile even though she never says a word. The giggling girls, the shy boys, the show-offs, the troublemakers—they are all special to me, and familiar, and dear.

English Instruction in Japanese Junior High Schools

Miho Tanaka Steinberg

Schools

Most foreign teachers who teach English in regular schools in Japan teach on the college and university levels. Many others teach in private English-conversation schools and in programs and classes sponsored by companies and institutions, but they are for adults. The number of native English speakers teaching on the secondary school level is decidedly small. However, I can think of three major categories in which they are sometimes engaged: public schools, private schools, and private English-conversation schools.

Formal English instruction in Japan begins in the seventh grade (first year in the lower seconday, or junior high school) in all public and private schools, although some private schools offer English at the elementary level. The Ministry of Education states that English is not a compulsory subject in Japanese lower secondary schools, but almost all of the schools offer English, and it is safe to say that Japanese upper secondary-school (high-school) graduates have had five to six years of English classes behind them.

Public Schools. The Ministry of Education subsidizes the hiring of native English speakers by the prefectures. They are known as Mombusho Fellows and they assist in materials development, demonstration classes, teacher training, etc., at the office of prefectural Departments of Education. Those prefectures that can afford several fellows arrange to have them conduct regular English classes in their respective school districts, while those prefectures with fewer fellows make other arrangements, such as having them make one visit during the school year to every class in the district, conducting special programs after school, and assisting with summer workshops for teachers.

In public schools the number of hours allotted for English in lower secondary schools has been 3 hours per week since 1980. Due to holidays, school programs, and various other activities, the actual number of instructional hours for English may be less than 2.5 hours per week throughout the school year. While the number of hours has been gradually decreasing from 5 hours per week in the 1960s to the present 3 hours, English is still part of the entrance examination for upper secondary school and for most universities. Furthermore, the content that must be covered during the 3 years has not been reduced accordingly. Therefore, it is inevitable that English teaching in schools reflects these sad conditions in both materials and methods. Upper secondary-school entrance examinations include problems in grammar, vocabulary, reading comprehension, and translation, but no oral production. Listening comprehension is included in the entrance examination in about half of the schools. Not suprisingly, most English classes are conducted with entrance-exam problems in mind. Many teachers feel they cannot afford the time to use the effective but time-consuming induction method. Games and skits that may be popular among students may also have to give way to more ''meat and potatoes''-type exercises, such as dictation, memorization of dialogs, and mechanical grammar drills in class. Interesting but time-consuming exercises are apt to be left for club activities or extra-curricular programs.

It is in this light that most of you must see your position. Indeed, you were told that you were going to be their important source of live English, that you would be asked to introduce aspects of your culture, that teachers would ask you for your assistance in this and that, etc. You are roaring to start. Such assistance would be desirable, welcome, and a godsend if time for such activities were added on to the existing schedule. Since this is not the case, Japanese teachers of English consider every minute spent on materials other than what is in the course syllabus to be a source of later hardship. The teachers are in a dilemma. They would love to have a native speaker visit their classes and motivate the students; they know that they, themselves, would benefit from such a visit. But they must consider the price they would have to pay; many may decide against rushing through the next lesson or having to give homework for what should have been covered in class. The result is that they decline your offer to visit them.

I gained an understanding of the magnitude of this problem when I visited a prefectural upper secondary school in Shiga Prefecture last spring. The principal surprised me by saying that his school was allotting 7 hours a week for freshman English (first year upper secondary school). He explained that with the decrease of English instructional hours in the lower secondary level, students were, understandably, coming into upper secondary level with lower English proficiency than before. Yet, the entrance examinations for colleges and universities are the same, if not harder. Upper secondary schools, therefore, have to bridge the gap. The principal felt that it was essential to increase the number of hours in freshman English to 7 hours to prepare students for the rest of the high-school English curriculum.

Private Schools. English instruction in private schools can be quite different from that in the public schools, for although they are under the jurisdiction of the Ministry of Education, they are not directly under the prefectural Department of Education (as are public schools). They come under the affairs of the governor's office. There is no office that oversees the English instruction in private schools per se. Theoretically, the principal is responsible for it, but in fact, the English curriculum is planned and carried out by the English teachers of each individual school. The teachers also decide on which textbooks to use.

Another way in which private school English programs differ from those of public schools is that in many of them—especially in Christian church-affiliated schools—native English speakers are on the faculty. I do not know of a school where all 5 hours or so of English are taught by the same native speaker. Usually one or two hours of aural/oral English taught by a native speaker are added on to the regular four or five hours taught by a Japanese teacher. A typical example of this is a Christian school I recently visited in Kanazawa City which offered 5 hours of regular classes taught by a Japanese teacher plus 2 hours of English-conversation classes taught by an American teacher—a total of 7 hours a week for all three grades of the lower secondary level.

Attending a private school can be one way to avoid stiff competition in the entrance examinations to the upper secondary level. Although the entrance exams are taken by all the applicants, those who have already been at that school for 3 years have a better chance of continuing on for 3 more years. For example, the schools at which I inquired said that 98-100% of the lower secondary-level students were promoted to the higher secondary level.

Under such conditions, English (or any other subject, for that matter) can be taught in a most pleasant way—without unnecessary tension or fear. The challenge that the teachers face here is one of motivating their students constantly.

Private English-Conversation Schools. English conversation is becoming increasingly popular as one of the many lessons—such as calligraphy, abacus calculation, and music lessons—to which Japanese children are sent after school and on weekends. Teaching conditions may be a bit different from the schools we have discussed above, for you may be facing a group of children of various levels and ages in one class, unless the administrator of the school is knowledgeable and sympathetic to language instruction. Even well-meaning administrators must sometimes consolidate classes in order to guarantee a profit.

If you are teaching at such a school, a hearty discussion on course objectives and teaching materials for these classes with the administrator is necessary to maintain quality instruction, especially in schools with small operations. Membership in professional organizations such as the Japan Association of Language Teachers (JALT) is important for any English teacher, but I recommend very strongly that teachers and administrators of these schools attend conferences and workshops to keep in touch with the latest teaching theories and techniques. High quality tutoring, after all, is the selling point of these schools. Also, meetings and conferences are very often the only times that teachers can exchange stories and problems with those in the same field, and this contact is very important for the mental health of isolated instructors.

Students

Your students range in age from 13 to 15 years. Most students were introduced to the English language for the first time when they entered the lower secondary school, although it seems that more children are being sent to private English-conversation schools when they are in about the fifth grade. Depending on where you are teaching (private or public, rural or urban schools), the number of students who have already been initiated into English will differ.

Since having English classes is a mark of becoming a junior high student, one can imagine the anticipation and eagerness with which students come into the English class the first day. When this eagerness is coupled with the positive attitude that the Japanese in general have about people who speak foreign languages, it seems that English teachers in Japan should have no problems in motivating their students to learn English.

Yet, it is a sad fact that most students lose their enthusiasm toward English very quickly. In a second-year class that I went to teach for a day last year, I posed the question of whether they liked the English subject. There was a resounding *"Kirai"* (We don't like it). A high-school teacher from the Chugoku area found that 78.9% of 201 technical high-school freshmen whom he polled said that they didn't like English (*Eigo Kyoiku,* December 1983). In both cases, the main reasons were that English "is difficult" and "is not interesting." I would guess that it is too difficult because they are required to memorize many words and sentences to get good grades on the tests; and it is not interesting because no immediate satisfaction stems from their learning. To have to study for an entrance examination looming in the future is deadly. It is also very discouraging since students do not have the opportunity to try out the English that they have learned on "real live foreigners."

Given such circumstances, a native speaker of English must keep up the students' enthusiasm in English if it has not already waned, or try to get it back for them if they have lost it. As a foreigner you are a step ahead of any Japanese teacher in that your students are curious and want to know about you even before you start. Use this to your advantage and talk about yourself and your country when you are reviewing vocabulary or structures.

Course Objectives

The following is an excerpt from *Teacher's Manual for Lower Secondary-School English Programs* (*Chugakko Shinkyoiku Katei no Kaisetsu*)

published by the Ministry of Education in October 1977. The manual groups the four main language skills as follows:
1. Listening, Speaking;
2. Reading; and
3. Writing.

The English course objectives for each grade are as follows:

1st Year 1. To be able to understand and produce short, easy English sentences.
2. To be able to read short, easy sentences.
3. To be able to write short easy sentences.

2nd Year 1. To be able to understand and express the general idea of things using basic English.
2. To be able to read and grasp the general idea of things written in basic English.
3. To be able to write and convey the general idea of things using basic English.

3rd Year 1. To be able to understand and express the essential idea of things using basic English.
2. To be able to read and understand the essential idea of things written in basic English.
3. To be able to express in writing the essential idea of things using basic English.

Linguistic activities through which the above objectives are to be attained are listed below:
A. Listening, Speaking
1. Listening to and understanding the topic of the speaker and getting necessary information.
2. Organizing one's ideas and verbalizing them without missing pertinent information.
3. Understanding the speaker and responding accurately to him/her.
B. Reading
1. Reading aloud accurately with clear pronounciation.
2. Reading aloud and silently, comprehending the content.
3. Reading aloud in a way that expresses the reader's understanding of the passage.

4. Reading and summarizing the passage.
C. Writing
1. Listening to sentences and accurately writing them down.
2. Organizing and writing passages without missing important information.
3. Comprehending a written passage and writing about it.

These activities are recommended throughout the 3 years of lower secondary school in order to achieve the respective course objectives listed above.

Textbooks

At the present time, the following five textbooks approved by the Ministry of Education are being used in Japanese lower secondary schools: *New Everyday English, New Horizon English Course, New Prince English Course, The New Crown English Series,* and *Total English, Revised Edition.*

In public schools the prefectural Department of Education conducts a review of the textbooks from which the school districts may select. The textbook committee of each district decides on a series that all the schools in that district adopt for a few years until the next review and selection takes place.

Private schools, as was mentioned before, do not have any restrictions as to what they can use so long as *one* of the five approved series is used. Therefore, regardless of what the public schools in their school district are using, the English teachers make their own choice for their schools. Native English speakers whom I asked were all using their own materials or were picking and choosing from a number of sources; the students did not have a separate textbook for the conversation classes, although there are many schools where they do.

Big, established, private English-conversation schools quite often have their own textbooks and materials, but the smaller, newer ones usually rely on the instructors for materials. Possibilities range from commercial ESL textbooks meant for use in English-speaking countries to materials that the teachers have written for their own students.

Teaching Oral English

The area in which native English teachers can assist the Japanese most effectively is in the area of oral English, both in aural comprehension and oral production. Although now there are many more occasions for the Japanese to hear English spoken by native speakers on radio, TV, and in movies than 10 years ago, these are by no means enough to influence ordinary students. Fewer still are the opportunities for them to use what English they have learned to communicate with a native speaker. This lack of contact with English speakers accounts for the fear most Japanese feel when they are faced with a foreigner. You will have been immensely successful if, through your association with the students, they can come to feel more relaxed with native English speakers.

Aural Comprehension. In general, it is more effective to begin with aural comprehension (understanding) rather than with oral production (speaking). Even in our native tongues, the scope of our understanding is far greater than that of our production. Infants, by the time they start to babble, have had hundreds of hours of training in listening, a fact that few people realize or apply to language teaching.

It is important for the teacher to know the difference between aural comprehension and oral production exercises. We must be aware that testing or evaluating aural comprehension ability through oral production is not only unfair but also misleading. A teacher cannot know whether a Japanese student who answers "To the balls" to the question, "Where did Cinderella go?" has 1) made a mistake in understanding that she went to *a ball,* 2) gotten the singular and plural noun forms mixed up, or 3) made a slip of the tongue adding /z/ to the noun accidentally. There is no doubt that the final goal is for the students to be able to carry on a conversation, which includes both understanding and speaking, but during the beginning stage the following exercises that do not rely on oral production to test comprehension are quite useful.

A.   Yes/No (Mm-hm/Uh-uh) Questions and True/False Statements

After telling a story, go over it using "inverted questions" (Yes/No questions):

    a. Did Cinderella work hard?
    b. Do you know this story?
    c. Did Cinderella have 4 stepsisters?
    d. Didn't her stepmother go to the ball?

The students can answer "Yes" or "No" chorally and/or individually. Another version of this is to get them to answer with the informal English "Hm-hm" (Yes) and "Uh-uh" (No.), which you have first taught them. These are invariably used by native speakers but no textbook touches upon them.

    These same questions can be presented as statements and the students can respond with "True" or "False" or by nodding or shaking their heads:

    a. Cinderella worked hard.
    b. You know this story.
    c. Cinderella had 4 stepsisters.
    d. Her stepmother didn't go to the ball.

B. Multiple Choice Questions

This is somewhat related to the previous activity except that there are more choices and this is the most common method that aural comprehension tests use. To the question "Where did Cinderella go?", you might give the following choices: 1) to the forest; 2) to church; or 3) to the prince's ball.

    You may give the choices orally or you may give them in writing. You must realize that in the latter case the students' reading ability is tested in this activity, and should make sure that the words used in these answers can be read with ease by the students. One way to reduce this problem is to give them the written form and then read it aloud to them.

C. Following Instructions

Many activities come under this category. The teacher gives the instruction and the students carry it out to show understanding of the message or instruction. For example, the teacher might say, "Go to the pile of cards on Toshio's desk and pull out the card *jump*. Take it to Miyoko." The student does not say anything but acts out what was said. In another exercise, the teacher might instruct the student to draw/write something on a piece of paper; for example, "Draw a circle the size of a 10-yen piece in the middle of the paper. Draw a triangle as large as possible in the circle.'' By examining the final figure, you will be able to evaluate your students' comprehension ability.

The following two exercises are also for aural comprehension practice. However, they require the students to write. Bearing in mind that these are listening exercises, you may want to disregard spelling errors. Joan Morley of the University of Michigan recommends strongly that the instructor explain the vocabulary, when necessary, before beginning an exercise.

D. Song (Activity 1 in Appendix I)

A sample exercise using *I've Been Working on the Railroad* is given here. You will be much more successful if you work on songs that students have requested. Encourage them to listen to the radio so that they can make a request with the correct title. Songs seem to make it easier for correct pronunciation and fluency and this is a great pace-changer. In this exercise, the blank gives the first letter of the missing word if it begins with a consonant but nothing if it begins with a vowel. You need a recorded tape unless you want to perform yourself. Although there are many ways in which this can be used, one is introduced here:

1. Play the entire song through once. Students listen with the exercise sheets in front of them.
2. Play the song line by line, stopping and giving the students a chance to write in the words.
3. Play the entire song again.
4. Go over each blank and discuss the word that is missing.
5. Practice saying the lines.
6. Play the tape over and sing along with the tape.

E. Space Puzzle (Activity 2 in Appendix I)

A space puzzle is a listening and writing exercise in which students write information in boxes on a piece of paper. When they have filled in enough spaces, they can guess the information in the remaining boxes. An exercise from Joan Morley's *Improving Aural Comprehension*, Unit 3, (University of Michigan Press, 1972) is presented in Appendix I to give you an idea of space puzzles you can make for your students at their levels. Follow the directions on the instructor's copy.

Oral Production. A native English speaker is usually expected to teach the correct pronunication of individual sounds that are difficult for Japanese: /θ/, /ð/, /r/, /l/, /d/, /i/, /u/, etc. Although some class time can be set aside for intensive drills on these sounds, I would like to stress the importance of other pronunication points that should be given due notice.

A. Stress Groups

Because the Japanese language has the "syllable-timed rhythm" where each syllable gets the same amount of time rather than the "stress-timed rhythm" that the English language has, most of your students will read the following sentence in a "putt-putt" fashion, giving each of the 13 syllables equal times:

Thé télévísión ín thís roóm ís nót véry bíg.

The eight different ways in which we can say this sentence by stressing a different word each time are all correct, but the most common way we might say this sentence is:

The télévision/in this roóm/is not bíg.

It would be very helpful if you would make it a practice to read through the reading sections of the text at least several times with students repeating after you in proper word groups.

The following are some items to bear in mind for they are frequently stressed mistakenly, even by the teachers:

1. *modals:*   Tóm/can pláy/ténnis.
   We do not usually stress a modal auxiliary (can, may, should, will, etc.) in this position. Stressing it would have an added meaning, such as "Contrary to what you think, Tom *is* able to play tennis."

2. *not:*   Í/did not ǵo/to schóol.
   Not can be stressed, but only when someone is saying the contrary (just as in the previous example). Drill the students not to stress the *not.*

3. Relative pronoun *that:*   The hoúse/that we paśsed/is Tóm's.
   Since *that* introduces a relative clause, there is a tendency to stress this intital word. You might practice this type of sentence omitting *that* at first and gradually bringing it in.

4. *Very, quite:*   I thínk/she sáng/very wéll.
   Stressing *very* in this situation will alter the meaning. In some

cases, it could be interpreted as condescending. Ordinarily, *very* is not stressed.

B.   Intonation and Fluency

Tonal variations of spoken English within a sentence also plague most students. So that students will be able to handle sentences as units with correct intonation, drill sentences using gestures (e.g. "No, I don't want it" by shaking your head, or "Please come" by beckoning). The students' attention will be on the gestures and their monotone utterances can quickly take on natural intonation patterns. Richard Via of the University of Hawaii advocates the following method. He gets the students to say the same sentence in different moods—"Say it as fast as you can," "Say it like a father," etc. This method will shift the students' focus away from *what* they are saying to *how* they are saying it, and quite often they get the intonation that you have been struggling to convey.

Choral repetition in large groups saves you time when you want to get the general idea of how the sentence sounds across to the students, but group work does not help students achieve natural fluency. I recommend that you always take time to give individual practice after drilling the children in groups.

Communication Exercises.   Students lament that English classes are boring. They are boring because the students cannot see any use for the sentences they are learning. The following activities have been successful because all of them involve students in requesting real information. The immediate goal of acquiring information (although some of the questions are admittedly contrived) keeps student interest high while some phonological point or grammatical structure is being drilled. Try them and have fun.

A.   Getting to Know You (Activity 3 in Appendix I)

In this activity, each student has a sheet of paper with nine boxes at the top and instructions below. Each box has a question, and students ask each other. The original version of this game for adults has 25 boxes. You can, of course, make a 16-box version. You can also vary the questions to suit your students. Let the students walk around in the classroom to ask each other questions.

B. One-sided Conversation Cards

This exercise recommended by Richard Via never fails to work. Write a short conversation (or have the students write one). Put all of A's items on one card and all of B's items on another card. The student must memorize each line and look at the other person when speaking the line but may then refer back to the card to memorize the next line. Don't number the individual items. This requires the students to listen to each other to make sure that they are using the correct response or comment. After they have done the conversation in this manner several times, vary the activity by changing the situation involved, i.e., same words, different types of people talking or different situations.

Sample dialog: A: Where have you been?
                   B: I was waiting out in front.
                   A: Didn't I tell you I'd meet you in here?
                   B: Yeah, but I forgot.
                   A: You do this every time we go out!
                   B: I can't help it; you always give me so many directions.

This could be acted out between:
a. Coach and a football player;
b. Couple looking for a reason to break up;
c. Shy girl and big man on campus who is interested in her;
d. Two thieves about to rob a bank, etc.

C. Where is the Post Office? How can I get to the Post Office?
     (Activity 4 in Appendix I)

Judy E. Winn-Bell Olsen's book *Communication Starters* (Alemany Press, 1977) has many interesting and useful communication activites. Downtown Map Exercise is an especially good one. After some preparatory drills students are paired and each pair is given two maps. The maps show the same streets and buildings, but eight different buildings on each map have question marks instead of names. There are two ways in which you can use this activity—asking for the location of a building or asking for the directions to get to a building. The former is easier and hence should be done first.

1) Before you divide the class into pairs, practice the following sentence patterns:

Building A is *on* Third Street.

Building B is *on the corner of* Main Street and Third Street.

Building C is *on the north-east corner of* Main Street and Third Street.

Building D is *across the street from* the restaurant.

Building E is *next to* the parking lot.

Building F is *between* the parking lot and the theater, etc.

2) Divide the class into pairs. Give Map A to one student and Map B to the other. Caution them not to look at each other's map.

3) Student A asks Student B where the hospital (the first item on the list below Map A) is. Student B gives him the information looking at his map. Student A labels the correct building on his map.

4) Student B next asks Student A where the sporting-goods store (the first item on Map B's list) is. A tells B, who then labels the building.

5) They take turns asking and answering until all the building are labeled.

The more difficult version is the one in which the directions to these buildings are given. For each separate direction, students should begin in the lower right corner at the place labeled "Start here each time." The basic instructions, such as "Drive (continue) ahead," "Turn right at the corner," and "———— is on your right (left)" should be drilled before you start.

D.   Strip Stories (Activity 5 in Appendix I)

In this activity the teacher types a story, one sentence per line, and then cuts the paper into strips so that each strip contains one sentence. The exercise was first introduced by Robert Gibson of the University of Hawaii. (See *TESOL Quarterly* Volume 9, No. 2, June 1973 for details.) Since then many different uses have been developed, but the original intent was to stimulate oral communication. This is how it is used:

1.   Select a story or passage which is the proper level for your students and has a logical (or chronological) order.

2.   Adjust the number of lines so that it fits your group(s).

3.   Type the lines with spaces in between.

4. Cut the lines into narrow strips.
5. Let each student choose one at random.
6. Have them memorize their lines.
7. Make them throw away the lines, or collect them for use with another group.
8. Sit back and let them reconstruct the passage.
9. Don't mention writing, and they generally won't either. (If they should, the answer is no.)

Stories can be used to reinforce teaching points, vocabulary, content, etc. Two samples are presented as Activity 5.

Considerations for Class Preparation

It is very rare that a native speaker teacher has a prescribed curriculum to follow except in private schools. You may be told that the class is now on, say, Lesson 6, but if you ask for specific instructions, "Onegai itashimasu" ("I'll leave it up to you") is what is usually said. Now feeling completely free and independent, you will go on your merry way only to find later that many teachers have a definite view of whether what you did was useful or a complete waste of time. In the light of the fact that you have used 1/3 of the weekly English-class hours, this concern is quite understandable. What, then, are the considerations that should go into preparing for a class? You might consider the following suggestions:

Step 1 Ask the regular English teacher, whose class you are teaching, what s/he would like you to do. If definite suggestions are made, consider yourself fortunate and work on them.

Step 2 If the teacher does not suggest anything concrete, ask what lesson the class is studying now. Ask whether the teacher would like you to 1) review the previous lesson(s), 2) do supplementary exercises for the present lesson, or 3) introduce the next lesson.

Step 3 If you must choose from among the above 3, it would probably be best to review the previous lesson(s). Regardless of the kind of class you will be conducting, it would be helpful if you note the particulars of the lesson on which you will build your lesson plans. The following is a sample (for *New Prince English Course*, Book 1):

Textbook: *New Prince*, Book 1   Lesson: 9   Section: 1
Title: Ellen no Tanjobi (Ellen's Birthday)
1. Aim(s) of lesson: Use of possessive pronouns, possessives
2. Content: Birthday party
3. Pronunciation Problems: /z/ in brothers, father's, yours
4. Vocabulary: Happy Birthday, tape, classical music, mine, yours, father's
5. Sentence Patterns: These tapes are mine.
                           Are those yours?
                           Those tapes are my father's.

Step 4 Your class will be doing something relevant to the lesson as long as your are dealing with 1, 2, 3, 4, or 5 (in the sample outline above) separately or in combination. I would suggest that you plan a lesson starting with listening activities followed by listening and oral production activities. (See suggestions under Teaching Oral English.) Prepare 3 or 4 different activities and, as much as time and situation permit, discuss them with the regular teacher. Asking the teacher to rank your activities as *A—Very useful, B—Useful,* or *C—Do it if you have time* will give you an idea of the teacher's priorities.

CONCLUSION

Those who are engaged in teaching English in the lower secondary schools are undertaking instruction at the most important and also the most interesting part of the Japanese students' English career, which spans from a minimum of 3 years to a lifetime. These instructors must try to accomplish feats of English teaching that most language teachers in the world would consider impossible. They must motivate the students; they must teach basic English that will be the foundation for the English courses to come; they must prepare students for entrance examinations, which are not necessarily good evaluations of what has been taught, etc.

And all this must be accomplished in only 3 hours a week for most of them!

That native speaker teachers have a definitely significant role in the current system is obvious when we hear the more fluent college students recount the excitement of the meetings or friendships with native speakers (teachers, in most cases) in their early teens that spurred them on. The current educational system in Japan is on the Prime Minister's list of items for immediate review, but it seems that the system will continue to produce students who lack oral communication proficiency until some reform takes place. The foreign teacher's task is to assist the Japanese English teachers in making their textbook come alive—by demonstrating how the English sentences introduced in them are actually used in English-speaking countries, and by being a sounding board upon which the students (and teachers) may practice those sentences.

APPENDIX I—ACTIVITIES

Activity 1 Song

I've Been Working on the Railroad

This song was chosen primarily because it is not covered by copyright. Your students, however, know a Japanese song with the same music, so you can use this exercise in class. Songs chosen by the students from the current best hits list will be more effective, however.

I've been w_____ on the railroad,
All the l_____ day.
I've been w_____ on the railroad,
Just to p_____ the time _____.
Don't you hear the w_____ blowing,
Rise up so _____ in the morn;
Don't you hear the c_____ shouting,
"Dinah, blow your h_____!"
    Dinah, w_____ you blow, Dinah won't you b_____,
    Dinah, won't you blow y_____ horn?
    Dinah w_____ you blow, Dinah, won't you b_____,

Dinah, won't you blow y_____. horn?
Someone's in the k_____ with Dinah,
S_____ in the kitchen, I k_____.
Someone's in the kitchen with D_____,
S_____ on the old b_____.
    Fee, Fie, Fiddle-ee I O,
    F____, Fie, F_____-ee I O,
    Fee, F____, Fiddle-ee ___ ___,
S_____ on the _____ b_____.

Activity 2   Space Puzzle

Who Plays the Guitar?

Five students from five different countries were studying English in the United States. They lived in adjoining houses. They planned to study in five different fields of study in five different cities. Each of the five had a different hobby.

	Red House	Blue House	Green House	White House	Purple House
Country					
Field					
City					
Hobby					

COUNTRY	CITY	FIELD	HOBBY
Turkey	San Francisco	Engineering	Dancing
Peru	Miami	Law	Soccer
Korea	Chicago	Business	Swimming
Spain	New York	Chemistry	Travel
India	Boston	Psychology	Playing the guitar

Activity 2   Instructor's Copy

Instructions

Look at the vocabulary at the bottom of the page. Repeat after me. (Oral practice.)

Now, look at the diagram. Notice that on the left side of the diagram you find *country, field, city,* and *hobby*. Notice that across the top of the diagram you find *Red House, Blue House, Green House, White House,* and *Purple House*. Listen very carefully, think, and write the answers. Listen to each statement. Find the correct square, write the correct word from the list below. Ready? Begin.

1. The student from the country of Turkey lives in the middle house. (Repeat.) Write *Turkey* in the correct square.
2. The student in the field of Engineering lives on the far right. (Repeat.) Write *Engineering* in the correct square.
3. The student who is going to New York to study lives next to the red house. (Repeat.)

BE SURE STUDENTS ARE WRITING IN THE CORRECT SQUARES!

4. The student who lives to the left of the blue house likes to play soccer, as a hobby. (Repeat.)
5. The student in the second house from the right—second house from the right—is going to study in Miami. (Repeat.)
6. The student from Peru lives next to the student who is going to New York. (Repeat.) There's only one space where you can write Peru.
7. The Law student lives next to the student who is going to Miami. (Repeat.)
8. The Law student likes to travel. (Repeat.)
9. The student in the second house from the left—second house from the left—is from Spain. (Repeat.)
10. The student who is studying in the field of Chemistry is from India. The Chemistry student is from India.
11. The student from Korea likes swimming. (Repeat.)
12. The student from Spain lives next door to the student in Psychology. (Repeat.)

13. The student on the far right is going to Boston. (Repeat.)
14. And last, the student who likes dancing as a hobby lives between the student who is going to Boston and the student who is going to Chicago. (Repeat.)

TEST

1. Who plays the guitar?
2. Who is going to study in San Francisco?
3. Who is going to study in the field of Business?

(From Joan Morley's *Improving Aural Comprehension*, University of Michigan Press, 1972.)

Activity 3   Getting to Know You

Do you come to school on foot?	Do you know what country Sydney is in?	Have you eaten at McDonald's?
Have you walked more than 10 km?	Do you sing in the bath?	Do you have fewer than 6 cousins?
Do you know who Mr. Nakasone is?	Have you ever talked with an American?	Have you ever seen an elephant?

GOAL: To fill in each box with one name.
RULES: You must write in a person's name *only* if s/he answers "Yes" to the question in the box.
You must have asked everyone in the room one question before you can ask anyone a second question.
You must have asked everyone two questions before you can ask anyone a third or fourth, etc.
You must be able to identify each person whose name you have written.
SCORING: 1 point for each name.
10 extra points for each time you have 3 names in a row—vertically, horizontally, or diagonally.

Activity 4   Where is the post office?

Instructions

You and your partner have different maps. *Do not look at your partner's map.* Ask your partner how to get to the places listed below, starting each time from the lower right-hand corner, where it says, "Start here each time." Write the name in the right place. Then let your partner ask you.

The places you want to find are:

the hospital   the department store   the hi-fi shop
the bank   the drugstore   the supermarket
the garage   the nursery

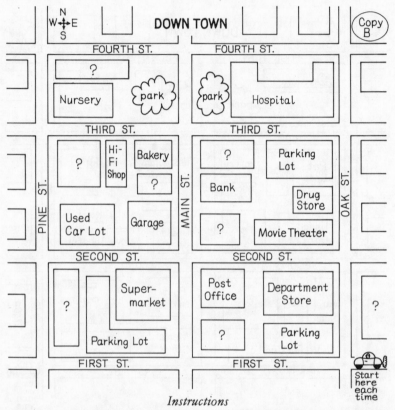

N
W + E
S

DOWN TOWN

Copy B

FOURTH ST.　FOURTH ST.

?

Nursery

park

park

Hospital

THIRD ST.　THIRD ST.

PINE ST.

?

Hi-Fi Shop

Bakery

?

?

MAIN ST.

Bank

?

OAK ST.

Parking Lot

Drug Store

Used Car Lot

Garage

Movie Theater

SECOND ST.　SECOND ST.

?

Super-market

Post Office

Department Store

?

Parking Lot

?

Parking Lot

FIRST ST.　FIRST ST.

Start here each time

Instructions

You and your partner have different maps. *Do not look at your partner's map*. Ask your partner how to get to the places listed below, starting each time from the lower right-hand corner, where it says, "Start here each time." Write the name in the right place. Then let your partner ask you.

The places you want to find are:

the sporting goods store
the men's store
the YMCA
the dress shop

the restaurant
the pet shop
the hardware store
the shoe repair shop

by Judy E. Winn-Bell Olsen. These maps first appeared in *On TESOL '75*. Reprinted with the permission of TESOL.

Copy for classroom use.

116

Activity 5   Strip Stories

I.   1. A man is lying in bed.
      2. While lying there, he lights up a cigarette.
      3. As he smokes, he picks up a book and starts to read.
      4. Reading always makes him sleepy.
      5. After reading a few pages, he gets very sleepy.
      6. He puts the book down and closes his eyes.
      7. He drifts off to sleep.
      8. His fingers go limp and the cigarette falls onto the bed.
      9. Smoke begins to rise from the bedspread.
     10. Flames begin to rise from the whole bedspread.
     11. The man wakes up.
     12. He is coughing violently.
     13. The man tries to put the fire out with a blanket, but he cannot.
     14. The man runs to the telephone and calls the fire department.
     15. The fire department arrives and begins to put out the fire.

II.   For *New Horizon* Book 3, Lesson 7
      1. Itaru Nonaka climbed Mt. Fuji alone on February 16, 1895.
      2. He climbed it because he wanted to build a weather station on top.
      3. He built a small weather station there during the summer of 1895.
      4. Itaru started working in the station alone.
      5. After a month, his wife came to help him at the station.
      6. He told his wife to go home, but Shiyoko stayed.
      7. They recorded the temperature, air pressure, and so on every two hours.
      8. In December Itaru became sick but they did not give up.
      9. On December 22, 1895, their friends came to save them.
     10. A permanent weather station was built on Mt. Fuji in 1932.

Appendix II — Sample Exercises for Review Lessons

SAMPLE 1 Textbook: *Total English Revised Edition*, Book 1, Lesson 14
            Content: Life in Canada and Australia

Sentence Patterns: 1: Which are the winter months?
2. Whose book is that? It is Akemi's.
3. Here is my album.

Prounciation: 1. Months of the year
2. /ɔ:/ *Au*stralia, *Au*gust, f*a*ll

A. *Months of the Year*
[Prepare flashcards with the names of the months in English on one side and in Japanese on the other.]
1) Go through the months of the year in unison in order from January to December. Watch out for the /er/ sound in Septemb*er*, Octob*er*, Novemb*er*, and Decemb*er* and the stress, e.g. Octóber, Novémber, etc.
2) Go through the months in order; this time students give the English as you flash the cards with the Japanese equivalent.
3) Now show those cards in random order to see if students can come up with the months in English. Use a real calendar and point to the months as the class calls out the names in English.

B. *Whose birthday is in January?*
[The word *birthday* has not been introduced yet in this book, but since the word is used in Japanese, you will not have much trouble. Use the correct pronunciation [bə́:rθdei] after explaining that this is the English way of saying /baasudei/.
Teacher asks: "Whose birthday is in January?"
[Students raise their hands.]
Teacher asks: "Keiko, when is your birthday?"
Keiko answers: "My birthday (It) is January 25."

C. *Keiko's is January 25.*
[Everybody writes his/her name and birthday on a card:]

Keiko
January 25

Takeo
October 9

Teacher: Takeo and Keiko, please change your cards.
[The two exchange their cards saying "Here's my card." "Here's mine."]

118

Teacher: Takeo, when is your birthday and when is Keiko's?
Takeo: My birthday is October 9 and Keiko's is January 25.
Teacher: Keiko, when is your birthday and when is Takeo's?
Keiko: My birthday is January 25 and Takeo's is October 9.

Of course, there is no inherent connection between birthdays and pronouns, so it is possible—and may sometimes be preferable—that you bring in a different content and review familiar vocabulary or sentence patterns. For example, you might want to talk about textbooks belonging to different students, introducing the exercise in the following manner:

Teacher: This is Tazuko's book and that is Toru's book. Is that Tazuko's book?
Class: No, it's Toru's.
Teacher: That is Mamoru's pencil and this is my pencil. Is this Mamoru's?
Class: No, it's yours.
Teacher: (to Masako) These are my shoes and those are yours. Are those mine?
Masako: No, they're mine.

Using objects whose ownership is not apparent at a glance—e.g., baby pictures, handkerchiefs, etc.—will make this exercise more exciting.

SAMPLE 2 Textbook: *New Prince English Course,* Book 2, Lesson 8
Content: International Dinner
Pronunciation: 1. there'll, it'll
2. have to / hæf tə /
3. You must hélp your mother.
You may úse my typewriter.
Sentence Patterns: 1. You may bring your own lunch.
2. I must bring something nice.
Shall I make fruit cakes?
3. You have to get up early.

A. *Pronunciation Practice* (Stress on the right word)
1. [Students repeat after the teacher]

Teacher: at the school cafeteria
  : have lunch / at the school cafeteria.
  : Let's have lunch / at the school cafeteria.
  : the cafeteria lunch.
  : don't like / the cafeteria lunch.
  : I don't like / the cafeteria lunch. (Continue in this way.)
2. Dramatic reading with the teacher taking the part of Taro, the class taking the part of Ellen. Try to have them look at you when they are talking. Give them time to look at the sentence *before* they start to say it.
Change roles.
Repeat this dramatic reading, dividing the class into halves, quarters, aisles, etc.

B. *must help, don't have to help*
[Teacher draws 2 figures on the board]

Tamiko

Midori

Teacher: Tamiko is Midori's sister.
Midori is younger than Tamiko.
Tamiko must do many things.
Midori doesn't have to do anything.
I will talk about Tamiko. You tell me about Midori.
1. Tamiko must clean the house.
Class: Midori doesn't have to clean the house.
Teacher: 2. Tamiko must help her mother.
Class: Midori doesn't have to help her mother.
Teacher: 3. Tamiko must make breakfast.
4. Tamiko must cook dinner.
5. Tamiko must get up at 6 o'clock.
6. Tamiko must make coffee for her father.

120

C. *Shall we — ?*
[Teacher reviews the many objects in a picture (or a box)—a sandwich, a ball, a piano, a camera, a fork, a napkin, a textbook, a bat, a towel, etc.]

Teacher: Class, we are going on a picnic. What do we need for a picnic? [Picks up or points to the first item: a textbook] Shall we take a textbook? Answer "Yes, let's," or "No, let's not."

Class: No, let's not.
Teacher: Shall we take some sandwiches?
Class: Yes, let's.
Teacher: Takeshi, you come up here and ask the class.
Takeshi: (to the class) Shall we take the piano?
Class: No, let's not.
Takeshi: (to Mieko) Mieko, your turn.
Mieko: (to the class) Shall we take a baseball and a bat?
Class: Yes, let's.

D. *May I borrow—?*
[Put up on the board things you want to do and things you need in order to do those things.]

Things you want to do	*Things you need*
1. type a letter	typewriter, paper
2. write a letter	pen, letter paper
3. ride a horse	horse, saddle
4. play music	guitar, piano, violin, etc.
5. play baseball	ball, glove, mitt, bat
6. make fruit cakes	sugar, eggs, flour, butter
7. play tennis	tennis racket, tennis ball
8. watch television	television set
9. drive a car	car

Teacher: Makoto, what do you want to do?
Makoto: I want to play tennis.
Sumiko, may I borrow your tennis racket?
Sumiko: Yes, you may. (*or* I'm sorry, I don't have a tennis racket.)
Toshiko: I want to type a letter. May I borrow your typewriter, Chieko?
Chieko: Yes, you may. (*or* I'm sorry, it's broken.)

121

Appendix III — Sample Exercises for Introductory Lessons

SAMPLE 1 Textbook: *New Everyday English*, Book 3, Lesson 11
Content: Body Language
Sentence Patterns: 1. I know *how old the man is.*
2. Tony *asked* me *to go* to the store.
3. Judy was *so* busy *that* she could not help Roy.

A. *Body language and gestures*
1. Yes   4. I don't know.   7. Good-bye
2. No   5. I   8. Good (Thumbs up)
3. O.K.   6. Come here.   9. No good (Thumbs down)

1) Have the students match your gestures with the meaning on the board.
2) Discuss each of them and see how the Japanese express such ideas.
3) Turn to the inside cover of the text and treat the gestures given there.

B. I know *how old the man is.*
[The students only hear this structure and reply to it—your goal is recognition only in the first exercise.]
1. Teacher (to Akio): Do you know how old Masaru is?
   Akio: Yes, I do. He's 15 years old.
   Teacher (to Motoko): Do you know how old Toshiko is?
   Motoko: No, I don't.
   Teacher (to Ken): Do you know how old Mr. Tanaka (the principal) is?
   Ken: No, I don't.
2. Teacher (to Saburo): Where does Jiro live?
   Saburo: I know where he lives. He lives in Ushita.
   Saburo (to Reiko): Where does Mr. Ota (the math teacher) live?
   Reiko: I don't know where he lives.

3. Teacher (to Goro):   What time does Eiko go to bed?
    Goro: I don't know what time she goes to bed.
    (to Eiko):   What time do you go to bed?
    Eiko   (to Goro):   At 10 o'clock.
    Goro: I know what time she goes to bed now. She goes to bed at 10.

SAMPLE 2   Textbook: *The New Crown English Series*, Book 3, Lesson 8
           Content: Jobs
           Sentence Patterns: 1. He *wants to work* in a restaurant.
                               2. She has a lot of work *to do*.
                               3. My mother works *to help* sick people.
                               4. *Why* do you want to be a nurse?

A. *Names of different professions*
    Introduce the following:
    [Even though the * words are not in the textbook word list, these seem to be easy enough to teach. *Carpenter* is introduced in this series as a family name, but the meaning can be taken up here.]

    Mr. Ueno works in a restaurant.   He is a cook.
    Mrs. Shimizu works in a hospital.   She is a nurse.
    Keiko works in a restaurant.   She is a waitress.*
    Mrs. Omura works in a hospital.   She is a doctor.*
    My mother works in a school.   She is a teacher.
    My brother works in an office.   He is an office worker.*
    My sister works in a television studio.*   She is an announcer.
    My uncle makes tables and chairs.   He is a carpenter.

B. I want (like) *to work* in a restaurant.
    Teacher: Taro plays basketball every day. He likes it.
              Taro likes to play basketball every day.
              I cook dinner every evening. I like it.
              I like to cook dinner every evening.
              Ken plays tennis every Sunday. He likes it.
              Ken likes to play tennis every Sunday.

My father plays the guitar and sings. He likes it.
My father likes to play the guitar and sing.
Emiko writes a letter to her penpal. She likes it.
Emiko likes to write a letter to her penpal.

Have the students repeat these sentences after you, making sure they understand what they are saying.

C.   I want *to close the window.*

Teacher:	The window is open. It is very cold.
	Shoko, what do you want to do?
Shoko:	I want to close the window.
Teacher:	You are very hungry. It is 6 o'clock.
	Tomio, what do you want to do?
Tomio:	I want to eat dinner. (I want to cook dinner.)
Teacher:	Your friend in America wrote a letter. It came yesterday.
	What do you want to do today, Momoko?
Momoko:	I want to write a letter to my friend today.
Teacher:	Akiko is very hungry. There is an apple on the table.
	Shigeru; what does Akiko want to do?
Shigeru:	She *wants* to eat the apple. (Beware of *s*-deletion in the verb.)
Teacher:	The window and the door are closed. It is very hot in here.
	Wakako, what does your sister want to do?
Wakako:	She wants to open the door and windows.

Strategies and Methods for English Teachers in Japanese High Schools

Thomas G. Gunterman

Working in/with the System

This section will explain how to adapt to the Japanese English teaching system in general, while at the same time making a personal contribution to the student.

Class Setting. Your role is to supplement the students' regular reading/translation class. Their regular class grades and progress are what they will be judged on when they try to enter college or apply for a job.

The number of students in your class will range from twenty to forty, depending on the degree of enlightenment of the administration. You will likely have any one group for only one or two hours a week. Often a Japanese teacher will be assigned to team-teach with you. I strongly recommend that you convince the department you are able to teach by yourself. As long as you are paired with another teacher, the students will look upon you as the lesser of the two teachers, a very frustrating position in which to be.

The administration will expect you to teach the students one or a combination of the three skills not taught in their reading class—listening, speaking, and writing. However, in the actual teaching, if you are allowed to work alone, you will encounter very little interference from the Japanese staff. This gives you rather a lot of leeway in interpreting your instructions into actual lessons, and is another reason to teach alone.

Texts and Materials. As in junior high school, the students' texts are decided by the Ministry of Education, the Mombusho. There is some difference in difficulty among the approved series, but the overall methodology is the same in all books. As far as I know, there are no texts written specifically for high-school use that don't follow the general Mombusho text reading/translation style. If you want to choose a text that uses other teaching methods, you will be forced to choose books that were written for commercial English schools. Your best bet is to get as many texts from as many different sources as possible for reference, and construct your own lessons from them.

Student Attitude and Ability. It is hard to tell what the level of your students will be. At best they will have a good intellectual grasp of basic English sentence structure and the present, present continuous, past, future (with *will*), and present perfect tenses. At worst they will not be able to count to ten or write the alphabet. Expect something in the middle with a sprinkling of both extremes.

For most students, you are probably their first foreign teacher. As a result, they are excited and you have their attention and cooperation. This initial excitement at having a foreign teacher will include the belief that becoming proficient in English will be effortless and easy. Your foreignness will make you popular. However, after the week or two it takes for them to find out that you are human, you will fall into the "adult" category in their minds, which is just slightly less negative than their "dentist's office" or "washing dishes" category.

Don't despair. You are different from the other teachers in the school. You can use that difference to your advantage, creating a situation in which, by comparison, the students will prefer your class to their other academic classes. Look at how the other subjects and classes are taught. With mind-cramping uniformity, they are almost all lectures with no student participation or anything to keep them awake but the vague desire to get a good grade and thereby a good job some time in the distant future. With competition like that, how can you fail to become one of the bright (well . . . less dark) spots in your students' school life?

Overall Teaching Goals. High school, of course, is an extension of junior high school. The overall three-year goal for the students is to pass the entrance examinations to the next level of education, college. In the academic subjects, teachers will use textbooks written for college entrance exams and thereby pace the class, treating college-bound students and students not going on to college to the same curriculum.

In contrast to junior high-school vocabulary lists, the high-school vocabulary lists contain words and idioms (which the students must learn) that are usually archaic, obtuse, and virtually useless. Although the first, and I believe correct, reaction is to throw away the standard text, it would do the students a great disservice to do so. They have to cope with the material in tests; they will be judged by how well they have learned the often useless phrases. No matter how distasteful the contents are to you, you can alleviate some of their suffering by helping them learn what their school system has chosen for them to learn.

A good primary goal would be to make sure the students know their junior high-school material. They will need it in their high-school classes, but in all likelihood their teacher will not bother to review it or check for any weak spots the students might have. This is where you can help out.

First, almost all junior high-school material, if arranged properly, can be used in everyday conversation. You can teach such functional words as ''who, why, what,'' etc. in a conversational setting and help the students indirectly in their reading/translation class by doing so. If students internalize the basics enough to use them in conversation, during tests, or in lessons, they won't spend time trying to remember the difference between ''why'' and ''when,'' and will be able to concentrate on such words as ''ubiquitous.''

Another way to help the students is to assist them in memorizing all the vocabulary they need to know. Admittedly, it would be an impossible task to try to teach every word. Supposedly they are required to memorize three thousand words in their three years of high school—three words per day except Sunday.

Avoid requiring the students to look up every new word they encounter in the dictionary. It is a time-consuming skill that is never tested. Spelling has its place but it is also not tested. Stress spelling only with the basic words. With the more uncommon words, stress reading fluency. Being able to read aloud helps pronunciation, which is tested in the examinations.

No matter what you are told your goals should be, remember you will be doing the students a great favor by helping to remove a bit of the drudgery and mystery surrounding the sometimes strange English they are taught. For your own education and development of empathy with the students, read a broad sampling of different college entrance examinations. Put simply, helping the students deal with their world and its requirements should be the primary goal of any teacher.

Helping Students to Organize.   Consider yourself, in part, to be the organizer of your students' studies. As mentioned earlier, help them deal with the Mombusho readers they must study in their regular class for the entrance examinations. You can help them streamline their studies in different ways.

One disadvantage of the Mombusho readers is that they have very few examples of the sentence structures, phrases, and idioms that they teach. The students are left without enough exposure to how these are used in other situations. Drills that you make, such as those used in the audio-lingual method, can compensate for this lack.

There will be a few one-sentence examples of the main points in each lesson. Choose a few that can be made into drills easily. One kind of drill is the substitution drill:

Text sentence:	They stood up so that they might see better.
Teacher:	Students:
He	He stood up so that he might see better.
put on glasses	He put on glasses so that he might see better.
moved closer	He moved closer so that he might see better.
hear	He moved closed so that he might hear better.

Another kind of drill that is easy to make is the guided construction drill.

Text sentence:	Living as we did near the ocean, we swam every morning.
Teacher:	Students:
in Japan/learn Japanese	Living as we did in Japan, we learned Japanese.
in a big house/ have lot guests	Living as we did in a big house, we had a lot of guests.
near the school/ walk to class	Living as we did near the school, we walked to class.

Some phrases are hard to make drills for. Simply giving more examples is beneficial.

Text sentence: We turned to the local government for the information.

Sample sentences: The little boy turned to his father for help.

He turned to the teacher for advice.

The child turned to her mother for comfort.

One way to save the students endless hours chained to the dictionary is to make a list of words that you feel comfortable with from their reader text. Leave out the words that you consider the least useful in normal conversation. Have a Japanese teacher write the Japanese translations beside the words and give the list to your students. A variation of this is to assign each student a certain page. The students then make a glossary of the words they find hard on their particular pages. Finally, they give their classmates the translations. This organization of time and effort will streamline the students' efforts. Once your Japanese is good enough, you can dispense with the above steps and go through the book quickly in class. Another technique is to pair students up so they can quiz one another on word meaning, spelling, sentence construction, etc. This frees you to work with individual students.

Don't be afraid to assign homework. It is an expected part of their school life and if students are jogged into studying more at home their English will benefit. Don't let the fear of correcting homework prevent you from assigning it. You can rotate homework-checking duty among the students.

Desired Attitude.   This section on attitude will be divided into three parts: attitude toward your work in general, toward the school and other teachers, and toward the students.

First, it is necessary to know as much about your job as possible. Find out how the school runs and how English is taught in other classes. Don't take another's word for how things are; look for yourself. In order to do all this (and this can't be repeated enough) *learn Japanese.* Of course, speaking and understanding are most important, but at least a minimal level of reading should also be achieved. Many school announcements are spread by memos and writing on the board. Being able to at least read that something is going on will help you function and will also earn the respect of the other teachers.

It is necessary to earn, and expect, respect from the other teachers. This respect will bear directly upon how you are able to work with students. You are not in Japan to revolutionize, change, or resist their way of teaching. On the other hand, keep your identity, values, and professionalism. You have a right to have some say in the classes you teach, the methods you use, or the text. If your questions and opinions are put mildly, and the answers you get are received in the same spirit, the other teachers will experience a pleasant lesson in cultural differences. That is one of the non-verbalized reasons you were hired. Neither rock the boat nor be a pushover, and you will have a long, enjoyable, and fulfilling stay in Japan.

The students are not apt to overwhelm you with their eagerness to talk or to try out the English you are teaching. They are, as a rule, shy and inhibited to the point of petrification. I have found that the best way to combat this is to adopt the Japanese custom of flattery. Drown them in flattery; throw truth to the winds: "You learn faster than anyone I have known." "You seem to have an ear for languages," etc. I have found that on a personal level it can be surprisingly effective, bringing out students who would be afraid to speak. Allow mistakes in the lesson. Don't spotlight one student until they show they can handle it. Loosen up in front of the class. Tell jokes. When the students know they will not be laughed at, they will begin to come out of their shells. Allowing a rather high noise level in class will work to good advantage when doing pronounciation practice and group drills.

Attitude can be summed up in these three ways: (1) Be enthusiastic about your work; (2) Be professional toward your fellow teachers; and (3) Be approachable to the students.

Discipline. If you have become friends with your students, minor infractions can be corrected by a stern talk or, if necessary, a good tongue-lashing; in the case of the latter, either language is OK. Knowing you as a cheerful person will make them eager to return you to that state when you start scowling and growling. However, it is necessary to be firm.

Most serious discipline problems can be avoided by the first impression you give to the students. From the beginning be sure to show them that you are in charge and are not a confused foreigner who does not know what is going on. If in doubt about the rules, make your own and enforce them with conviction. It will be something to laugh about in the future if you go overboard, and the students will forgive any excesses; they have seen worse.

Insist that the students call you by your last name. That is how they address the other teachers and you deserve the same respect and courtesy. The biggest problem in this case is that you will also have to train the other teachers to address you properly in front of the students. They, even more than the students, will tend to consider you their token foreigner and not a real teacher. The students pick up such an attitude very quickly. If not remedied, the student whom you have just chastised for being disruptive in class will go to his favorite teacher who will proceed to undermine any authority or discipline you have established.

Remember that you have absolute power in the classroom and are expected to use it to control your class. Do not expect to take a truculent student into the principal's office for a three-way interview. The student will be able to out-talk you and the principal will wonder why you don't just haul off and hit the kid and be done with it. Physical force isn't encouraged, but neither is it taboo. In dealing with discipline problems, use your judgment, remembering your own values and also those of the country you are in.

There are many in-class punishments, or "consequences" as we say in this age of enlightenment, available to the teacher. For the student who forgets his book, standing up for a certain amount of time may encourage him and his classmates to be more attentive. For the student who didn't do the assigned homework, extra study time after school might help. Discipline is up to you.

Curriculum and Departmental Proceedings. Participate and learn as much as you can about how the English department is run. Quietly give your opinion when it seems appropriate. Every so often departments go through a period of self-evaluation or a time for rearranging the curriculum. At these times there is a chance to contribute your opinion and also a good chance that it will count.

You can try to change the textbook you have been required to use. You may be able to have your classes changed to the morning rather than after lunch. The department may even be willing to start new programs, such as a typing program, or study-trips abroad.

Every department has a budget. As you are a foreigner, it may be assumed that you are not interested in such inner workings of the school and you may not be told of it. Again, find out. Work out your own budget for things that would help you teach, and present it to whoever is in charge. These items could range from cardboard and colored felt pens to overhead projectors and graded English readers for a department library. These is no harm in asking for some funds to buy a few reference books for yourself and the department, or a year's membership in JALT. Schools will often pay for a business trip or two, and you can go to a couple of conferences. The trick is to go out of your way to learn what is available. Just remember to ask politely, be reasonable, and accept any refusal graciously. . . then try again next year.

Strategies and Methods

Here I give some general examples of how you can supplement the students' regular lesson. I encourage you always to look for other ways. While supplementing is important, developing your own course of study is also necessary. I have found the following strategies and methods to be successful. It is by no means a complete list. You have to pick and choose what suits you best.

Conversation. Many times you will be asked to teach a conversation-only class. The Japanese teacher will be the students' main English teacher, the one who teaches them how to get into college. This automatically relegates you to a "sub" position, an unimportant position in the students' minds. You won't be considered a vital part of their education; you are a one-hour-a-week break from the real stuff. That is a tough position to be in. The following are some suggestions on how to go about teaching in such a situation.

The students expect this class to be lighter and more fun than their regular English classes. To a certain extent, these expectations should be met; it will be a head start in the job of getting them motivated.

However, it is necessary to have a solid base for the class. This can be in the form of an appropriate conversation text, which may be hard to find, or writing your own units. Create mini-dialogues of conversations the students might use in their everyday life, or ones you would be likely to have with them if you met them in the hall. For example:

A: How are you doing?
B: Pretty good.
A: Where are you going?
B: To chemistry class. What about you?
A: I'm going to the faculty room.
B: Oh . . . well, take it easy.
A: See you later.

A simple dialogue like this could be a regular feature of the class, with its introduction, practice, performance, and obvious variations. The students could be held responsible for memorizing, and performing from a Japanese translation, one dialogue per week. You can test them on a selection of the dialogues during the school mid-term and final exams. This kind of consistency will give the class the right amount of legitimacy for the students while giving you time to do games, songs, or other pleasant activities.

Most students want to learn how a real native speaker speaks. Another good objective that will complement simple dialogues is to teach the linkage between words in normal conversation.

A Japanese will often say that an English native speaker speaks too fast for him to understand. The problem many times is not that of speed, but rather that words are linked together, forming a whole new word. "Gonna" is as much a different word from "going to" as "jail" is from "penal institution."

The most bothersome linkages are not that many, and they appear in the most basic English phrases. Here are a few of the linkages that I have found useful:

Did you	Didja

$$\left.\begin{array}{l}\text{Who}\\\text{Why}\\\text{What}\\\text{etc.}\end{array}\right\}\text{did you} \qquad \left.\begin{array}{l}\text{Who}\\\text{Why}\\\text{What}\\\text{etc.}\end{array}\right\}\text{dja}$$

have to	hafta
want to	wanna

$$\text{What}\left\{\begin{array}{l}\text{do}\\\text{are}\end{array}\right\}\text{you} \qquad \text{Whacha}$$

As you can see from the examples, the linkages each person chooses will reflect his own dialect. Dialects are a fact of life; don't be shy about teaching them yours. Make up your own spelling to reflect the pronunciation. The phonetic alphabet is not tested on entrance examinations, so it is not necessary to teach it.

Culture. Presenting lesson units on your country's culture, customs, and holidays is a welcome break for the students. This can be done by telling them anecdotes of your own high-school years. Tell them how your classes and schedules differed from theirs, about drive-in movies, school proms, coming to school in a car. Using the following guidelines will enable you to give a long talk that the students will understand:

1. Mentally arrange the speech beforehand so it will be smooth and easy to follow.
2. Hand out a word list of the difficult words you will use and their Japanese meanings.
3. Use body gestures and diagrams as much as possible.

Pictures and slides of your hometown, your family, your childhood, and your friends will keep their attention for a long time. One way to keep them in suspense is to bring a picture to class and to start talking about it while just showing them the back. Only turn the picture around when you are finished.

It is unlikely that you will have one room set aside for your English classes; you will move from one to another. However, if you are on good terms with the homeroom teacher who is in charge of the classroom in which you teach, you can decorate the walls with pictures and posters from back home. As the physical environment is usually not considered important by the administration, any break in the usual drabness is appreciated by the students. The posters and pictures can be incorporated into drills and sentence samples.

Take advantage of all the national holidays from back home and celebrate. Again, this can be done after the usual short educational lecture. If you are an American and want to have a watermelon party on the Fourth of July, get the students to pitch in some money. Most classes have a self-regulated class fund to which everybody contributes. If you don't teach one whole homeroom class with an independent fund, tell the students what kind of party you would like to have, what you need to buy, and ask how much they are willing to help. They are used to the process.

Read letters from home to your class as much as decency allows. Let them know how life feels to a person a long way from home. Ask your family to send postcards every so often.

Discuss with the students what you enjoy about Japan and what you find difficult to adapt to. However, be careful with stereotyping; the students have enough stereotypical images already.

Dictation. Dictation is an age-old method used in teaching languages. Probably because it conjures up images of stylus and clay tablets, dictation is not often mentioned or used anymore. I have found it to be a useful tool if used under certain restraints and for certain purposes. All it requires is a pencil and paper. I rediscovered dictation one day when I walked into class, realized that I had forgotten my text, and was faced with a roomful of students to whom I had given a long and serious lecture the day before on coming to class prepared. I've been using it ever since.

The danger with dictation is that it doesn't take much time before the students are terribly frustrated. With this in mind, keep it light. Dictation should not be a spelling test. It is best used as listening practice, a review of what they know. Following are some guidelines to consider:

1. Use words and phrases that you are sure the students are comfortable with.
2. Keep the sentences, and also the entire exercise, short and fast-paced. Ten sentences is a good-sized unit.
3. Use the same words and phrases several times in the exercise.
4. After every sentence or two, give the correct answer on the board.
5. Speak at normal to fast speed. If done slowly, dictation becomes a spelling test.
6. If the students are still asking for one more repetition after the third time, the sentence is probably too hard and should be shown on the board.
7. If you know some of the words you want to use are a bit difficult to spell, write them on the board for the students to refer to.

When combined with modern technology, dictation can be a useful homework assignment. I have never met a Japanese student who didn't have access to a cassette tape recorder at home. I have also never heard of a school that didn't have a language laboratory, an unused dinosaur which every self-respecting school has spent money on. Have the students bring a blank tape, find out how to work the machines, and you can simultaneously record as many tapes as there are booths. The assignment can be from one night's worth to a whole summer's worth.

Diary. Diaries and journals make up a large portion of Japanese ancient literature. The custom of keeping accounts of day-to-day events is still popular. Even homeroom classes have a homeroom diary. The advantage of a diary in English teaching is that there is so much repetition of basic phrases such as "I went to bed at 10:30," "I'll go shopping tomorrow," and "I have to study for a test next week." These phrases will become second nature to the student and serve as a basis for his knowledge of simple grammar structure.

The daily entries should be kept short in the beginning so you are able to correct the common errors. Since the same mistakes will be made by a large number of the students, the corrections can be done on the board. It is a good idea not to be too critical of mistakes at first. Encourage the students to write as much as possible.

Admittedly, keeping a diary for some can be a very grueling chore. Rather than get into a struggle with the few students who gradually stop turning in their notebooks, diary-keeping should be limited to one month or to one day per week.

Games. "Games" seems to be the category into which all the bits and pieces of other methods are put. To the student they give the impression of making work seem like it isn't; to the teacher who has used them ad infinitum, it is a word that has lost its once lighthearted, joyful meaning. The following are some games that students enjoy. Their objective is to develop the students' ability at word recognition, spelling, and sentence construction.

Hangman is an old standard. Keep the drawing simple: head, trunk, arms, legs. Insist on a time limit for each guess. Words must come from a selected part of the book. The guesser may not look at the book while guessing.

Concentration is a common card game. Choose a list of about twenty-five words and write each word on two cards. Turn the fifty cards face down on a table and mix them up. The students try to match two cards with the same word. They are allowed to flip over only two cards per turn. After a turn, the exposed cards are replaced face down again in their original places. The above is the simplest variation. To add a little more difficulty, write one card in English and the other in Japanese.

Group spelling with cards is a rowdy game that can usually be heard too clearly in the next classroom. Two groups of fifteen to thirty students are needed. Get two sets of thirty cards. Write one letter of the alphabet on each card. Make an extra E, T, R, S, since there are many words with two of those letters. Distribute one set of letters among each team so that each student has one or two cards. To play, call out a word, and the members of each team that have a letter in that word run to the front of the class and spell the word by holding up their cards in the correct order. The fastest team gets a point. A variation of this game is to write words on the cards and construct sentences.

The last is also a card game I thought of when watching the game called "Hyakunin Isshu." I simply substituted English for Japanese. The cards are spread face up on the table with sentences written on them. When one of the sentences is read, the first player to grab the matching card gets a point. There are obvious variations with either words or sentences read in English or Japanese.

Singing. I will leave the argument as to whether or not singing is beneficial to language learning to others. It is, at worst, fun for the students and enjoyable if you like to sing. The following song is a good activity for the one class you are scheduled to teach after the final examinations or the day before summer vacation. The variation is a must. Teach the students "My Bonnie Lies Over the Ocean."

My bonnie lies over the ocean,
My bonnie lies over the sea.
My bonnie lies over the ocean,
Oh, bring back my bonnie to me.
  Bring back, bring back,
  Oh, bring back my bonnie to me, to me
  Bring back, bring back,
  Oh, bring back my bonnie to me.
(The variation is to have them sit down or stand up every time they sing a word that begins with a "b.")

Extensive Reading. Your students will very rarely be in a situation in which they must use English. In class it is impossible to put them in, or create, all the situations in which they will need English. One remedy for this is to have them read books in English extensively.

They will already be reading in their regular class, if muddling through a page a day, looking up every word in the dictionary, can be called reading. That kind of reading is called intensive reading and is a sure killer of any motivation or enjoyment the student might feel toward reading in English.

On the other hand, extensive reading is enjoyable reading well within one's level of comprehension. It is the kind of reading that doesn't require a dictionary; in fact, using a dictionary at all should be actively discouraged. There are many graded readers published for this purpose. Graded readers are stories printed at predetermined levels of difficulty, from beginning to advanced, usually according to word difficulty. Some points to be careful about are:

1. Make sure the interest level of the book is appropriate to the age group you are teaching.
2. When surveying a book to determine its difficulty, check the idiomatic level as well as the vocabulary level.

A certain amount of coercion will be needed to get the students to read anything at all. However, keep it as pressure-free as possible; this is supposed to be pleasant reading. Keeping a file of each student's short book reports should be sufficient. The goal is to get the students to read as much as possible, happily, with quantity taking precedence over quality. As mentioned in *Curriculum and Departmental Proceedings,* petition the department to put aside a certain amount of the budget for these graded readers.

Pre-Post Testing.   The students only get feedback on how they are progressing in their regular classes twice a semester, when they have midterm and final examinations. These tests are very intense and are not conducive to quiet self-evaluation and reflection. They are usually discouraging. Pre-post testing fulfills the students' need to be able to see how much progress they have made. It also forces you, the teacher, to think clearly about the goals of the lesson.

To make a pre-post test, decide what your objectives are. Write questions whose answers will reflect whether your objectives have been met or not. The test can either be for a single lesson or a whole semester, a decision which will affect the length of the test. Give the test before you start teaching any of the material; if the students do badly you know that you will be teaching them something they don't know. Scoring this first test is optional. The important thing is to keep it for future comparison. After the lesson or unit, give the same test again. The results of this second test will let the students know how much they have grasped of what has been taught. The results will also tell you if you have followed and achieved the objectives you set.

Speech Contests. There are usually speech contests several times a year in most prefectures. Take advantage of them and give your students a chance at glory and fame. Speeches, if edited well to insure good English, are remembered for a long time and help fluency.

Since it is not possible to have all your students enter a contest (because of sheer numbers), organize an in-school contest as a preliminary. Again, if the number of students is too great, reduce it further by having an in-class competition, choosing the best four to represent their class. Ask other English teachers to help judge. Beforehand, prepare simple judging cards to make evaluation easier. Posture/gestures, voice/intonation, and pronounciation are three easily understood categories that can each be given a value of one to five points. Winners are decided by the highest total.

Sample Lesson Plan

The preceding methods and strategies can be used in writing lesson plans. The following lesson plan will reflect the supplemental role you have in relation to the students' regular class.

First, ask for the teacher's supplement to the reader the students are using. Each text has a supplement in which the grammar is explained in depth (in Japanese). Even if you don't read Japanese yet, it will be easy to tell which parts of the passage the authors of the text want emphasized; those parts will be listed separately. Decide which phrases and words you wish to emphasize.

The text sample I have chosen is from the *Vista English Series,* one of those recommended by the Mombusho. This series is one of the less difficult.

The Reader Text

No garden lover can fail to be charmed by the gardens of Japan. They are so different from anything in the European styles. The Japanese garden is not just an arrangement of flowers and plants, formal or informal, but the creation of a miniature landscape. Art is hidden by art. Trees and bushes, rocks and ponds, little streams winding round refresh the spirit with their gentle naturalness, but they have all been carefully placed. Some gardens are made up of silver sand and rocks, expressing rivers and hills, or sea and islands. Japanese gardens are designed to show the essence of nature within a small space.

The authors recommend that these phrases and words be taught:

No garden lover can fail to
be charmed by
so
not just . . . but
creation of a miniature landscape
Art is hidden by art
streams winding round
refresh the spirit with their gentle naturalness
but they have all been
carefully placed
expressing

The following are the points I will choose for this sample. Which particular points to choose are up to you.

Idioms / Grammar Points

fail to	be charmed by

Vocabulary

arrangement	plant
miniature	stream
rock	hill

Next prepare a pre-post test that features these points. It is not necessary to test every time; a few samples will do.

Pre-Post Test

I. Rewrite the sentences, keeping the original meaning.
1. Yumiko didn't do the homework.

_____

2. The flowers charmed the young lady.

_____

II. Fill in the blanks with the words below.
1. The boy threw a _____ at the dog.
2. A small mountain is a _____ .
3. A small river is a _____ .
   arrangement, plant, stream, miniature, hill, rock

A lesson must include: 1) review of material studied previously, 2) introduction of new material, 3) performance practice of the new material and, 4) evaluation/feedback of the performance. The following lesson plan, based on the above passage from *Vista,* is the sort that I have used in my classes with some success. It features the four important elements of a lesson, though not in the same order. This plan would require one fifty-minute period to complete.

Lesson Plan

1. Administer the pre-post text. Collect it without correcting it.
2. Introduce the text.
   A. Read the passage aloud.
      Have the students read along with you the second time.
      Very briefly, drill the pronunication of the difficult words.
   B. Assign one line per student.
      Each student looks up the difficult words in his line.
      The students then each read their line aloud, giving the translations of the unknown words.
   C. Introduce the six target vocabulary words.
      Have the students work in pairs, quizzing each other on meaning and spelling.
   D. Give more drills and examples of how the target idioms/grammar points are used in sentences:
      fail to:
      Hanako failed to bring her books to school.

I failed to pass the test.
She failed to give her mother the message.
be charmed by:

    Teacher: The little puppy charmed the children.
    Students: The children were charmed by the puppy.
    T: His songs charmed us.
    S: We were charmed by his songs.
    T: The baby charmed the grandparents.
    S: The grandparents were charmed by the baby.

3.   Change pace by choosing an activity not directly related to the text: Have the students practice a mini-dialog.

    A: What are you looking for?
    B: My bus pass. You haven't seen it, have you?
    A: No. When did you lose it?
    B: I'm not sure. I used it this morning, but. . .
    A: You'd better tell the teacher. He'll announce it over the PA.
    B: Yeah, good idea.

Use the time for diary-writing. While each student is writing his own entry, move around the room helping individuals with spelling, sentence construction, etc.

Give the students in-class reading time for their extensive readers.

4.   Assign homework. Below are some possible assignments:

Memorize the mini-dialog for performance the next class period. Each student must include four gestures in performance. Write a book report on the extensive reader.

5.   Administer the pre-post test again.

Conclusion

The above lesson plan may seem rather long for a mere fifty-minute class. To finish in the allotted time, it must be kept at a very fast pace. This will also keep the students awake. After a few weeks, they will become used to the different activities and will be able to proceed quickly.

There will be times when nothing in the reader text seems worth teaching. In such cases, center the lesson around activities such as those suggested in steps 3 and 4.

During class, speak only English. When you begin learning Japanese, it is very tempting to practice, or show off, what you have learned. Barring some preliminary translation at the beginning of the year, the students will soon be able to understand all of the usual commands you give in English.

Bibliography

Bamford, Julian. "Extensive Readers: Best Hits EFL." *The Language Teacher* (publication of the Japan Association of Language Teachers), 8:4,5,6 (April—June, 1984). These three numbers have very good articles and information on starting your own extensive reading program. Included are lists of books available and reviews.

Madsen, Harold S., and J. Donald Bowen. *Adaptation in Language Teaching.* Newbury House Publishers, Inc., 1978. Short of writing your own text, you will never find one that fits all your needs. This book gives very good guidelines for adapting the text you are stuck with.

Seido Language Institute. *Modern English: An Oral Approach.* 1978. This ten-book series is the ultimate in audio-lingual drills, which is its biggest weakness as well as strength. Geared toward adults who have already graduated from a Japanese high school, it can be used as reference or adapted as a text for limited use in high school.

Stevick, Earl W. *Teaching and Learning Languages.* Cambridge University Press, 1982. An all-around reference book for doing what the title states. There are plenty of examples, plenty of theory, and it is written in an easy-to-understand style.

English Education in Japanese Universities and Its Social Context

Hal Eugene Hansen

THE JAPANESE POSSESS a low estimation of themselves as speakers of English. At the same time, public opinion maintains that the average university graduate reads English competently, and that he or she is relatively well informed about "Western Culture," though supporting evidence is scarce. The harshest criticisms of Japanese English education come from non-Japanese, who frequently find communication with Japanese awkward and difficult, and from those sections of Japanese society whose contact with other peoples calls for foreign-language competence. On the whole, other Japanese, including educators, do not feel the same pressing need for foreign-language education reform. As a result, publications in English, whether by Japanese or others, misrepresent the degree to which policy makers, teachers, and the public feel the need for change. Yet, the level of discontent with the present state of affairs is not insignificant.

Most critics of the present system have tried to lay the blame at the feet of teachers, their methods, their materials, and their teaching philosophies. University professors tend to criticize high-school English education because students are unable to follow university level courses in English. High-school teachers generally believe the fault lies with the university entrance-examination system, which exercises a very strong influence on high-school instruction. The public is inclined to blame both of these groups. Who is responsible? Probably no one and everyone. It is difficult to imagine a radical change in the effectivness of foreign-language programs in Japan without a correponding change in the values and organization of the society itself. Significant and meaningful improvements are possible, but they require a rigorous and frank analysis of the current situation beyond the classroom, and a willingness among teachers to experiment and to learn from one another's experience. With this paper, I hope to direct attention to the social dynamics of the English educational setting, and to report on an ''experiment'' taking place at the Kobe University of Commerce.

English Education: The Setting

No man is an island; neither is a teacher, nor a student. We all live and act in a social environment that profoundly shapes our goals, expectations, motivations, and values. Most discussions of English programs in schools and universities focus on the classroom—the teacher-student interaction, the instruction materials, the course objectives, and teaching philosophy. English instruction cannot be improved without an understanding of the dynamics of the classroom. However, this, by itself, is not enough. The classroom is but one element in a network of groups and institutions whose distinct and occasionally contradictory interests affect the nature and effectiveness of the educational process. Students and teachers alike are keenly influenced by forces that have nothing to do with the classroom.

Peter Strevens has suggested a four-part analysis of the educational setting, consisting of The Learner, The Teacher, The Language Teaching Profession, and The Community (Strevens 1978). These he orders in the following way:

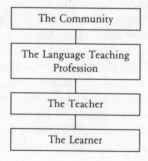

In the language learning/language teaching (LL/LT) process, a change in the learner is the object of the process. The flow diagram therefore suggests The Learner as the final component. On the other hand, The Community defines the importance of language learning, and authorizes and pays for the establishment and operation of foreign-language programs in schools and universities through taxes and tuition. Thus, it initiates the process, which proceeds through The Language Teaching Profession and The Teacher, and culminates in The Learner. Certainly, the LL/LT setting is more complex than this rudimentary outline indicates. The model will serve, however, to organize the analysis to follow.

The Community. Strevens distinguishes two elements within the community: the public will, and administration and organization. The public will may be interpreted on two levels. The first corresponds to the consensus at a particular time that a certain language or languages should be learned. At present, the public will supports the study of English for six years in junior and senior high schools, and two years at university. On the second, less tangible level, the community creates general levels of expectation for the language-learning achievement of its citizens. Strevens points out that the generally high level of achievement of students of English in Sweden results more from the fulfillment of high expectations than from excellent language teaching. Strevens does not go on to say that these expectations are intimately related to the need and opportunities for using the foreign language once it has been acquired. The situation in Japan is contradictory in the sense that while learning English has been strongly supported on an official level, community expectations are extremely low, as are those of the majority of students and professors. This can hardly be surprising when one considers the proportion of the 450,000 annual graduates from universities and junior colleges who will have the need or even the opportunity to utilize their English language skills. Beyond the relatively superficial level of English competence and knowledge about other countries necessary to be considered educated, Japanese on the whole have little incentive to master English or any other foreign language. In fact, too much contact with or sympathy for a foreign culture can have a decidedly negative effect upon the standing of a Japanese within his own culture.[1] The learner's willingness to study a foreign language, his persistence, and what he hopes to gain from his efforts are fundamentally affected by the attitudes, prejudices, perceptions, and fads which constitute his community's situation—what we might call the sociolinguistic setting.

Administration and organization exercise an equally important influence on the LL/LT situation. The national and local governments, or governing boards in the case of private institutions, provide the framework of organization within which learners and teachers come into contact with one another. These various bodies furnish buildings, employ professors and instructors, establish curricular guidelines, and oversee teacher training and certification. However, their contributions can be inadequate, resulting in overcrowded classes, insufficient time, poorly maintained facilities, unrealistic objectives, and the like. Of course, these organizations have limited funds, and must make difficult decisions. These decisions, however, have major consequences for the LL/LT setting.

Class size continues to be one of the most vexing problems in Japan. While conversation classes may be limited to twenty or thirty students, the mainstays of Japanese university English instruction, Reading and Composition classes, contain anywhere from 40 to 100 students or more. This phenomenon is not so surprising when Japan's average per student spending on higher education is compared with North America's or Western Europe's.

As noted above, English education has on the whole been strongly supported in Japan. Pressures to reduce the current level of support are growing. Along with the perception of minimal return on the society's investment of time and money, the more subtle and powerful national self-assurance of Japan's political and business leaders has contributed to a recent reduction in the number of hours of English instruction in the junior high schools (Usui 1983). Many of these leaders seem to feel that non-Japanese should learn Japanese. The eventual effects on university-level English education are impossible to predict.

The public will may also conflict with the policies of the administration, as appears to be the case at the moment. The reduction of English class hours in junior high schools has not been well received by teachers or parents. Why this is so may have more to do with their concern respectively about their jobs and their children's university entrance examinations than with their devotion to foreign language education. Whatever the reasons, objections to the present policy have received little response from the authorities. The history of educational policy from the Meiji era to the present has been one of control from the top: the Ministry of Education has never been terribly responsive to the public will.

Additional complications arise from the interaction between the public will and administration and the interests, expectations, and organization of the next component, the language teaching profession.

The English Education Professional. "The language teaching profession" is something of a misnomer, especially in reference to members of college and university English departments in Japan. Perhaps "English education profession" is a more accurate term, for it encompasses English literature and linguistics, the focus of most of its membership. There is a strong sense in which "English educators" are scholars first and teachers second. This reflects the university system which values, encourages, and rewards scholarship, especially publications, in the form of promotions to higher academic status, or even to more prestigious institutions. Superior teaching receives no such consideration; in fact, an overly zealous devotion to teaching may be interpreted as a dereliction of duty to scholarship, and as a silent criticism of colleagues who are less circumspect in their devotion to teaching responsibilities.

The Japanese call their promotional system *"Nen ko joretsu,"* meaning "order in ages," or seniority. Once a young scholar has been hired, he or she has essentially received tenure. (Note that non-Japanese hired as foreign instructors or lecturers are subject to a separate system.) The speed with which promotions are granted will depend largely on the quantity of scholarship, rather than on its quality, as Japanese scholars are most reluctant to criticize or evaluate the work of colleagues. The quality of a scholar's research will have a greater impact on his ability to move to a more prestigious institution. From the Japanese point of view, the seniority system "implicitly recognizes" the professor's skill and experience as a teacher (another manifestation of the reluctance to evaluate), and thus equates ability with age. The absence of institutional values in support of teaching, not to mention incentives, permits a good deal of indifference to the classroom. Individual professors can hardly be held responsible for these attitudes, for they are sanctioned by the community and rewarded by the organization.

This phenomenon has two negative effects. On the organizational level within each department there is little incentive to consider or discuss departmental goals, organization, minimum competence levels, testing, evaluation, work loads, and so forth. These constitute issues on which there is little agreement. Tradition allows each professor to follow his or her own preferences. To some degree education is thought to rest upon a set of beliefs that distinguish the teaching of each individual professor. These beliefs are largely a private affair, not subject to public discussion. Moreover, the superior-subservient vertical relationships that characterize university organization place a professor closer to his lecturer, assistant (frequently a former student), and students than to any of his fellow professors, unlike the United States or England, where minor differences of individual rank tend to be ignored, allowing for the formation of a more functional group based on "colleague identification" (Nakane 1973, pp. 39-40).[2] These considerations, combined with the time, effort, and trauma that would be necessary to establish a consensus on any of these issues, give rise to a disjointed, even discordant series of courses linked nominally by the term "English." The organizational problems simply outweigh the beneficial effects of a well-managed, well-organized program on the LL/LT process, in view of the relative indifference toward teaching, authorized and encouraged by the system. The second negative effect, that on teaching methods, will be discussed under The Teacher.

The university constitutes a semi-independent social system with its own internal values, goals, and incentives. These do not necessarily correspond to, and in fact frequently conflict with, the community's expectations and public policy. With respect to English education, the community expects students to be able to use English after eight years of study (even though it may not highly value this ability). This point was made by Mr. Wataru Hiraizumi, member of the House of Councillors, who proposed that only five percent of all high-school students be allowed to study English intensively as an elective subject, and that English be removed from college entrance examinations, because so much time and money had been wasted in teaching English ineffectively. Most university professors and lecturers, however, do not wish to become "practical English" instructors, occasionally condescendingly referred to as "skills trainers." There is even a lingering disdain for a "scholar" with a comfortable facility in a foreign language, though this is changing. The reasons are complex.

A university professor owes his position and prestige to his specialized knowledge. "Anyone" can become competent in a foreign language; not just "anyone" can comprehend Wordsworth or Shakespeare (though it remains to be explained how either can be deeply understood without a thorough mastery of the spoken language). That "scholarship" is valued more highly than "teaching" can hardly be surprising, for this is so at virtually every university in the world. What does surprise is the *degree* of indifference to practical skills displayed by many university English professors in Japan. The causes are to some degree political and historical.

In 1854, Japan was forced at gunpoint and against her will by the United States to open her doors to Western commerce and influence. The Meiji leaders, by 1869, had deposed the Tokugawa government under the slogan "expel the barbarians," with the public justification that the Tokugawa government was unable to do so. In the process, these leaders formulated a prudent policy for dealing with foreigners that might be crudely summarized: "If you can't beat them, join them until you can." The modern Japanese university grew out of this policy; it was conceived as an arm of the state. Its role was not to pursue "truth for truth's sake," but rather to introduce Western technology through translations. The modern Japanese university is the product of translation (Nagai 1971, p. 59). University "translation culture" served to protect Japan from Western cultural imperialism, and from what authorities believed to be "dangerous" social and political ideas. This was accomplished through censorship, an emphasis on technical translations, and the interpretative process of translating Western ideas into Japanese images, metaphors, and thought patterns, frequently leading to transformations in the ideas themselves. Thus, translation contained a subtle but powerful ideological component that served to protect and reinforce the growing sense of national identity. (For example, how terms like "individualism," "freedom," "rights," "equality," and "justice" were and are translated into Japanese in classroom exercises, and to what degree do the emotive and intellectual content of their Japanese "equivalents" differ from their English meanings and associations?) To the degree that translation continues to serve this ideological task, it undermines the potential contribution of foreign-language education to the cultivation of a more internationally minded populace.

The translation method has a long and distinguished history within the Japanese university. Virtually all Japanese professors have been educated using it. Most of them take deep pride in their foreign-language accomplishments. They feel that "if it was good enough for us, it's good enough for them," meaning the younger generation. Just as Europeans and Americans defended the translation of Greek and Latin as an important mental exercise, many Japanese maintain a similar status for English. Perhaps most importantly, the translation method stands as a symbol, in a sense sacred, of the traditions and spirit of the Japanese university itself. It is a ritual shared by all educated Japanese, and whatever its faults, it represents a rite of passage, considered by many English professors to distinguish the Japanese university experience. As a result, there is a strong, inarticulate, emotional attachment to the translation method.

Face-to-face contacts between Japanese and non-Japanese are relatively recent phenomena. These have rarely been officially encouraged or highly valued, except on a technical or commercial level. Even today, these contacts, along with the study of foreign languages, are publicly justified on utilitarian grounds. The well-traveled Japanese defends his "cosmopolitanism" to his countrymen as a "sacrifice" on behalf of his company, and indirectly, the welfare of Japan. Most non-Japanese hardly know what to make of the lack of more than a superficial level of curiosity and interest in "foreign" cultures, histories, and ideas displayed by many educated Japanese, both at home and abroad; this is due only in part to "Japanese reserve." These attitudes, which appear to be changing among the younger generation of Japanese (to the great dismay of the adult public), are deeply seated. They serve to reinforce the view that "practical English" is shallow and unnecessary.

Lastly, the war period and occupation played an undeniable role in the development of the older generation of English scholars. During the pre-war period and throughout the war, English study was discouraged. Even the reading of English books in public invited criticism, if not attack. Private study provided the only alternative. Moreover, after the war, English fluency generally indicated an undesirably close association with the American Army of Occupation. These factors further reinforced the emphasis on reading.

Against this background, the profession's attitudes toward "practical English" can be more easily understood. English department members want to establish their "academic credentials" by divorcing themselves as much as possible from what they, and colleagues in other departments, consider to be the business of junior and senior high-school teachers—teaching basic, practical language skills. Many professors also rightly criticize the low intellectual level of most commercially available "practical English" texts and programs, which were largely designed for the second-language rather than the foreign-language market. The establishment of educational linguistics as a legitimate academic discipline may well contribute to an easing of both of these problems. The differences between the values and goals of the community/public authority and the profession are substantial. The resulting friction is aggravated by the inability of the two groups to reach a common ground due to a lack of understanding of the other's values and interests. The profession must recognize the reluctance of the community's financing authorities to support "more of the same" in the form of larger full-time professorial staffs, when teaching needs might be more effectively met through a program supplemented by qualified part-time instructors and native-speakers. On the other hand, the community must understand the importance of scholarship to the life of the university, and not be too quick to undervalue the educational background and training of competent language instructors and professors. Scholarship and teaching go hand-in-hand in effective university communities.

The Teacher. Teachers and their methods, materials, and teaching philosophies constitute the most visible elements in the LL/LT situation, and therefore are most frequently cited as "weak links" in the network of factors that determine the effectiveness of English education in Japan. We can see that this view is short-sighted. This is not to say that teachers as a group bear no responsibility for the current situation. However, "finger-pointing" does not serve to improve this situation, nor does it help us to understand the organizational and institutional mechanisms of socialization that shape the thoughts and actions of individual teachers. It is to these mechanisms and processes that we should turn our attention.

Language teachers, to be effective, must command a wide range of abilities and techniques, in addition to possessing various personal characteristics. Three requirements essential to being even an adequate language teacher are a non-discouraging personality, adequate classroom command of the language being taught, and adequate presentational skills as a teacher (Perren 1968, and Strevens 1977). There are currently many more college and university language staff members who fail to meet even these minimum criteria than those who do. Why do these shortcomings persist?

Educational psychologists have long recognized the effects of teacher expectations on student achievement. Students whose teachers expect little from them are predisposed to learn little. It is not so much the case that "language educators" possess *discouraging* personalities; it is rather more accurate to say that they have *discouraged* personalities. The inertia of student indifference would stifle Sisyphus himself, to say nothing of the average well-intentioned mortal. Young teachers are often enthusiastic and idealistic about their work. However, the frustration encountered by those who single-handedly strive to improve the attitudes and heighten the abilities of their students, and this within the space of an hour-and-a-half per week, quickly deadens their enthusiasm. Colleagues provide little vent for these frustrations, for, as we have seen, these issues are essentially private and rarely discussed. Retreat into academic research, valued as it is, also typifies, in a very real sense, an escape from the desperation of the classroom. The automatic passing of substandard and indifferent work represents an institutional grace bestowed upon professor and student alike. The result is that neither teachers nor students, with few exceptions, expect much of themselves or each other.

As for adequate classroom command of English, the number of university and college faculty members unable to speak, understand, or write English at an acceptable level is dwindling, thanks to increased opportunities for contacts with native speakers and members of third countries who use English as a lingua franca, through mass media, travel, and study abroad. The root of the problem lies deeper, for a very small percentage of those professors and instructors competent to do so actually use English in their classes. This is intimately related to the third criterion, adequate presentational skills as a teacher.

The grammar-translation-lecture method is still overwhelmingly the predominant method of language teaching in Japanese universities and colleges today. In a sense, it has become sanctified by tradition as "the Japanese method." No other country devotes so much time to translation as a method of modern language teaching. Though it has never been shown to be a particularly effective method of learning anything except "translation," and even this is disputed, its roots are deeply embedded in the history and traditions of the Japanese university system. Not a few English professors hold that the ability to translate is the standard by which all English education should be judged. This is, however, gradually changing.

For the majority of university teachers, translation represents an easy way of conducting a class, a method that students already understand. It requires virtually no time for preparation, simplifies testing, and facilitates classroom management. There are, of course, professors who spend a great deal of time preparing for their translation classes. The point is that one can get by with very little preparation, and many do, especially after several years of experience. That English is not used even by those able to do so is due in part to their perplexity as to how English might be taught through its use, which derives from a lack of training. It is also quite natural for anyone to be reticent to teach countrymen in a foreign language that one does not command to the same degree as one's own. Planning, preparing, and conducting effective language classes all require significant amounts of time and energy. In view of the fact that the university neither rewards nor encourages this kind of effort, can anyone seriously fault individual teachers for not adopting new methods that are more demanding than the old? Moreover, in an atmosphere where faculty cooperation is unusual, a single professor, however dedicated, can scarcely affect student habits and attitudes. Even students find translation classes an easy, if uninteresting, way to get their credits.

The Learner: The learner is central to any model of the LL/LT situation. Highly motivated language students will learn in spite of low community expectations and support, and despite poor teaching, methods, and materials. The problem is that these very conditions almost invariably lead to low levels of perceived success, and to high levels of frustration, which in turn undermine motivation. The average student wants to get his English credits. He or she would like to learn English as well, but not at the cost of hours of study. Moreover, six years of junior and senior high-school English have convinced most that the payoff does not justify the investment.

The motivational factors affecting language learning must be viewed within the context of undergraduate education in Japan. Students have to divide their time among some twenty-plus separate courses per year, in addition to which, many work at part-time jobs from 15 to 40 hours per week. Students almost unanimously agree that "university is not serious," "club activities are more important," and that "university is the only real vacation" sandwiched into a life otherwise absorbed in the competition of the high-school student and the obligations of the salaryman. There is a certain truth to this that cannot easily be ignored.

Japanese undergraduates undergo a socialization process that over-shadows the importance of intellectual training. This system seems to function relatively well in "producing" competent, malleable salarymen for government service and industry. Just as students know "something about" economics when they graduate from a university of commerce, they know "something about" English. However, what they know has virtually nothing to do with a functional ability to use English in any way, including the ability to read it. Whereas with respect to economics, the student will be expected to learn what he needs to know in the company, this is not necessarily the case with English. Yet it is threatening and probably unfair to English faculty members to judge them by a standard different from that used to evaluate members of other disciplines. Many of the educational problems outlined above are not unique to English departments; most can be generalized to the university system as a whole.

From a historical perspective, it is also important to keep in mind the degree to which the university student population has changed since the pre-war period. Prior to World War II, the Japanese university system was very elitist, consisting of just 2% of the college-age population. Today, that figure has grown to just under 40%. The intelligence, motivation, and post-graduation promise of average college students in 1985 is by no means comparable to that of their counterparts in 1935. It is not uncommon for U.S.-occupation reforms to be held responsible for many of the ills of the modern Japanese university system, including those of English departments. Professor Shoichi Watanabe of Sophia University, in his widely publicized debate with Mr. Wataru Hiraizumi (mentioned above), argued that the fault did not rest with traditional principles of Japanese English education, but rather with an insufficient degree of effort on the teacher's part (Watanabe 1982). Both of these views, however, fail to take account of what every teacher knows—that the best student will probably learn no matter what the teacher does, unlike most of the other students in the class. That students before the war managed to learn English under the pre-war system, or in the "traditional way," constitutes no argument that today's students should therefore be able to do so too; they are not comparable students populations. The evidence is heavily weighted against these propositions. Almost every human being can and does learn natural language; the question is how to facilitate this in the classroom.

English Education: A Discussion

The following ten factors are commonly associated with below-average achievement in the LL/LT setting (Strevens 1978, 1979): 1) unwilling learners; 2) low expectations of success; 3) unattainable aims and objectives; 4) unsuitable syllabus (or no syllabus); 5) confusion between language learning and the study of literature (or, recently, linguistics); 6) physical, organizational, and psychological shortcomings; 7) insufficient or excessive time or intensity of tuition; 8) poor materials not compensated for by good teachers; 9) inadequate teacher training; and, 10) incompetent class teaching and lack of interest in learners.

One need search neither long nor hard to find most of these inhibitive factors present in one form or another in most university English programs in Japan. As we have seen, the problems are complex, and firmly embedded into the social and institutional framework of the LL/LT setting. To place the blame at the feet of either teachers or students is unfair and unhelpful. The community, the profession, the teacher, and the student form a network of values and interests whose organic functioning has brought the current situation to pass.

What can be done? The analysis provides an awareness of the magnitude and complexity of the issues. The realist might simply shrug his shoulders and conclude that English education will improve if and when the acquistition of English becomes needed and valued by the community. The answers, though by no means obvious, are clearer than are the means and processes by which they might be achieved. The ideal situation would be to reverse those factors associated with LL/LT failure. This would require the community to alter its attitudes toward foreign languages and cultures, and to provide more opportunities for English-language use. The funding authority would be forced to consider institutional recognition and rewards for conscientious teaching. The profession would need to come to see that good teaching does not preclude scholarship, that teaching can be an enjoyable, rewarding experience under the right circumstances, and that pedagogical management constitutes an essential element in any successful language program. Individual teachers would have to receive proper training. They would have to see the need for experimentation and cooperation with their colleagues, for both information sharing and emotional support, and to taste the pleasure of success in the classroom. Students would need to see language learning as useful and meaningful, to have heightened expectations of themselves and their teachers, and maybe even come to see that all learning is not goal-oriented in the narrow sense, but that education can improve the quality and enjoyment of their lives.

English Education: An Experiment at the Kobe University of Commerce (K.U.C.)

In April of 1980, K.U.C. hired its first full-time foreign instructor, a graduate of the school's Master of Economics program who had grown up in Japan. During the course of the year, he made friends with the Japanese Associate Professor who was responsible for the school's language laboratory classes. The foreign instructor regularly gave assistance to his Japanese colleague in transcribing taped news programs intended for L.L. use. As a result of this collaboration, they decided to coordinate their L.L. and Current English classes during the 1981–82 academic year. The Japanese instructor introduced T.V. news in his L.L. class, and the foreign instructor discussed the contents with the same students in his classes. Though no standardized testing was done, both instructors felt that the students from the coordinated class displayed more progress in their overall ability to understand and use spoken English than students in their uncoordinated classes, though these students were exposed to the same amount of instruction.

These two, along with a recently appointed Associate Professor who had received his Ph.D. in the U.S., befriended me during my first year at K.U.C. We shared many of the same frustrations, and thought something could be done about them. One evening, we mapped out what we felt to be the essentials of a successful program, and developed a proposal that we viewed as a manageable first step toward creating a genuine English program.

Our decision was motivated by our desire to do better. We felt the present system lacked conviction, effectiveness, and direction. We wanted to expand the cooperation which had begun the previous year. Yet, we wanted to limit the amount of proposed change for two reasons: first, we did not want to take on more than we could handle, for this first step was a new experience for us; second, we wanted to present our proposal to our colleagues as a reasonable experiment—we did not want to threaten them. Therefore, we decided to rearrange the curriculum for 80 first-year students of the department of Marketing and International Trade. We chose these students because they take more English than students in other departments; furthermore, the four of us were already largely responsible for their instruction. Our strategy was to place more emphasis on spoken English in the first year, and to *use* English in all their classes.

We divided the two Current English classes into four, consisting of 20 students each, plus repeat students. These are intermediate level courses, beginning with a rapid review of basic structures and vocabulary, using relatively elementary materials. They are taught by the two foreign instructors in English, using the same methods and materials, and coordinated with L.L., where corresponding listening-comprehension exercises are carried out. We are using recently videotaped materials—largely interviews and news stories having to do with simple but unusual subjects, such as an interview with a blind Japanese student about his trip to England. These are introduced in L.L. and reviewed and discussed in Current English. Emphasis in these smaller contact classes is placed on encouraging interaction with the teacher and among the students in English. Reading, the third class, is designed to emphasize extensive reading of an intermediate-level text, whose contents the students summarize in Japanese in advance, then discuss in English in class. Both L.L. and Reading are comprised of 40 students plus repeats, and are taught by the two Japanese Associate Professors. Language seminars are elective courses, lasting three semesters and consisting of 25 students. The seminars reflect the interests of the individual instructors—at present, basic economic theory and American Civilization. English texts are provided, and English is used in class discussions and testing.

We initially approached the chairman of the English department as a group and outlined our proposal and its rationale. He was cooperative, and helpful in anticipating potential problems and objections. We then broached the subject individually with other members of the staff. The major obstacle turned out to be covering the two newly created classes, scheduling, and redistributing teaching assignments. Virtually all members of the department were supportive in getting the department of General Education and the Curriculum Committee to assent to the changes. This in no way implies that they saw this project as an attractive alternative for themselves.

K.U.C.'s Program for First-year Students
of Marketing and International Trade

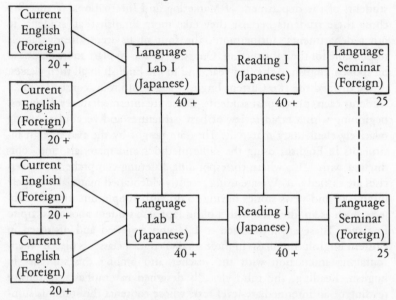

At the conclusion of the first year of our program, we decided to continue our project, and to extend the program to sophomore Marketing and International Trade students for the 1983–84 academic year. A Japanese professor and a part-time Japanese instructor agreed to join the project. Reading II, L.L. II, and Composition, each consisting of 40 students plus repeaters, continue the methods of, and are based on the levels achieved during, the first year of the program.

Composition classes and Reading II classes are designed to be parallel in the sense that the subject matter revolves around similar business and economic topics. The objective is to deepen and expand the students' knowledge of fundamental business and economic terms in English. Students in both sections cover the same materials. The composition text is designed to give students practice in organizational skills, both in reading and writing, through a series of exercises requiring graphic representations of short written texts, and alternately, written descriptions of graphically presented information. It includes a certain degree of problem solving in which English is the medium rather than the object of

K.U.C.'s Program for Second-year Students
of Marketing and International Trade

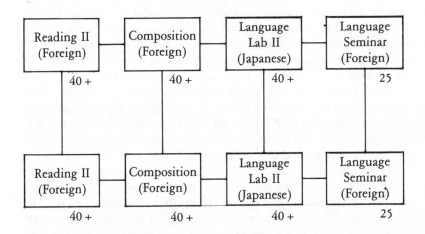

study. Reading II emphasizes extensive reading skills. Students receive chapter-long assignments each week. In class, students take short quizzes designed to check their comprehension of key terms, concepts, and information contained in the texts, and review the major points through a series of questions and answers. L.L. II has come to stress public speaking. Students regularly make short prepared presentations. Language Seminar is simply a one-semester continuation of the seminars begun in the first year.

The Approach

Language "input" represents the quantity of the target language to which the learner is exposed through listening and reading. Language "intake" corresponds to that part of "input" that can be understood or used by the learner. Our basic approach to language teaching has followed the well-documented observation that language learning/acquisition is directly related to language "intake" (Winitz 1981). This means that students must be exposed to abundant contact with the target language, and that this "input" has to be appropriate to their capabilities and interests. How this can most effectively be achieved is the subject of wide-ranging debate; however, it is clear that the usual, virtually total absence of English from the classroom and the incredibly meager speed of classroom translation, totaling some 40–50 pages per year per reading class, results in learners who hardly know what English is.

Furthermore, first- and second-language research increasingly has demonstrated the central importance of meaning in language acquisition (Snow and Ferguson 1977; Fletcher and Garman 1979). This research strongly suggests that learners pay attention to meaning rather than form in natural settings, and that teachers should do so too. (*See* Widdowson 1978; Winitz 1981; Wells 1981). Language is an instrument of communication. Reading serves as a tool for getting information and provides a means of enjoyment. Languages are naturally acquired when used in these ways. When learners perceive English as real, useful, and stimulating, they are motivated to learn. This necessitates attending to meaning.

These two principles, maximizing "intake" and attending to meaning, constitute our basic approach. To this end, we have attempted to increase substantially the amount of exposure to spoken and written English, to tailor this exposure as much as possible to the students' abilities and interests, and to attend to the meaning of discourse, rather than to its grammatical and lexical detail.

In reading classes, this has meant the transition towards more extensive reading, and the cultivation of a tolerance for a certain amount of ambiguity. This tolerance is essential in the early stages of reading, for without it, reading directly in the foreign language is impossible (Rivers 1968). Thus, we assign the students a lengthy passage that they are required to read before class. To insure that they do so, they are either required to summarize the passage in Japanese, or their knowledge of the passage is tested at the outset of each class. Classtime is then devoted to a discussion of the contents, including the most essential vocabulary, the basic facts, the writer's point of view, and a critical analysis. The discussion is directed in English by the teacher, though in some classes the students are occasionally allowed to respond in Japanese. Thus, the students receive exposure to oral English in class, and are forced to deal with the written text directly outside of class. We believe that over time, students will be discouraged from "reading via translation" due to the sheer quantities of time required to do so. In at least some cases, this appears to be happening.

Likewise, all classes in the program are conducted in English. In order to facilitate this, we think it prudent to expose entering students to a core class, Current English, which is small enough to allow the instructors to "break the ice," to cut through the students' fear of actual contact with English, and to start them on the road to thinking in English. Though 20 students or fewer represent the ideal class size for all forms of foreign language education, we believe it to be absolutely essential in the initial English contact class.

Language Laboratory I is coordinated with this core class in order to effectively double student exposure to the structures and vocabulary of the contact class. We conceive it not only as a means of increasing classtime exposure to English, but also as a place to test student progress through listening comprehension and short dictation quizzes. This weekly testing is designed to movitate students to utilize and review outside of class the aural materials on cassettes with which they are provided.

The objectives and contents of Composition, Reading II, and L.L. II have been outlined above. We have attempted to establish a relationship between Reading II and Composition along the lines outlined by Henry Widdowson (1978, 1979). Our methods, syllabus, and materials are by no means fixed. We expect they will change, even as we, our students' needs and interests, and the community's values and goals change. More basic to the success or failure of language programs than the pedagogical approach is the process by which they constitute, alter, and renew themselves.

When my colleagues and I at K.U.C. first decided to work together, we felt that K.U.C.'s English "program" consisted of a disjointed, even discordant series of courses linked nominally by the term "English." Few of us were privy to what our colleagues were doing with our students in their classes, not to mention what they had done the year before, or planned to do in the upcoming one. This prevented any sort of coordination, which in and of itself virtually condemned our individual efforts to ineffectiveness, if not to total impotence.

Intensiveness of language learning increases the productivity of each hour of instruction (Strevens 1977). This can be demonstrated best with a diagram depicting a learning curve.

Hypothetical Learning Curve

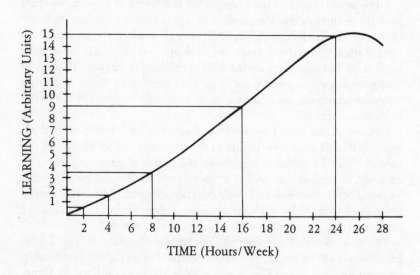

Little learning seems to take place when exposure/study time adds up to less than three hours per week. Doubling the exposure/study time more than doubles learning. Learning curves differ widely, depending upon the LL/LT setting; however, the phenomenon is generally recognized. Though our General Education English ''program'' allotted first-year students as many as four one-and-a-half-hour classes, we felt the differences in content, level, and approach among the classes produced the net effect of one-and-a-half hours per week, repeated four times, rather than the intensified effect of an integrated six-hour program (plus home study).

For this reason, we believed the only possible, practical solution was to make a cooperative effort. We decided to begin with a small step, not only to allay the fears and to enlist the cooperation of our colleagues, but also to give ourselves a chance to get our feet wet without the threat of drowning. Moreover, we realized that genuine, lasting changes would take years to effect, and that one-shot enthusiasm generally consumes itself impetuously.

Given differences of age, experience, personality, and outlook, along with the academic tradition of autonomy described above, many of our colleagues quite naturally disagree with us about what constitute the most important elements of an English program and why they are important. Yet, if we are to develop a genuine English program, and to manage it effectively, we must arrive at a functional underlying philosophy from which pedagogy derives its purpose and content. If we are to arrive at a workable agreement at this philosophical level, and thereby permit ourselves to cooperate, coordinate, set common standards, and so forth on the pedagogical level, we must engage in a political process with colleagues. The understanding and eventual active participation of these colleagues is essential to achieving even the rather limited hopes of our present endeavor. We will have to be willing to seek compromise in the interests of the whole. This is in its essence a political process, the art of the possible. To the degree that we intransigently insist on doing things our way, we aggravate the problem we strive to cure.

The most essential tool in this interchange with colleagues is the art of persuasion. How can one be more persuasive than to demonstrate the effectiveness of one's views? "Showing" is not only the most effective form of persuasion, it is undoubtedly the least offensive one. "Telling" a hundred times is not so good as "showing" once, nor is it so prudent. It is therefore our intention to do our best to demonstrate the merits of an organized program to our colleagues, and to encourage them to join in our efforts.

At the same time, we will be forced to adopt the approach of the overall program to the views, interests, and abilities of these additional collaborators. We must be as prepared to learn from them as they are from us. The essential point is cooperation, not a particular set of goals, methods, and materials. However, to render cooperation possible, we must arrive at some level of compromise, however tentative, as to the goals and objectives of our common endeavour. This constitutes a slow and exceedingly complex process, one that has only just begun.

The Outlook

One obvious shortcoming of this discussion of the K.U.C. program is the absence of hard empirical evidence demonstrating the effects of this experiment on student performance. In our defense, the time and effort required to reach the present stage of development have been substantial. We have not as yet arrived at a satisfactory level of coordination among ourselves, nor have we been able to locate and develop wholly appropriate materials for our courses. We are steadily making progress in these directions.

All participating faculty members agree that second-year International Trade and Marketing students are much more comfortable with oral English than second-year students in other departments, and that as a group, they have significantly higher expectations concerning their overall English workload. However, this much is taken for granted by non-participating faculty members as well. Their concern is with reading, writing, and translation skills. Given the foregoing discussion, it is clear that a study of reading skills should be our first priority. If it can be shown that not only speaking and listening comprehension proficiency, but also reading competence, have developed as a result of the program, it will merit more serious attention. However, launching into an empirical study prematurely may not only lead to erroneous conclusions (due to the program's rather primitive stage of development and the participating staff's relative inexperience), it may also be politically deadly. In this kind of setting, the experimenter is not only testing an hypothesis, he is also testing his ability to carry out the experiment according to plan. We want to avoid testing an unpracticed execution of a good plan. Hopefully, we will be able to carry out a reading study soon. We do already know that students in the program are reading a good deal more material than other students, and they are able to grasp the essential information, as reflected in their weekly tests.

Whatever the outcome of our testing, the realistic prospects of our experiment's developing into a permanent program are slim, as are those of the realization of its hoped-for beneficial effects on student motivation and learning and on teaching-staff morale. The LL/LT setting, as sketched above, is foreboding. What effective institutional rewards and values support these efforts? Why should our colleagues sacrifice their ''peace of mind'' for such a project? Why should the present collaborators continue to do so? And what will happen if we do manage to graduate students with a basic proficiency in oral and written English, and who possess a desire to develop it? Will the society provide them with recognition and with opportunities to do so, giving students still in school reason for taking their English studies seriously?

Indeed, the outlook is far from encouraging. For such a program to work, virtually everyone within the department would need to give his active support. This would mean that each had come to see the merits of a coordinated program and to understand that teaching preparation time had not increased significantly. The students would have to elevate their expectations. Under present conditions, this would in practice mean that students would perceive their employment opportunities to be enhanced due to the overall reputation of the school's English program, or as a result of some certification, provided by the university and widely recognized throughout the local business community, of the students' English proficiency. These are the minimum requirements.

Should our little project fail to grow and prosper, it will not have been a failure, for it will have helped us to clarify the problems, and comprehend the limitations of the current LL/LT setting. As dedicated English educators, we feel that we can and should do better. Yet, as this paper should make abundantly clear, much of the current debate over, and criticism of, teaching methods, materials, and goals misses the point. Larger and more powerful forces are at work, and their existence cannot be ignored.

Notes

1. Children returning to Japan after several years abroad are widely reported to suffer from identity problems. This often results in a radical rejection of everything foreign, including their willingness to speak the language they have acquired. Reischauer has suggested that English-education reform has been hindered by the feeling that changes might erode the Japanese sense of their Japaneseness, an effect of the more general fear that Japan will lose its identity in the flood of influences from the West. (Reischauer 1977, pp. 408-10.)

2. This is no way implies that major differences in rank among departmental

members of English and American universities are ignored, though in some institutions this may be the case.

Bibliography

Fletcher, Paul, and M. Garman (eds.), 1979. *Language Acquisition.* Cambridge University Press.

Jansen, Marius B. (ed.), 1965. *Changing Japanese Attitudes Toward Modernization.* Tokyo: Charles E. Tuttle Co.

Koike, Ikuo, M. Matsuyama, Y. Igarashi, and K. Suzuki (eds.), 1978. *The Teaching of English in Japan.* Tokyo: Eichosha Publishing Company.

Matsuyama, Masao, 1978. "Entrance Examinations: College Entrance Examinations and English Education in Japan," in Koike, *et al.,* 1978.

Nagai, Michio, 1971. *Higher Education in Japan.* Tokyo: Tokyo University Press.

Passin, Herbert, 1965. *Society and Education in Japan.* New York: Columbia University.

Perren, G.E. (ed.), 1968. *Teachers of English as a Second Language: Their Training and Preparation.* Cambridge University Press.

Reischauer, Edwin O., 1977. *The Japanese.* Tokyo: Charles E. Tuttle Co.

Rivers, Wilga, 1968. *Teaching Foreign Language Skills.* University of Chicago.

Snow, Catherine, and C. Ferguson (eds.), 1977. *Talking to Children: Language Input and Acquistion.* Cambridge University Press.

Strevens, Peter, 1979. *Conditions for Success in Language Teaching.* Oxford University Press.

_____, 1978. "The Nature of Language Teaching," in Richards, Jack C. (ed.), 1978. *Understanding Second and Foreign Language Learning, Issues and Approaches.* Rowley, Mass.: Newbury House.

_____, 1977. *New Orientations in the Teaching of English.* Oxford University Press.

Usui, H., August 18, 1983. "English Teachers 'Tunnel-Visioned,' " in the *Daily Yomiuri,* Tokyo, p. 7.

Watanabe, Shoichi, August, 1982. "Daigaku no eigo-kyoiku wa kore de ii no ka?" *Eigoseinen* (The Rising Generation), Vol. 128, No. 5, pp. 254–255.

Wells, Gordon, 1981. *Learning Through Interaction: The Study of Language Development.* Cambridge University Press.

Widdowson, H.G., 1979. *Explorations in Applied Linguistics.* Oxford University Press.

_____, 1978. *Teaching Language as Communication.* Oxford University Press.

Winitz, Harris (ed.), 1981. *The Comprehension Approach to Foreign Language Instruction.* Rowley: Newbury House.

Addendum: Finding a College Position

[Hal Hansen wrote his essay to illustrate the interaction of society and education at the college level, and to describe his school's program. He did not include information about finding work in colleges, so the editor has added these comments.]

College teaching positions in Japan may pay slightly less than a combination of company and private lessons, but annual salaries are high (between three and six million yen), teaching loads are generally low (except at universities of foreign studies, where salary is computed on hours taught, which vary from term to term), and pay is for twelve months though teachers may be required only to appear on campus ninety days a year.

Every national university has at least one, and sometimes many more native speakers on the teaching staff. A rough estimate of the number of full-time positions may be found by multiplying the number of junior and regular colleges by two. However, because the rewards are so great for full-time foreign teachers, some schools put most of their classes in the hands of part-timers. Although part-timers may be given preferential treatment when full-time positions open up, an outsider with better credentials may displace an experienced part-timer in such a case.

The qualifications required, for the best jobs in particular, are quite high. Public colleges require an M.A. in a relevant field (though there are exceptions), and in the major urban areas they can often find Ph.D.'s willing to compete for available slots. Furthermore, whenever possible, colleges will rely upon contacts to secure foreign instructors. Therefore, graduates from schools that have hosted visiting Japanese scholars have an advantage with certain Japanese schools. Job seekers presently studying outside of Japan should remember to make as many contacts as possible among Japanese scholars while working toward degrees.

On the other hand, schools do interview candidates who send in unsolicited resumes from time to time. February is an ideal time to send such applications—if a school needs a teacher in that month, it may compromise earlier demands. Because of time restraints, this sort of application can be made more successfully in Japan than from outside of the country. The most common way for a foreigner to make his or her way into a department is by teaching part-time for a year or two. Submitting an application for part-time work may bear fruit more quickly than trying for a full-time position.

Teaching part-time or full-time at a high school is a good way to improve a curriculum vitae and make contacts. Membership and participation in organizations such as JACET (Japan Association of College English Teachers) are likewise valuable for contacts. The American and English Literature Societies of Japan have local and national meetings. Their monthly lectures are usually in Japanese, but native English speakers with degrees in literature will probably be able to give a talk in English if they join and persevere. For further information, contacting the English department in a nearby university will probably be productive, though interest in finding work should be subordinated to love of literature when asking to join. When the proper chance presents itself, job seekers should give their name cards to college teachers with the information that they are interested in college work.

One of the best ways to learn about available college work, indeed about any teaching work, is by making friends and keeping up contacts with native speakers of English holding such positions. Often a teacher will have to supply a replacement if he or she moves to a more attractive position within Japan. However, applicants without proper credentials will face a difficult time no matter who their contacts are. Fortunately, Temple University's Japan campus offers work leading to an M.Ed. in teaching English to speakers of other languages, with course offerings both in the Tokyo and Osaka areas. Those teachers seriously considering long-term employment in Japan would be well-advised to enroll in such a program.

C.B.W.

Teaching Oral English in Large Classes

Richard E. Freeman

THERE IS NO GREATER STRAIN placed on a teacher's love of teaching than having to teach oral English in a large class. The joy of teaching can easily turn into a nightmare. The feeling of accomplishment so easily achieved in a round-table situation of half a dozen students can change to a sense of futility and frustration in a class ten times as large. A teacher can feel he is literally drowning in a sea of faces.

But all need not be lost. As many teachers have learned, often slowly and painfully through trial and error, it is possible not only to manage a class of 50 or 60 students, but actually manage to teach; not only to suffer through what seemed at first glance an impossible situation, but actually to look forward to the joy of it; not only to survive, but to thrive.

This paper presents the teaching experiences of many years that have culminated in this happy state of affairs. It does not propose a single teaching method, of which there are many that can achieve much the same results, but a teaching philosophy around which a teaching system has been developed. The methods used have changed over the years, and no doubt will continue to change and develop in the future. Even old methods are revised from time to time, for the system is not and, indeed, must not be static. In fact, the dynamics of variation and change are at the very heart of the system and the philosophy.

Philosphical Approach

In its simplest form, the philosophy of the system is based on the concept that certain aspects of a subject cannot effectively be taught. This is most easily observable in the arts. It is easy enough to teach the techniques of painting or writing or music and the like, but the practitioners of such arts become artists, poets, and musicians mainly through their own efforts. They learn by doing. Many, in fact, are self-taught.

In varying degrees, the same can be said of the natural and social sciences as well. Mathematics, biology, history, economics, philosophy, to name only a few, can all be taught. But simple acquisition of knowledge relating to these disciplines does not make one a mathematician, scientist, historian, economist, or philosopher. These are on another order of magnitude, a level that can only be reached through lonely individual struggle.

In language learning, the student can be taught the pronunciation and meaning of words, the rules of grammar, sentence patterns, intonation, and so on, and yet remain a deaf mute as far as being able to understand and speak the language. In fact, as we all know, the most proficient speakers are often those who learned without any instruction at all, by simply being exposed to the language.

If we accept this thesis, whether we totally believe it or not, the teaching situation becomes vastly improved. Instead of being faced with the impossible task of trying to teach 50 or 60 students to speak a foreign language, on a schedule of only once a week, we set ourselves the challenging but feasible task of providing a language-teaching environment in which the student more or less teaches himself.

Motivational Approach

The first and most important step is to try to instill or maintain learning motivation. Without student motivation, there is no practical or philosophical method that will support a teaching program.

In Japan, fortunately, most students have at least a vague desire to try to "master" English. This is the beginning of motivation. If "English Conversation" is a required subject, the desire for a good mark will be a strong motivation. If the course is elective, the motivating force that inspired the student to take the course in the first place must be periodically reinforced.

Motivation can be instilled in many ways. The enthusiasm and interest of the teacher play no small role. Enthusiasm is catching. A student naturally wants to please a teacher who is enthusiastic and takes a personal interest in him. It is difficult, of course, to take a personal interest in each of 60 students, but the teacher can exhibit his interest in them as a group, and if he can do this with enough enthusiasm, it can reach their hearts as individuals.

Competition is always an effective motivational force, so that providing opportunities for competition is one of the most valuable aids the teacher has. The competition can be on an individual or group basis. In Japan, especially, group pride is a potent force and can be nurtured through competition to create strong motivation. Games and contests are the natural outlets for such competition, but almost all classroom activities can be aimed in this direction if the teacher keeps motivation on the front burner of his mind.

Teaching Goals

Along with motivation, the teacher must keep his goals in mind. His ultimate goal is to produce students who can communicate in the language as effectively as a native speaker. Of course, under the time limits imposed by the length and frequency of university oral English classes, the chances of achieving this goal are as remote as the chances of teaching a chimpanzee to sing. In fact, it is well to keep in mind that the student is unlikely to reach this goal no matter how long and diligently he studies. It is well to remember this so as not to waste time unduly striving to achieve perfection in any single aspect of the language learning process. Of what use is it, for example, for a student to be able to pronounce the initial "r" perfectly if he cannot put three words together into an intelligible sentence? Of what use is it for him to memorize 10 sentence patterns out of the infinite number possible, when it makes no discernible improvement in the pattern of his broken English?

This ultimate goal serves as our north star, guiding us to our destination. It keeps us on course or gets us back on course when we get bogged down in trivialities and lose sight of our aim.

Our immediate practical goal is to achieve the highest level of fluency of which the student is capable in the time available. Fluency means having facility in the use of the language. It means speaking smoothly and effortlessly. It implies a level of grammatical and pronunciation correctness that permits the listener to understand the speaker effortlessly, too. We do not define grammatical or pronunciation correctness in absolute terms, only in terms of fluency and comprehensibility. Indeed, the level of fluency that some students are able to attain in the time available is painfully slow and tortured and only barely comprehensible. But whatever progress is to be made in achieving fluency is up to the student. The role of the teacher is to provide the language environment that permits the student to try his wings, so to speak.

Language-Learning Environment

The first requirement of the language-learning environment is that it be in the language being learned. This means that the teacher and students should rely entirely on the language being learned for all communication. This concept is being questioned in some quarters, and other ways are being explored, but there are so many persuasive arguments in favor of this system that there is hardly room for discussion of any other.

One of the most important reasons for insisting on this requirement is the practical one of holding down the noise level in large classes. If 50 or 60 students working in groups or pairs are permitted to use their own language, the resulting uproar plays havoc with the target language, as well as with the teacher's sanity.

At the other extreme, there is a risk that for the first week or two, especially in classes in which the students have poor ability in the spoken language, the teacher may be met with a deafening silence when he tries to get the class to speak in the target language. This can be overcome by giving the class a conversation assignment that they can easily handle. Details will be given later.

One of the main pedagogical reasons for insisting on the students and teacher using the target language only is based on the psychological phenomenon of the brain (and body) being able to rise to the occasion called for. We have read of women finding superhuman strength to lift a car or other heavy object from a trapped child or husband, and the brain likewise becomes superalert and receptive to communication in a foreign language when forced to. On the other hand, it can lose all ability in this regard when it knows there is an interpreter present. In other words, if the student knows that the teacher (or his classmate) will explain in his own language everything that he cannot understand in the target language, his brain will cease to make an effort and he will not be able to understand anything in the language being learned. This phenomenon has been observed too many times for there to be any question about it. The teacher who has given into the temptation to facilitate communication with the students by speaking in their language has certainly observed the deterioration in the students' ability to understand him in the target language thereafter.

Another reason for insisting on using the target language only is the obvious fact that time consumed in speaking the student's language is time taken away from his exposure to the target language. For this reason, some teachers even give the students "English names" because considerable time is consumed referring to the students' names plus the title of respect. With English names, they are being exposed to English sounds and the time is no longer being wasted. The more difficult the name-sound, the better, for in the process of hearing English names over and over, they will learn the difficult sounds.

For Japanese students, names containing the troublesome r/l, th, and f/v sounds are the best, although for the class as a whole, all sounds that are difficult for Japanese should be included. Along these lines, a dictionary of names can yield, from the beginning of the alphabet alone, such appropriate names for girls as the following: Adele, Aileen, Alice, Althea, Alva, April, Arlene, Athena, Avis, Barbara, Belle, Beryl, Beth, Beverly, Blythe, Carla, Carol, Cathleen, Clara, Clarissa, Cynthia, Dolores, Dorothy, Edith, Eleanor, Elizabeth, Emily, Evelyn, and Faith. Likewise for boys are such names as Aaron, Adair, Alan, Albert, Alexander, Alfred, Alvin, Andrew, Anthony, Arthur, Arvin, Averill, Avery, Baird, Barry, Bert, Bill, Brian, Bruce, Burton, Byron, Calvin, Charles, Charlton, Christopher, Clarence, Claud, Clive, Clyde, Colin, Corey Craig, Curtis, Darrell, David, Derrick, Devin, and Douglas.

An added benefit in using such names is to familiarize students with the first names of English-speaking people, many of whom use first names more often than family names in relating to one another.

In small classes it is well to take a little time to choose the most appropriate name for a particular student, in terms of matching it for rhythm and euphony with his family name, as well as for suitability with his personality. For large classes, it would be too time-consuming to do this and there seems to be no alternative but to assign the names arbitrarily, or to put them in a hat and let the students choose them by lottery.

If it is decided to give the students English names, it should be emphasized that the names are merely nicknames and are not intended to replace their own given names. The rationale for using English names should be carefully explained to the students so as to ward off possible suspicion that it is some sort of imperialistic plot.

Student Orientation

Indeed, for the success of the program, it is necessary to explain the plan and procedures, as well as the rationale, of the program to the students in order to enlist their cooperation and support.

The orientation should be comprehensive, beginning with a self-introduction by the teacher that includes an outline of his philosophical approach. The rationale for using only English in the classroom should be given along with the assurance that it is not as difficult as it seems. If it is the first time they have experienced such a system, they should be told that it may be difficult at first but that they will soon get used to it and be rewarded with the pleasure of knowing that they can take part in an all-English-speaking environment.

It is usually necessary to impose a system of punishment for transgressors of the rule prohibiting use of the students' language in the classroom. Some teachers collect anywhere from a token ten yen or so for each time the student uses his own language up to substantial amounts. Others have him memorize a dialogue or poem or record an exercise on a tape. There are endless possibilities and the students usually accept the punishment in good humor. If the teacher senses grumbling or stirrings of revolt at the idea of punishment, he can appeal to their maturity and put them on the "honor" system to speak English only. If the honor system fails, the students will then accept a system of punishment.

But the teacher should not let himself be put into the position of being the lone watchdog for the system. It is almost impossible for him to find the culprits in a large class without the cooperation of the students. Also, monetary collections should be for a good cause, such as a Christmas party, so as to gain everyone's cooperation. If the students do not cooperate, the teacher must resort to group punishment or even class punishment if he hears someone speaking other than the target language, but cannot be sure who it is. The threat of group punishment should encourage everyone to remind the forgetful ones not to speak in their own language.

In the beginning, the teacher should give a short grace period for forgetfulness, and in fact he may continue to be lenient when it is a mere matter of forgetfulness. But he should crack down severely on flagrant violators, in the beginning especially, if he hopes to see the system work. If the teacher is too lenient in the beginning, he will find it very difficult to be firm later. If he is firm in the beginning, the class will fall into a routine use of the target language that will make it seldom necessary to use punishment. Moreover, transgressions then can be mostly ignored, or transgressors merely given a warning.

In the orientation, the teacher must set forth the goals he has in mind for the class. He should explain to the students that in the class time available, it is not possible to "master" English, but it is possible to achieve some level of fluency that will permit them to communicate their thoughts.

The only way to achieve fluency in speaking, they should be told, is by speaking. And it is obvious that in a large class it is not possible to obtain fluency by each student taking turns speaking with the teacher. This would work out to only a minute or so of speaking for each student.

With these preliminary remarks, the teacher should then introduce the plan of having the students work together for much of class time in groups and pairs. This will permit each student to devote as much as half the class time to developing his own fluency.

The teacher should be prepared for the possibility that some students will not like the plan, especially if this is their first exposure to such a system. For one thing, they are used to the lecture system in which they are spoon-fed information by the teacher. They do not take lightly to the idea of being left to their own resources.

But a more serious objection to the plan is based on the not totally invalid complaint that they have to listen to the broken English of their colleagues.

The answer to this, of course, and it must be reiterated from time to time, is that the goal of the program is to improve their fluency, not their hearing ability. The only way to improve fluency, it may be necessary to repeat, is by speaking, and although it may be ideal to have a native speaker of the language as the listener, it is hardly necessary. Anyone can serve as the sounding board as long as he understands the language.

Some students will bemoan the fact that without a native speaker listening there will be no one to correct their own grammatical and pronunciation errors.

Again the answer to this is that even if they were engaged in a man-to-man conversation with the teacher, it would make little difference. For one thing, it is extremely difficult for the teacher to catch and correct the mistakes without interfering with the speaker's train of thought and flow of language. Moreover, even if he were able to do so, correcting errors in this way is almost wholly useless for improving the student's speaking ability, for such errors are already deeply ingrained in his speech pattern and cannot be changed without great effort, such as drilling the corrected pattern a hundred times. Obviously, a conversation cannot be conducted under such circumstances.

It might be well to mention at this point, also, that there seems to be a certain amount of built-in prejudice among some Japanese about speaking English with a fellow Japanese. There is a bias in favor of Caucasians that is manifested in the reluctance of conversation schools to hire, for example, second- or third-generation Japanese-American English teachers, or indeed teachers of any other race than white, regardless of the person's English speaking ability.

English is an international language of many dialects, none of which can claim to be better than another. Some say that even Japanese English is due respect rather than disdain. For practical reasons, one should try to learn to speak the dialect or dialects that are most easily understood by speakers of all the other dialects. But to be a truly international man, one must be able to understand as many of the dialects as possible, which skill can only come from listening to or engaging in conversation with speakers of other dialects. For one's own fluency of expression, it is sufficient to engage in conversation with anyone who can understand the language. Being partial to a particular race or nationality is undignified and unbecoming to someone hoping to become an internationalist.

But to become an internationalist, as a matter of fact, it is not necessary to speak English like a native. There are very few, if any, Japanese who need to master English to that extent. The need is merely to communicate effectively. Effective communication is possible on many levels, even with gestures and body language.

The best way to improve hearing ability, the students should be told, is with a tape recorder and a collection of a variety of tapes with their transcriptions. When they cannot understand something, they can refer to the transcription. Listening to FEN, for example, may be too slow a process, because there are no transcripts for the programs. There are various tape sets on the market now with transcriptions of actual interviews and conversations.

If the students seriously want to improve the correctness of their speech, again the most effective way is with a tape recorder. In this case they should get a good set of drill tapes with a variety of transformation drills, not only simple substitution drills. If they should practice with such tapes diligently for two or three hours a day or more, they would surely improve. A month of such effort, for example, would be far more effective in this regard than a one-month visit to England or America. And much cheaper, although not as enjoyable, of course.

One speech, of course, will not be immediately or permanently persuasive and the ideas must be reiterated from time to time. At the same time, it should be pointed out to the students that although they will largely be engaged in conversation with one another, the teacher, in fact, will be circulating from group to group or from pair to pair to give them such aid as they need or desire. The teacher will be immediately available for their personal instruction at all times.

After all, the great advantage in using the group method for teaching oral English in large classes is the very same advantage offered by the language laboratory, namely, that the students work largely on their own, thereby leaving the teacher free to help individuals (or groups) who most need help, or those who can benefit most from the teacher's personal attention.

It can also be mentioned, however, that if some students feel strongly that the time spent listening to the Japanese English of their colleagues is a waste of time, they can turn the practice into a useful exercise by imagining in their minds, or on paper, the correct way of phrasing what their classmate was trying to say. The teacher, in fact, can offer to evaluate such written efforts for the listener's own sake, as well as for the benefit of the speaker.

Student as Teacher

In this regard, the students should be encouraged to help one another as much as possible. There is a saying in English (perhaps in Japanese, also) that is useful for reminding them that helping others can be mutually beneficial: "The best way to learn is to teach." Numerous examples from personal experience can be used to prove the truth of this statement and will probably touch on experiences the students have had themselves, such as being asked a question by a younger brother or sister and having to go to the encyclopedia for the answer.

There are many exercises in which the student can serve as teacher. If there are pattern drills in the textbook, for example, a student can serve as drill instructor. The student doing the drill closes his book while the student teacher keeps his book open to give the cue words and to check his partner's response.

If there are dialogs with a running translation in the textbook, the student teacher may read his part in the original English, but his partner must try to reproduce his part by referring to the translation only. Of course, the student teacher, as necessary, helps his partner to give the correct rendition from the translation.

If the dialogs are not translated, this method can still be used by having the student teacher read his part in the original English and then cue his student with an oral translation of the student's part (making an exception to the rule of not speaking Japanese in class). The student, with his textbook closed, then tries to render his lines in English from the student teacher's oral Japanese translation.

Of course, prior to such an exercise, the two students should both read the dialog two or three times in the normal way so that later when they try it from translation, it is not so much a translation cue as a memory cue.

The students can even be paired as teacher and student for answering comprehension questions on the text. This is a more difficult role for the student teachers but generally they can rise to the challenge. The procedure consists of the student teacher working from the textbook and the student keeping his textbook closed. The student teacher then reads one of the comprehension questions in the text. The student tries to answer from his memory while the student teacher searches for the precise answer in the text.

If the student cannot answer the question, the student teacher should be instructed to try to draw out the answer from the student's memory, not to tell him the answer too quickly. He should first try to give him a hint as to the answer by reminding him of the situation or related facts. As a last resort, again making an exception to the no-Japanese rule, the student teacher may give the student the answer in Japanese and ask him to render it in English.

Of course, the classroom teacher in the meantime is circulating from pair to pair to help the student teacher, and the student teacher should be urged to call for the classroom teacher's aid at any time. Occasionally the student teacher is not sure of the correct answer even though he has access to the textbook, and at such times the classroom teacher can whisper the answer in his ear.

Generally the students take their responsibility as "teachers" very seriously and do the job well, but the classroom teacher periodically should try to inspire them to "be good teachers." Again, there is a saying in English which helps to keep their minds focused on this aim: "If the student hasn't learned, the teacher hasn't taught."

As a follow-up to this concept, the classroom teacher can hold the student teacher responsible for the student's learning. Thus, when the classroom teacher later checks the entire class in a review of the day's work, he can turn to the student teacher and give him a mock scolding when his "student" fails to answer the classroom teacher's question. Of course, the class will laugh when they realize the teacher is only half serious, but there will be an element of seriousness remaining that will serve to keep the student teachers on their toes.

Incidentally, when the students are paired for answering comprehension questions, the student teacher is not expected to be able to judge the grammatical correctness of the answer, only its factual nature. But to some extent the students can help each other achieve grammatical correctness. Often they can hear the mistakes of others while being unaware of their own. Again, in teaching others, they learn themselves, so it is useful for all concerned to help develop this awareness.

A useful classroom exercise in this connection is to ask all students to try to catch the errors of a student speaking in front of the class. This serves a double or triple purpose. For one thing, it increases class interest and focuses the students' attention. For another, it turns the problem of "wasting time listening to broken English" into a worthwhile exercise, and third, it makes the students aware of errors that may occur in their own speech.

In the pairing of students of unequal ability, the saying "The best way to learn is to teach" again comes into play. It is well for the student of lesser ability to be the teacher first. In the process of "teaching" he will learn. Then, when they switch roles, the student of lesser ability will be better able to do the drills or answer the question, since it becomes a matter of review for him. At the same time, it lessens the teaching burden on the student of higher ability.

The dictum "If the student hasn't learned, the teacher hasn't taught," with mock scolding of the student teacher when his student fails, is also extremely useful for changing the attitude of the student of higher ability who at times is resentful of being paired with a student of low ability. Often this policy turns his resentment into a challenge to try to teach the poorer student. The dictum also calls for praise for the student teacher when he does well, and the classroom teacher should not neglect this aspect of it.

Pronunciation Practice

In a large class, it is virtually impossible to have much fruitful pronunciation practice. As a matter of fact, on a once-a-week basis, there is little observable improvement in pronunciation at the university age level regardless of pronunciation practice efforts.

Moreover, under the goals of this program in which attaining fluency is of primary importance, there is no requirement to have perfect pronunciation. The question itself of what constitutes perfect pronunciation is becoming more and more unanswerable, especially as all English dialects gain increased recognition.

The operating concept is "comprehensibility." If the student's pronunciation is easily comprehensible, it is considered satisfactory. Of course, there is a great difference between "comprehensible" and "easily comprehensible," and pronunciation efforts are directed to narrowing this gap.

Naturally the teacher's dialect serves as guide for pronunciation practice, and pronunciation problems peculiar to the Japanese are the ones mainly attacked. And although under this program there is no great stress put on pronunciation, it is extremely important to point out to the students that this is due to the order of priorities in the time available, not to any denigration of pronunciation. Good pronunciation is intimately tied to fluency and easy comprehension. Poor pronunciation may be comprehensible, but it is not pleasant to listen to, and an

English-speaking person is likely to try to avoid engaging in conversation with someone who has poor pronunciation.

In light of this, it is essential that the teacher try to determine the particular pronunciation problems of each student and inform him of them. Then the teacher should tell the students that their pronunciation defects are already deeply ingrained in their psyches and that to correct them will take a great deal of personal effort.

It so happens that two of the biggest pronunciation problems for the average Japanese are also the most easily correctable. These are the sounds th and f/v. The reason they are so easily correctable is that their pronunciation is so highly visible. With a mirror the student can easily see his mistake, which is certainly not true of the r/l sounds, for example, and many others. With a few minutes of instruction, almost every Japanese person of whatever age can learn to pronounce these sounds correctly. The fact that mispronunciation of these sounds is so prevalent is not due to inability of learners to produce them correctly, but to forgetfulness. During a pronunciation practice drill, for example, a teacher can obtain almost 100 percent correct rendition of th or f/v, but in "free conversation" later he can consider himself lucky to meet with even a 20 percent success rate.

So the burden goes back to the student, and since these particular sounds are so visible in their production, even the student teachers can be taught to be aware of them and to point them out to their charges. Few other problem sounds of English can be entrusted in this way to student teachers.

In asking students to be alert to these particular sounds, the teacher should at the same time stress their importance. For one thing, some of the most important and frequently used words in the English language are comprised of these sounds, namely: this, that, the, them, those, than, then, their, there, thing, think, thought, three, third, thirty, Thursday, mother, father, brother, month, fourth, fifth, seventh, five, love, very, and "fine, thank you." It is always good for a laugh when the teacher demonstrates the pronunciation horror of "Hine, sank you."

The teacher should mention, secondly, that of all the problem sounds in English th and f/v mispronunciations are the most serious for the very same reason that they are easiest to correct, namely, that they are so highly visible. Thus when someone says "Hine, sank you" instead of "Fine, thank you," it not only sounds bad, but also looks bad. When the r/l in "girl" for example, is mispronounced, it merely sounds bad. We can see nothing amiss.

For these reasons, the sounds th and f/v are given special emphasis in the course, and the students are urged to make a special effort to correct themselves and to alert their comrades to their pronunciation lapses in these sounds so their comrades can correct themselves.

Periodically, the teacher should give exercises to keep everyone aware of these errors and to maintain their skill in observing them. Thus, when a single student is speaking in front of the class, the teacher, for variation, can ask the listeners to note pronunciation mistakes, rather than grammatical errors. Then the teacher should call on individuals at random to read the list of mistakes they noticed. It is not unusual for the person called on to mispronounce the words himself as he is reading them, thereby giving the teaching point double impact.

Organizing the Class

The most effective way to organize the class is to divide the students into permanent groups, with from four to six students in each group. Six is probably the ideal number, provided the seats can be arranged to form at least a rough circle.

The easiest way to form the groups is to have the students write their names on slips of paper, count the slips and divide by six to determine the number of groups, and distribute the slips at random in the appropriate number of piles of six. Next, give a letter name to each group, determine where each group should sit, call the name of one member from each group and have that person call the names of the other members.

If the class is coeducational, the teacher may want to have the groups balanced as to sex (to the extent possible) in order to facilitate the reading of dialogs, for example, that have roles for both males and females. In group activities such as singing, also, it is well to have both male and female voices, if possible.

After the groups have been organized, the teacher should have each group leader write the names of his group's members on the front of a 3 by 5 card (or larger), and have the members themselves write their names, addresses, and telephone numbers on the back of the card.

It is advantageous to have a group leader and an assistant leader for each group. It is probably best to have the students choose these leaders themselves, although it is sometimes difficult for them to do so, especially when all are strangers. One workable procedure is to have the students first introduce themselves within their groups. Each student should speak, in English, of course, for no less than two minutes nor more than three. If the teacher should neglect to mention that they should introduce themselves in English, it is not unusual for some groups to do it in Japanese. When this happens, it is always good for a laugh when the teacher interrupts the activity by clapping for attention and mentions this neglected point.

After the students have been able to evaluate one another, they should try to choose a leader. Their tendency is to choose the leader by *"jan ken pon"* or by lot, but this should be discouraged or even prohibited. The teacher should try to persuade them that it is for the good of the group to try to choose the best person for leader. It should be mentioned that the best leader is not necessarily the best speaker of English, although this is the person they most often choose. Actually there are "leader types," apart from language ability, and if they can choose such a person the group is more likely to develop esprit de corps. Tales of interesting activities of previous groups can be mentioned to encourage them. Under strong leadership, in fact, groups in the past have organized various kinds of activities even outside of class, in the manner of small "ESS" clubs. There have been groups which met daily at lunch time to continue discussions started in class. Groups have attended English-speaking activities together, such as "open house" celebrations at American military bases.

To encourage this group esprit de corps, the teacher can take group photographs and attach them to the group cards. This is an excellent way to help him remember the students. He can have an extra copy made for the group leader, or lend the group the negative so they can have copies made themselves. He should also have the members of the group exchange names, addresses, and phone numbers. It may also prove useful to devise a system for communicating with the class quickly. There may be an interesting television program he would like them to watch, for example, or an interesting outside English-speaking activity, such as the open-house event mentioned previously, that will take place before he meets them in class again. It would hardly be possible for him to phone all the students to inform them, but it would be possible for him to phone, say, the leaders of Groups A and B. Group A leader would then phone two people, namely his own assistant leader and the leader of Group C. Group B leader would phone his own assistant leader and the leader of Group D. The assistant leaders would phone two members of their own group who in turn would phone the others. Group C and D leaders would inform the other groups, on down the line. Very quickly the entire class could be informed.

Of course the best laid plans of mice and men are sure to go awry, so there must be a way to check to see if all members of the class have been informed. The best way to do this is to have the last person in the last group finally phone the teacher to report that he has been informed, and to repeat the message to make sure it has not been garbled.

Of course, this sort of interest in the students on the part of the teacher is effective in maintaining their own interest and enthusiasm, which in turn makes the class interesting and enjoyable for the teacher.

Group Activities

Group Singing. There are countless group activities to keep the class always interesting and interested. One of the best is group singing, for not only is this entertaining to the class, but the students are obliged to practice outside of the classroom. Any activity which can get them to use English outside the classroom is a plus.

An amazing phenomenon in Japan is that in a group of six students chosen at random, there is almost surely someone who plays the guitar. If there are ten groups in the class, at least half of them will probably have a member who can play the guitar, without any effort being made to distribute the guitar-playing students equally among the groups. Groups without a guitar player may turn up another instrument, such as a flute. Or a pianist who will record the accompaniment on tape to play on a tape recorder. The one or two groups without such musical talent may also use a tape recorder with background music supplied by one of their favorite singing groups. There have also been groups with marvelous a cappella singing.

The fact is that almost any group of six Japanese students can sing English songs beautifully if they will take the time to practice. Some groups, of course, will not do so and their lack of effort will show. The teacher must try to encourage their best effort.

A recent idea that has served well in encouraging their best effort is to record their singing. The teacher brings in a tape recorder with a microphone and keeps one tape for each class. The groups take turns singing, one or two groups performing in front of the class each week. They may chose the songs themselves and seem to have no difficulty getting copies of sheet music. If possible, the teacher should advise them as to troublesome points of pronunciation before they learn the song, since pronunciation and intonation practice are the greatest benefits realized from singing English songs, and the opportunity should not be missed to take advantage of it.

One problem that has not been solved to date is how to involve the rest of the class profitably when a particular group is singing. They sit in the role of passive listeners, being unable usually to understand the lyrics since the logistics of trying to provide copies of the songs to everyone is prohibitive.

Some songs are not worthy of study, but some songs with meaningful (and grammatically correct) lyrics could be studied if the teacher wishes to take the additional time necessary. One way would be to use the song as dictation practice for the class. The group that sang the song could be sent around the room to check on spelling and the like. Or the ones who sang the song could take the dictation on the blackboard so that the students at their desks could check their mistakes. It is not unusual for the ones who sang the song to make mistakes when trying to write it from dictation.

Self-introduction. One of the most useful ways for the teacher to get to know the students is to ask them to write a self-introduction. If he does not want to take up class time with writing, he can ask them to do it at home and bring it in the following week. But a student's writing ability is a good gauge of his speaking ability, and if the teacher feels it would be useful to have such an evaluation, it might be worthwhile to take 30 minutes or so and have them all write their self-introductions in class. If they are allowed to write them at home, the teacher has no way of knowing whether the students worked on them for minutes or hours and loses an important basis of comparison—the time element.

To expedite their writing, the teacher should give the students as much help as possible. For one thing, he should assure them that it is not a writing test, and that there is no need to worry about grammar and spelling. He simply wants to get to know them, he should say, so that the more they write, the better. Then he should fill the blackboard with topic suggestions and tell them they may write on all, some, or none of these. They are suggestions only.

One good way to present the topics is to group them under various headings such as present, past, and future. Under "present" could be listed such cues as hobbies, pastimes, clubs, family, pets, daily activities, your room, your house, your classes, social life, university life, abilities, likes, and dislikes. Under "past" could be listed childhood, home life, schools, experiences, memories, illness, injuries, and trips. Under "future" could be listed such categories as hopes, plans, ambition, dreams, next Sunday, next summer, after graduation, marriage, and children.

Under the category "miscellaneous," a broader range of subjects may be suggested, such as fears, concerns, problems, your character or nature, introvert, extrovert, optimist, pessimist, philosophy of life, and politics.

After they have finished their written self-introductions, it is a good idea to have the students, with these thoughts still fresh in their minds, give a more comprehensive oral self-introduction within their groups. Each student should be able to speak for at least four or five minutes, but whether he can or not, a question-and-answer session should follow. It is relatively easy for the students to answer questions posed by fellow members of their group. And in the process they all get to know one another better.

Intensive Interviews. A natural follow-up to the self-introduction and question-and-answer session is an intensive interview. The students in the group pair up and interview each other in depth. Most students need assistance in this, so the teacher can provide interview questions for them to use with the caution that they not use the questions mindlessly but adapt them to the individual and add their own questions as necessary.

Again such questions are conveniently divided into the categories present, past, and future. A selection from each category follows:

Present

1. Where do you live? Do you live in a house or an apartment?
2. When is your birthday? What do you do on your birthday? Do you get presents and have a cake?
3. What is your favorite possession? When or how did you get it?
4. What do you do in your free time?
5. Do you have a boy (girl) friend? Do you go on dates? Where do you go? How often do you date? Who pays?
6. How often do you watch TV? What are your favorite programs?
7. What kind of tape recorder do you have and how do you use it?
8. Are you a night-type person or a day-type person? What time do you get up and what time do you go to bed?
9. What do you spend your allowance for? Are you satisfied with the amount? What would you like to buy right now?
10. Can you cook? Do you cook? What do you cook?
11. Do you get along well with your parents? Do you feel a generation gap between you and them? What do you do that they don't like?
12. What's your father's occupation? What kind of a man is he?
13. What do you do when you are alone? Are you sometimes lonely? How do you overcome your loneliness?
14. Do you belong to any club? If not, why not? If so, why did you join that particular club?

Past

1. When and where were you born? Do you know the day of the week? Do you know the time of day? Do you believe in astrology?
2. What was your most unforgettable experience in primary school?
3. Who were your most unforgettable teachers and what do you remember about them?
4. What is the happiest memory of your childhood?
5. What is the most frightening experience you have ever had?
6. Did you collect anything? Do you still have the collection?
7. What food did you like and what did you dislike? Do you still have the same likes and dislikes?
8. What was the most unforgettable book you have ever read?
9. How did you happen to attend this university?

10. Have you ever had a part-time job? What, when, and where?
11. What were you like when you were a child? Fat or thin? Quiet or talkative? Shy or outgoing? Sad or cheerful? Studious or lazy? How would you describe yourself now?
12. Have you changed in any of these ways since you were younger?

Future

1. What are you going to do when you go home?
2. Do you usually plan your vacations and other activities? How far ahead do you usually plan them? Do you keep a daily schedule?
3. Are you saving any money? What are you going to spend it for?
4. To what level do you want to be able to speak and understand English? Are you willing to spend the time and effort necessary to master it? Or will you be content merely to be able to communicate?
5. What kind of job would you like to get when you graduate?
6. Do you think you will marry a fellow student? Why or why not?
7. In what ways would you like the relationship you have with your marriage partner to be different from the relationship your mother and father have with each other?
8. What do you hope to achieve in your life?

There is another interesting category of questions that might be called "speculative." These are sometimes useful when the interviewee is non-communicative or leads such an uninteresting life that the interview is not very interesting. Of course, the interviewee still may give uninteresting or "I don't know" type answers, but the questions themselves add interest to the interview.

Speculative Questions

1. What would you have done if you hadn't been able to enter this university?
2. What would you have done if you hadn't been able to enter any university?
3. What would you do if you had a million yen?
4. What would you do if you had one thousand million yen?

5. What would you do if you could live until you were 500 years old?
6. Where would you live if you could live anywhere in the world?
7. What would you do if you were the Prime Minister of Japan?
8. What would you do if you were the Education Minister?
9. What would you do if you were the president of this university?
10. What would you do if you could speak English like a native?

Reporting. A natural follow-up to the interviews is to have the interviewer report his findings to the other members of the group. This is more difficult than introducing himself and represents a progression from speaking in the first person to reporting in the third person. After the report, the other members may ask the interviewer additional questions about the interviewee, and the number of questions he can and cannot answer is a good gauge of the success of the interview. The teacher, of course, will also ask questions, and knowing this in advance, the student will make a greater effort to get an in-depth interview.

Since the students already know their partners to some extent from the self-introductions, a little more difficult interview would be one in which the members of one group interview the members of another group, and then introduce their new acquaintance to the members of their own group.

Impromptu Speeches. Progressively more difficult are impromptu speeches. The teacher provides each group with a selection of speech topics from which the speaker chooses one and speaks for two minutes. Actually, the student chooses one slip sight unseen from several presented. On his slip are two topics, and he has one minute to choose one of them and to prepare his speech. He then speaks for two minutes. Afterward, there can be a group discussion of the topic, or the group can elect to go on at once to the next speaker.

The paired topics from which the speakers choose usually consist of one personal subject and one general subject. Following is a sampling of the paired topics:

1. Coffee Shops
   Why I Like (Don't Like) Summer
2. Automobiles
   My Best Friend

3. My Grandparents
   How to Get Enough Exercise
4. Women's Fashions
   My University
5. The Ideal Home Life
   My Favorite Japanese Novel
6. The "Omiai" System
   If I Had a Million Dollars
7. The Most Unforgettable Person I Ever Met
   Women's Liberation
8. Something I Don't Like
   The Population Problem

Prepared Speeches. It is debatable whether impromptu speeches or prepared speeches are more difficult. The former may be more demanding, but the ordeal is over in a short time. The latter may be easier but involve a great deal more time and effort. The teacher may begin by first assigning personal topics, such as those for impromptu speeches, then later the more general topics. Still later he can assign even more difficult subjects, such as "Mercy Killing is Justifiable," "All Members of a Society Should Be Educated," or "Consistency is a Desirable Trait."

Again it is often profitable to have a group discussion of the topic after the speech.

Debates. On a higher level of difficulty are debates. The group forms two teams and follows much the same procedure as a formal debate. There are three members on each team, one of whom gives the presentation, another the rebuttal, and the third the summation. Judges often can be obtained from groups that are unable to form two teams because of absences.

Again, debating can begin with simple subjects such as:

1. Night is more fun than day.
2. A bicycle is better than a car.
3. It is better to be single than married.
4. It is better to be blind than deaf.
5. TV news is better than newspaper news.
6. It's better to be too hot than too cold.
7. Too fat is better than too thin.

Later, the students can debate the more traditional subjects which involve domestic and international problems.

And, of course, interest in the debates reaches a peak when two groups debate before the entire class, with a three-man team from each group. Students from disinterested groups can serve as judges. The teacher can confirm or dispute their judgment.

Textbook Work.   Despite the wealth of activities possible without a textbook, Japanese students feel rather lost without one. Therefore, it is advisable to have a textbook. The textbook can serve as the framework around which the course is built, although it may be used only a third of the hour. The best textbook is one that contains a variety of materials on current topics of interest to the students. It is well to have dialogs that the students can act out in pairs. As mentioned previously, the dialogs can also be used in a student teacher/student situation, with one student trying to reproduce his lines from cues given by the student teacher.

It is useful to have drills and comprehension questions in the book so that the students can work in the same way, one acting as teacher and the other as student.

There can be competition between the groups by having individuals from each group perform the dramatic skits from memory. The applause of the class decides the winner.

Games.   The best games for language learners are oral word games such as guessing games and action chains, but there are few of these that can be successful without the supervision of the teacher, so they are best played with the class as a whole, in competition between groups. Pencil and paper games can work well in unsupervised group activities. Puzzles and quizzes are good, but if they are too difficult they take too much time. But since the first team to answer wins, there is pressure on the group to "think in English" rather than take time to translate the idea into Japanese first. The following serves as an example:

> If the statement, "There are more dogs in the U.S. than there are hairs on any one dog in the U.S.," is true, then is the statement, "There are at least two dogs in the U.S. with exactly the same number of hairs," true or false? And why? (Answer: True. The number of dogs exceeds the possible variations in the number of hairs they have.)

There are many games that can be played in competition between groups with the teacher supervising or conducting the game and the rest of the class watching or cheering, or, it is hoped, competing mentally. One game will suffice here as an example:

> This is an action game which tests the students' hearing ability. Two chairs are placed in front of the room and labeled "true chair" and "untrue chair." The two groups line up about two meters from the chairs. The teacher makes a statement, such as "It's raining today." If this is not true the first student in each line rushes to sit on the "untrue chair." The successful student scores a point for his team. The teacher than makes another statement, such as "The lights are not on in this room." The students second in line rush to sit on the chair matching the statement.

This game is suitable for all ability levels, with the teacher adjusting the statements according to the average ability of the class.

Outside Activities.   Whatever outside English-speaking activities the teacher can cajole or even force the students to take part in are to their benefit. Many of them can be persuaded to attend outside activities such as the previously mentioned U.S. military base open-house events on the American holidays Independence Day (July 4) and Labor Day (first Monday in September). They are not inclined to attend plays or discussion meetings, even when these are free. And they always must be forced to take part in one of the most interesting activities they can experience: an interview with an unknown foreigner.

Sometime this assignment is given as punishment for speaking Japanese in the classroom, but it is better to simply make it a class assignment. The students are told to get a tape recorder with fresh batteries, a tape, and a microphone, and to go together to the heart of Tokyo and interview a foreigner. This is an appropriate follow-up to the interviews they practiced with one another in class.

There are many places they can go to, such as international hotels, parks, and even English-speaking schools and clubs. They are urged to try to find tourists, if possible, who are less jaded than oldtimers and who will even consider the interview an interesting experience.

They should be urged to avoid routine questions such as "How do you like Japan?" and "Did you eat sushi?" and instead try to learn something a little more worthwhile, such as facts about the foreigner's country or way of life. Conceivably, they could come across a person who could give them practical answers to questions in their own field of study.

The students are asked to submit a written report with their tape to the teacher. The report should consist of a general introduction, the questions asked (identified as to speaker) in the order asked, and a transcription of the most interesting replies (to total 150 or so words).

The teacher may receive too many tapes to be able to listen to them all, but guided by the list of questions, he can peruse the most promising answers and perhaps find replies that are worth sharing with the entire class.

General Class Activity

It is well to end the class with some activity that involves the entire class together. Often the activity can be combined with taking attendance, although with the group system it is a simple matter to take attendance by visiting each group. Also, the teacher may prefer to take attendance at the beginning of the class.

At any rate, calling the roll can be made more profitable by having the students reply with something other than "here." It could be a good way to learn the students' individual pronunciation problems, for instance. One week the students can be asked to respond, "Fine, thank you," to test their pronunciation of "f" and "th." The following week they can be asked to say something like "really religious" to check "r" and "l."

Or the teacher can test, or at least give practice in, hearing comprehension by asking the students questions. After the summer vacation, for example, it would be appropriate to ask them how they spent it. To keep the roll call moving along at a fast clip, the teacher should ask only questions which can be answered yes or no. And to maintain student interest, he could ask each student a different question. If it is a large class, especially, the students are kept in suspense, of sorts, wondering if the teacher will be able to think of enough questions to go around. A sampling of questions for 50 students follows:

1. Did you have a nice summer vacation?
2. Did you go outside of Japan?
3. Did you earn any money?

4. Did you study in the library?
5. Did you speak English to anyone?
6. Did you get married? (Always good for a laugh.)
7. Did you cook anything?
8. Did you make any new friends?
9. Did you send summer greeting cards?
10. Did you visit your hometown?
11. Did you meet any members of your group?
12. Did you get drunk?
13. Did you have a birthday?
14. Did you get a job?
15. Did you see a tie-breaking home run?
16. Did you get a haircut?
17. Did you watch any English-language programs on TV?

It is possible to surprise the students every week with a call for a different response. In fact, instead of merely noting the attendance, the teacher can give the response a grade, based on a scale of, say, 5 excellent, 4 good, 3 fair, 2 poor, and 1 very poor. If over the weeks the student makes no improvement in his pronunciation of "th," he would be marked accordingly. If the teacher collects enough of these oral grades, it would be unnecessary to give a final examination.

It is a good policy to give all group activities scrutiny in front of the class. Thus, the members of one or two groups, by turn or at random, should come to the front of the class and demonstrate their dialogue performance, or their interviewing techniques, or introduce someone they interviewed, or repeat their self-introductions, or give impromptu speeches, or do any other activity which they have been practicing in their group. The teacher could use the occasion to give them grades.

It is also a good time to have competition between groups: the inter-group debates or quizzes or games. And the class day should be topped off with group singing.

It is rather absurd to have to give a written examination in a class supposedly striving for oral fluency, so the teacher should make every effort to avoid this, if possible. The only way to avoid it, however, is by evaluating class work frequently and recording it faithfully. The need to evaluate the students and to give them a final grade is the one task that makes teaching English in large classes less than a perfect joy.

Useful Books

1. *3500 Names for Baby;* Dell Publishing Co., 1969.
2. *Language Teaching Games and Contests,* by W. R. Lee; Oxford University Press.
3. *English Teaching Forum,* Vol. XII, Oct.-Dec., 1974, No. 4.
4. *New Movements in the Study and Teaching of English,* edited by N. Bagnall; Temple Smith, London.
5. *The Gift of Language,* by Margaret Schlauch; Dover Publications, Inc., N.Y.
6. *Mainline Progress A & B,* Teacher's Book, by L. G. Alexander; Longman Group, Ltd., London.
7. *Teaching and Learning English,* by Raja T. Nasr; Longman, London.
8. *English Teaching Extracts,* by Donn Byrne; Longman, London.
9. *Simple Audio-Visual Aids to Foreign-Language Teaching,* by Lee and Coppen; Oxford University Press.
10. *Teaching English as a Second Language,* by Mary Finocchiaro; Harper & Row, New York and London.
11. *The Foreign Language Learner,* by Finocchiaro and Bonomo; Regents Publishing Co., New York.
12. *Games and Parties for All Occasions,* by Kemmerer and Brickett; Denison & Co., Minneapolis.
13. *New Ways to Learn a Foreign Language,* by R. Hall; Bantam Books, New York.
14. *Teaching English as a Foreign Language,* by P. Gurrey; Longman.
15. *Language Teaching: A Scientific Approach,* by R. Lado; McGraw-Hill, New York.

Teaching Opportunities Outside of the Japanese Educational System

Richard Evanoff

IT IS SOMETIMES PERPLEXING, even to those who have been teaching English a number of years in Japan, why the demand for what might be termed "extra-curricular" English instruction in Japan is so high. In addition to the large number of English courses offered in the standard curriculum of nearly every Japanese secondary school and university, a great deal of time, effort, and money is spent studying English in private, non-academic settings by Japanese of nearly all ages and ability levels, from pre-kindergarten children to retirees. As a result, the teaching of English has become a profitable business in Japan. In order to help satisfy the high demand for extra-curricular English instruction, a variety of private enterprises have come into being that employ a large percentage of native English speakers as instructors. This article explores the range of employment opportunities such enterprises offer the foreign teacher.

First comes a description of the general market for extra-curricular English instruction in Japan. The next section outlines some of the more common institutional arrangements that presently exist in Japan to meet the demands of that market. The final section focuses on the individual teacher, giving special attention to the qualifications necessary to be successful in this field.

The Market

Required courses in English were introduced into the Japanese educational system following the Second World War and, with the obvious exception of children who are just beginning to learn the language, nearly everyone the foreign teacher will be expected to teach in the extracurricular language market in Japan has previously studied English in junior high school, high school, and quite commonly also at the university level. In spite of this, the formal education of most Japanese has done relatively little to enable them to carry on a normal conversation in English. It is precisely for this reason that the demand for courses in English conversation, and particularly for courses taught by native speaking teachers, is so high. The majority of English courses offered in Japanese schools and universities concentrate almost exclusively on grammar and translation, giving the student little or no opportunity to practice speaking the language in a conversational setting. In order to make up for this deficiency many students wish to take additional conversation lessons. The lessons most desired are those that simply give the student a chance to practice speaking the English he or she has previously studied in textbooks.

Because students must take the initiative to study English extracurricularly, they are usually highly motivated. It is, after all, their own time and money that is being spent. Their motives for studying, however, often vary. Persons still in school may think that additional lessons in English will enable them to perform better on school tests and college entrance exams. Young people may study with the hope of enhancing their future employment prospects, persons already working with a view toward being given more responsibilities in their companies. Housewives may join a neighborhood English class as a chance to get out of the house and meet new people. Others may pursue English as they would a hobby. There is, however, a genuine desire on the part of most students to learn how to communicate well in English and to learn about the cultures in which it is spoken. Those who speak English well are almost universally admired in Japan. Yet nearly everyone—even the best of speakers—is self-deprecatory about his or her own ability to speak English. There always seems to be room for improvement, and this is perhaps why additional study is so highly valued.

There is also a considerable market in Japan for teaching English to children, though many positions in this field are open only to Japanese nationals. Some parents feel, for a variety of reasons, that it is better for children to study English with a Japanese teacher who can explain matters thoroughly to the pupils in Japanese. Others, however, believe that studying with a foreign teacher gives children certain advantages, especially in such areas as oral comprehension and pronunciation. The special difficulties of teaching a foreign language to children and the advisability of being able to conduct portions of the class in Japanese have led some foreign teachers to steer away from positions that involve teaching children. However, a few schools have developed quite sophisticated programs for teaching English to children that have been especially designed to be taught by foreign teachers.

The market for potential students in Japan includes persons of nearly all ages and levels of ability. What is surprising is that the demand is so high and that there are in fact so many persons who are interested in learning English and, moreover, willing to pay for the opportunity of studying with a foreign teacher. As long as this demand remains high there will be a need for foreign teachers to teach English extra-curricularly in Japan.

Institutional Arrangements

Language Schools. The most common institution for teaching English extra-curricularly in Japan is the private language school. Since language schools are private enterprises not accredited by the government, there are virtually no regulations that stipulate how they should be run or what kind of curriculum they should provide. No two are alike. Some cater to certain kinds of students, such as children or businessmen. Others attempt to teach the whole spectrum of students, from children to adults, beginners through advanced.

Most language schools have been founded by individual entrepreneurs, both Japanese and foreign, some of whom were previously teachers in other schools. A few schools have been spawned from businesses in related fields. Still others are the branches of internationally-operated language institutes. As with anything else, a language school cannot be judged by external appearances, nor even by the reputation it might enjoy. A prestigious and expensively furnished school may in fact be less concerned about its students and teachers than a school operating out of a one-room apartment.

Language schools typically recruit their students by advertising their services in newspapers, on billboards and posters, and through home-delivered handbills. Anyone willing to pay the required tuition is accepted as a student. There are no entrance requirements and no one is ever turned away. Most schools charge a monthly tuition fee. Some may charge an additional entrance fee when the student begins studying at the school. In arrangements of this type the student may take lessons for as long as he likes and can stop whenever he chooses. Some students attend a class for only a few months; others may continue for years. Less commonly, a school may charge a set fee for a specific course that extends over a fixed period of time. A few schools charge for a certain number of hours of instruction that the student can attend whenever he wishes by prior appointment. Regardless of the method of scheduling and payment, however, the emphasis in nearly every school is on having the students continue to study—and to pay tuition—for as long a period as possible, either through keeping the students involved in a class that runs indefinitely or through getting them to sign up for a new course when the current one ends.

The fact that language schools are operated within the context of the free enterprise system puts a certain amount of pressure on the teacher. Because classes are purely voluntary and the students may quit at any time, the teacher must strive to make his classes interesting and relevant to the students' needs. In some cases this may compromise the quality of the instruction the teacher is able to offer. Usually he cannot, for example, assign homework that is dull, no matter how valuable it may be from an educational standpoint. In most language schools, however, the classroom environment is fresh and stimulating both for teachers and students. The teacher is free from most of the bureaucratic pressures that are usually associated with teaching positions at accredited schools. The teacher is thus free to devote his full attention to his students. Some schools give the teacher a great deal of latitude in choosing how he will conduct his classes, leaving him the freedom to develop his own methods and style. Other schools have particular methods they want their teachers to follow and will usually give them adequate training in those methods.

Teachers are typically paid monthly according to the number of hours they have actually spent teaching. Hourly wages vary considerably from school to school, making generalizations about what a prospective teacher should expect to receive difficult. However, anyone asked to accept less than ¥2,500 per hour would probably be able to find something better with a little extra perseverance. Wages above ¥5,000 would be rare. For schedules involving only a few hours of teaching a week, such as company classes (described below), wages would typically range between ¥4,000 and ¥6,000 per class, sometimes even higher. When considering wages, however, one should also take into account other modes of compensation that might be offered by some employers, such as free room and board. One should also inquire into how much will be expected from a teacher outside of the classroom—frequently little or no compensation is given for time spent preparing for classes, attending meetings, acquiring additional training, helping with school-sponsored activities, and so on. It is not uncommon for some employers to take advantage of employees in such matters.

In determining schedules, some schools offer their teachers a minimum guarantee. This means the school guarantees the teacher that he will be able to teach a certain number of hours per week at a certain wage over a certain period of time. The teacher may in fact be asked to teach more hours than his guarantee indicates, but he at least is assured that he will receive a certain minimum income each month. At other schools, the amount of income one receives is directly related to how many classes the teacher is able to keep together. If enrollment in a particular class sinks below a certain level the class will be disbanded. It will then be up to the school's discretion whether or not the teacher will or can be given another class in its place. In schools using this system, successful teachers are generally kept well supplied with classes and students, while the schedules of less successful teachers may simply be allowed to diminish to the point of virtual non-employment, perhaps without ever formally dismissing the teacher. In some schools, it is not uncommon for the teacher to be asked to share some of the responsibility for keeping the number of students in his classes at an acceptable level.

A typical teaching load is twenty classroom hours per week for a "full-time" teacher. The nature of the market necessitates that nearly all of this be scheduled in the late afternoon and early evening. With the exception of so-called housewives' classes, which are usually held in the morning or early afternoon, few teaching schedules can begin before 3:00 P.M. At a school that teaches the entire range of students, a typical schedule might include three or four children's classes in the late afternoon when the children have finished regular school, a junior high-school and/or high-school class in the early evening, and to end the day an adult class over by no later than 9:00 or 10:00 P.M. Classes usually meet once a week. Thus, a teacher finds himself teaching different classes and students each day, sometimes even at different locations. This variety is appreciated by many teachers, especially since they may be teaching the same students for a number of years.

In theory, schedules and modes of payment are all set out in advance in what is almost always a one-year, renewable contract. In practice, however, the terms of the contract are seldom followed strictly, giving the employer a great deal of flexibility in how he wishes to deal with his employees. Frequently this flexibility works to the teacher's advantage. The employer can, however, still dismiss a teacher at any time, provided there is sufficient reason. Conversely, a teacher can quit his position if he feels the terms of the contract are obviously not being fulfilled. The purpose of the contract is less to protect either of the parties involved than to satisfy the demands of immigration officials who require the contract as evidence that a foreigner can support himself while living in Japan. Every foreigner working in Japan must also have a sponsor who agrees to take legal responsibility for him while he is residing in Japan. This sponsor can be either a private Japanese citizen or the company one works for. Since many foreigners have no Japanese acquaintances willing to sponsor them, the school one teaches at will usually offer to act as sponsor. One should be aware, however, that some schools may on occasion use the sponsorship as a form of coercion, especially to prevent teachers from taking on side jobs at other institutions.

The atmosphere at the majority of schools is personal and friendly. Because most schools are small, it is easy to become acquainted with other teachers, nearly all of whom will be from English-speaking countries. The larger schools also employ Japanese as staff and secretaries. If the school has a manager, he will usually be Japanese. Most foreigners lack the language ability and knowledge of Japanese business customs to move into managerial positions, which in any event usually pay less than teaching positions. Some, however, may be given responsibilities supervising or training other teachers. Ultimate authority usually rests with the owner of the school. In some schools there are well-defined policies explaining a teacher's rights and responsibilities. In other schools policies are pretty much left up to the personal whims of the owner. And, like owners of any small, private company, some tend to be authoritarian, while others attempt to foster a democratic atmosphere in which teachers are allowed to play a part in the decision-making process.

Though one's income can be quite high, depending on the school and the number of hours a teacher is willing and able to fit into his schedule, teaching at most language schools offers one little job security, few opportunities for advancement, and, from the standpoint of Japanese society, absolutely no prestige. A majority of the people who teach at them are persons who plan on staying only temporarily in Japan and who use the employment to support themselves while they are here. The transient nature of the work force has led to a corresponding unwillingness on the part of many employers to make long-term commitments to their employees. Fringe benefits of any sort are rare and retirement programs are almost unheard of. Still, a few persons have made quite successful careers out of teaching at some of the better schools. Others have used their work at a language school to supplement income from other activities, such as writing or teaching at a university.

Language schools are viewed by many Japanese (and sometimes by the people who work for them) as being more interested in the tuition fee than in the quality of education they provide. It is unfortunate that many schools deserve this reputation, especially given the positive contribution that language schools in general are capable of making to English education in Japan. The Japanese are becoming increasingly selective in where they will spend their money to study English and it is likely that in the near future only those schools having sound educational programs will be able to survive. Competition has insured that there are presently quite a few good schools employing qualified teachers in Japan, but unfortunately there are also a number of schools whose practices and educational standards remain questionable.

Company Classes. Many Japanese companies encourage their employees to take lessons in conversational English. In some cases, the ability to communicate in English is essential to the employee's job. But even those who in their present work have little occasion to use English will often be encouraged to study English should the need arise later. Some employees will take their own initiative to study English in order to be considered for some special job within their companies, such as an overseas assignment. Other employees will have been specifically directed by their companies to take a course in conversational English.

A few large companies have their own English-language programs. Foreigners who teach at these companies are hired as full-time employees. They usually put in a forty-hour week, with some of the time being devoted to other language-related tasks such as writing business letters, working on promotional material, etc. Salaries for such positions are about the same as those for a typical teaching load at a good language school, although the amount of time actually spent working is usually more. One advantage, however, is that a foreigner who is hired as a full-time employee in such companies is often given the same full range of fringe benefits that Japanese employees receive: a guarantee of life-time employment, retirement and health benefits, semi-annual bonuses, housing allowances, and so on. What one gains in security one may lose in flexibility, however, since most such companies will not let their teachers teach elsewhere. Some teachers may have considerably higher incomes, even when fringe benefits are taken into consideration, teaching the same number of hours at a variety of high-paying part-time jobs. Other teachers may for cultural reasons find it difficult to adjust to the working atmosphere of a Japanese company.

The majority of companies do not have such extensive language programs, however. Most will simply hire a teacher to teach one or more classes on a part-time basis, usually in the evenings. The average hourly renumeration for such classes is probably the top in the English-teaching business. But because it is almost impossible to construct a full schedule out of such classes, most teachers use them to supplement income from other sources. Some companies will also have special intensive seminars, such as a refresher course to prepare employees for a trip abroad, which offer temporary, though often lucrative, employment.

Most companies realize the part-time nature of the teaching jobs they are offering and usually have no objections to a teacher teaching elsewhere. However, most are also reluctant to act as sponsors for a foreign teacher's visa. Instead of organizing their own classes some companies will have contracts with language schools to provide a teacher for English instruction. The teacher may be paid a slightly higher wage than he would normally receive for regular classes in the language school, though the school will, of course, also take its cut. Other companies will simply encourage, and sometimes pay for, their employees to take lessons at a language school, typically one which specializes in teaching businessmen.

Teaching Independently. Teachers who have some experience teaching English in Japan frequently start their own classes independent of any language school or company. Even those who have full-time jobs elsewhere will sometimes organize a few classes of their own, not infrequently taught right in the teacher's home. Some teachers in Japan support themselves entirely from the income they receive teaching independently. Others eventually expand their home-operated businesses into full-fledged language schools with rented locations and hired teachers.

Teaching independently offers the potential of making a higher income than one could make working for someone else and, of course, the freedom to be one's own boss. The risk involved is surprisingly low, considering how little money is needed for an initial investment. All one requires is space to teach in, which can be one's own home if necessary, and teaching materials. In the case of adults little more than a small blackboard and a teacher's copy of the textbook is necessary. With children one can make many of the teaching materials by oneself or purchase them cheaply from a supplier of educational materials.

Besides using newspaper ads and shopping guides, one of the most successful methods of advertising is to have copies of a handbill printed up that the teacher can distribute himself to houses in his neighborhood. The handbill might include a brief listing of the teacher's qualifications, a map showing where the classes will be conducted, and a chart showing the classes he plans to offer, with information on the time, ability level, age level, and tuition of each class. Besides offering classes, the teacher may also wish to advertise for private lessons. The advantage of classes over private lessons though is that as the number of students per class increases so does one's hourly income. However, most students prefer classes limited to not more than eight students. It is therefore difficult to hold a class together that is larger than this, and of course, also more difficult to teach.

One aspect of teaching independently is that, like any business, one is under continual pressure to keep a steady flow of income coming in. Students come and go and the teacher must advertise frequently to keep the classes from disintegrating. It usually takes a year or more for a teacher to fill out a schedule that will support himself entirely without income from any other source. Many teachers, of course, simply do it a few hours a week as a side job.

Any teacher who wishes to teach independently should first receive permission from the immigration authorities. Usually there are no complications for anyone already teaching in Japan. Complications do arise, however, if one plans to use his independent teaching as his sole source of income. First, since he will not be teaching for any company or institution he will need an independent sponsor, in most cases a private Japanese citizen. Second, in order to prove that he will not become a public burden, he may be required to show that he is in fact capable of supporting himself by teaching independently. It is also advisable for anyone teaching independently to consult with the nearest tax office to see what procedures to follow for paying taxes. Depending on the size and nature of the operation, one may also be required to obtain a business license.

The Individual Teacher

It is not very difficult for anyone, regardless of educational background or experience, to find a teaching position in Japan if he is a native speaker of English. There are relatively few foreigners teaching extra-curricularly in Japan who have specific training or experience in teaching English as a foreign language. While some teachers acquire excellent teaching skills during the course of their employment, and while many schools expend a great deal of effort training their teachers, the general quality of extra-curricular teachers in Japan remains rather low. There is such a high demand for native English speakers as instructors that in many schools and companies being a native speaker is the only qualification that really counts. Because it is so easy to find a teaching position, there are many unqualified foreigners teaching English in Japan who are little more than long-term tourists with little interest in or aptitude for teaching as a profession. The Japanese public, of course, is aware of this situation and students have recently become more discriminating in choosing their teachers. Yet for better or worse, being a native speaker is one factor taken into consideration by nearly every school when hiring a teacher. Qualified teachers who are not native speakers of English will have a more difficult time finding employment. On the other hand, some teaching positions, often those related to teaching children, are advertised as being open only to Japanese nationals. Few schools or companies require their foreign teachers to be able to speak Japanese, although teachers will often be encouraged to study the language after arriving in Japan.

Most visas that permit one to teach in Japan require the person to have a bachelor's degree; the field of study is not specified. There are other visas, however, such as those for spouses of Japanese citizens, where a degree is not required. With regard to schools and companies, hiring practices vary. A bachelor's degree is generally preferred, but in some cases not absolutely necessary. A few schools and companies will hire only teachers having degrees in teaching English as a second language. Most schools, however, will accept a degree in any field, even the sciences, though some preference may be given to degrees in education, the social sciences, or the humanities.

Regardless of one's college major or area of specialization, a successful teacher in Japan must be conversant in a variety of subjects, since the interests of his students may be quite varied. A broad educational background with some travel experience is extremely useful, as is a friendly, outgoing manner and a natural curiosity in learning about others. Conversation classes provide an opportunity for genuine cross-cultural communication to take place. In the course of giving his students listening practice, a teacher can tell his students much about his own country and culture and, while prompting his students to speak, he can ask them questions about Japan and Japanese customs. A foreign teacher should in fact be quite familiar with various aspects of Japanese culture. In extracurricular English classes, establishing good rapport is extremely important. Being able to create a relaxed yet stimulating atmosphere is an essential precondition of any successful class.

Most schools and companies advertise openings for teaching positions in the classified ad sections of English-language newspapers. Unlike positions at most universities, personal connections are not particularly crucial. Sending unsolicited resumes or applying uninvited directly at the school or company rarely results in an interview. Some schools, especially those in remote locations, will recruit their teachers directly from English-speaking countries. In most cases, however, a school will not consider an applicant unless he is already in Japan and readily available for an interview.

Interviews usually proceed according to the same rules observed in the West, although if the interviewer is Japanese the prospective teacher should be aware of the different cultural perspectives that may come into play. Since one cannot usually know in advance the amount of previous experience a Japanese has had in dealing with foreigners, generally it is best in such a situation for the prospective teacher to let the interviewer take the lead, answering questions briefly and politely. He should not try to "sell himself" on the basis of his qualifications or past achievements, which to the Japanese may sound like bragging. Schedules will usually be discussed after qualifications. Once the interviewer is satisfied that the prospective teacher is suited for the position, he will indicate this decision by stating how much the position pays. The interviewee may be given very little time to decide whether to accept or reject the offer, so one is well-advised to have decided beforehand what is and is not acceptable. Saying one "needs some time to think it over" may be interpreted as a polite way of saying one is not interested.

By the standards of most English-speaking countries, hiring practices in Japan can at times seem somewhat discriminatory. The distinction made with regard to native speakers and Japanese nationals has already been mentioned, though some would argue that such a distinction is justified and not discriminatory. Unfortunately, however, native speakers of Oriental ancestry are sometimes discriminated against simply because they do not "look foreign." Neither is it uncommon for job openings to be quite openly categorized according to sex.

The best opportunities for finding employment, at least in terms of the variety of openings available, are still in large cities and their environs. However, many big cities—Tokyo and Osaka in particular—have become saturated with foreigners, with the result that competition for the best positions is stiffer. Company classes are almost exclusively limited to the larger cities. There has recently been an increase in the number of language schools operating outside of major cities, however, especially those which specialize in teaching children.

Conclusion

There is such a wide variety of extra-curricular teaching opportunities open to the foreign teacher that he must be discriminating with regard to where and how he will work. There are almost no rules of thumb for determining in advance the character of a particular school or job situation. A teacher may immediately find a position in a school or company he likes. Or he may wish to work in several different situations before deciding which type of work he is best suited for. Many teachers feel more secure having their eggs in different baskets, and it would not be unusual for a single teacher to be simultaneously pursuing a variety of teaching options. A highly motivated teacher who finds a teaching environment that is comfortable for him will be able to make a significant contribution to the teaching of English in Japan.

Bibliography

Various newspapers, particularly the *Japan Times,* the *Asahi Evening News,* and the *Mainichi Daily News,* carry articles related to teaching English extra-curricularly in Japan. Most books on the subject deal more specifically with teaching methods than with the environmental factors discussed in the present article. One of the best sources of information, however, with regard both to the general teaching situation in Japan and to specific teaching options, is to simply talk with teachers who have already spent some time teaching in Japan.

Teaching English to Japanese Adults

Richard Evanoff

ONE SOURCE OF FRUSTRATION for many foreign language teachers who teach English to adults in Japan is the genuine difficulty many students seem to have in carrying on even a simple conversation in English. What usually makes the frustration even greater is knowing that any adult who has gone through the Japanese educational system has been obliged to study English a minimum of six years in junior high school and high school. A great deal of frustration—for student as well as teacher—can be avoided, however, if a prospective student's present capabilities are honestly assessed before he enters the classroom and if, on the basis of that assessment, he is then offered a course of study appropriate to those capabilities. In this article I would like to redefine the traditional divisions between the levels "beginning," "intermediate," and "advanced" in a way that will make them more relevent to the specific teaching situation in Japan. Then I would like to discuss some of the methods that can be used to teach adult students at each of the respective levels.

Determining Levels

Adult students in Japan are primarily interested in English-conversation classes, with a strong emphasis in the minds of most students being placed on the word "conversation." To carry on a meaningful conversation in English requires a variety of skills. Basic speaking and hearing skills are, of course, essential. A speaker's pronunciation, intonation, and accent must be within acceptable ranges if he is to be readily understood. He must be able to speak the language with a reasonable degree of grammatical correctness. His speech cannot simply be a disconnected string of vocabulary items. The basic sentence patterns in which the English language is spoken must be thoroughly mastered. Moreover, the individual must be able to recall these sentence patterns with a fair amount of speed and accuracy. Prolonged hesitation and stumbling make one's speech uninteresting and difficult to follow. A speaker must not only be able to use these patterns as a means of expressing his thoughts; his thoughts themselves must be conceived in terms of these patterns. That is, he must be able to think in English. He cannot formulate what he wishes to say in his own language and then attempt to translate from that into English. In a conversation a person must also, of course, be able to understand what is spoken to him and know how to respond in an acceptable manner. He should have some feeling for the idiomatic nuances of the language, as well as a basic understanding of the rules by which conversations in English are typically governed. He must therefore have some appreciation of the social contexts in which English is spoken. He must be aware of certain culturally-conditioned attitudes towards language, such as the high value that English-speaking cultures place on expressing oneself clearly. And if he is to become what would be regarded as a good conversationalist, he must be capable of "keeping up his end of the conversation."

This list, of course, could be greatly expanded. It is selective in that it singles out precisely those skills in which most Japanese schools provide very little training. Speaking itself is given scant attention in the typical curriculum. Whereas most modern texts on language teaching, particularly those advocating the audio-lingual method, emphasize the primacy of the speaking skill and stress the importance of using it as the basis from which other skills, such as reading and writing, can be acquired, more traditional teaching methods are typically employed in Japanese schools. Teachers in many Japanese junior high schools and high schools tend to concentrate a disproportionate amount of attention on reading and writing, the teaching methods most favored being those that involve detailed grammatical expositions and translation. The students thus spend a great deal of their time acquiring rules about how English is constructed rather than a functional ability to actually use the language as a means of communication. Speaking in class, if it is done at all, is usually

little more than a variant way of doing what would otherwise be a written exercise of the more traditional type.

Such is the formal preparation that most students have received prior to their first lesson with a foreign instructor. Yet, despite the relative uniformity of the Japanese educational system, the foreign teacher will immediately notice vast differences in the speaking abilities of his students. Some will barely be able to respond to even a simple question, while others (though considerably fewer in numbers) may be immediately prepared to discuss a variety of social, political, even philosophical issues. There are a variety of reasons as to why these differences exist. Some students have, of course, retained more of what they have been previously taught, and some are simply better at applying what they have learned to a conversational situation. Others may have had special experiences, such as travel to English-speaking countries or friendships with native speakers, that have contributed to their ability to converse in English.

When organizing classes it is naturally important that students with similar abilities be grouped together. It is unfair to expect a student who has difficulty constructing simple sentences in English to participate in a philosophical debate, and it is just as unfair to expect a person with excellent conversational skills to endure the amount of drillwork that is necessary in any beginning class. However, a much wider range of factors than those that are typically considered must be taken into account when determining how students might be grouped together into appropriate classes. In many adult classes students are grouped together on the basis of factors that are, for the most part, irrelevant. As has been seen, the number of years a student has previously studied English gives little indication as to his or her ability to perform well in a conversation class.

Even less reliable are judgments made on the basis of how much a student is capable of understanding, whether written or spoken. Most foreign-language students—regardless of the language they are studying—understand more than they are capable of reproducing. Their ability to read and understand a text will usually be considerably higher than their ability to write something of similar complexity. With regard to oral skills, their ability to understand what is said to them will in most cases exceed what they are capable of saying in response. Students, as well as teachers, are sometimes misled in thinking that because everything printed in a conversation textbook can be readily understood, the text

must therefore be too easy. Putting the students in a situation where they must be able to freely reproduce the patterns drilled in the text usually cures any misconceptions of this sort.

Perhaps the least reliable guide to a student's true capabilities is the student's own opinion of himself. When asked, nearly every Japanese student will, out of modesty, classify himself as a beginner, even if he or she is in fact quite good. Privately, however, many students may actually overestimate their abilities. They may feel, as many of their former teachers undoubtedly told them, that conversation is something that can be easily "picked up" once one has paid his dues in the grammar and translation class. Nothing could be further from the truth, of course.

Written examinations may have some limited value in that they can assess the student's general competence with regard to such items as grammar and vocabularly. But one will usually find—and this is especially true for Japanese students—that performance on a written test has little connection with a student's ability to communicate in spoken English. While it is true that anyone who is able to converse well in English will probably be able to do well on a written test, it is not equally true that everyone who does well on such a test will be competent at conversation. Carefully constructed oral tests might be somewhat more useful, though these are not generally available, the teacher usually being obliged to construct his own.

Relying on some objective standard, such as any of those just mentioned, naturally seems fairer in determining a student's level than using subjective ones. However, a student's present knowledge of the English language, measured by whatever means, should never be the sole criterion by which students are grouped together into classes. There are a number of other factors, in fact quite subjective and therefore more difficult to evaluate, that nonetheless should also be taken into consideration.

One such factor is motivation. Nearly every student will claim that his or her goal is to be able to speak excellent English, but the acid test, of course, lies in how much time and effort the student is actually willing to spend both inside and outside of the classroom pursuing this goal. What passes for a conversation class is sometimes little more than a pleasant chat over a cup of coffee. The atmosphere is extremely relaxed, the pace is slow, no advance preparation is required on the part of the students (or teacher!), no homework is ever assigned. Students who wish to participate

in a class of this sort should of course be separated from those who are more serious in their intentions and more willing to put in the necessary time and effort which learning a language well requires.

Another factor is personality. Some students are naturally shy and hesitant to speak freely; others are more open and aggressive. Some students become easily embarrassed when a simple mistake is made. They often speak slowly and deliberately, lapsing into total silence when they are uncertain of the correct form a sentence should take. Others will quickly try to express themselves in a number of different ways if their first attempts fail. The teacher may notice that some students need to be continually prodded and encouraged before they will say anything at all. While it is true that many Japanese students remain somewhat reserved and hesitant and constantly need to be drawn out, a few will simply bubble over with enthusiasm, sometimes unfairly monopolizing the classtime.

One last, but very important factor, is how well the student is presently able to carry on a simple conversation in English. Many, if not most, Japanese students have been so conditioned to learning their English through textbooks that the first time a foreigner actually tries to communicate with them in the language they may either become so nervous that they are virtually speechless or simply gape at the foreigner as if he had come from an alien planet. Many students seem to express genuine shock that anyone would ever expect them to actually use any of the English they have learned in high school and elsewhere, and at first many students honestly may not want to carry on a conversation with their teacher in English, even after class. Some students seem, and in fact are, more content to keep their noses buried in a textbook. It is only with a great deal of effort that they can be broken of this tendency. But the procedure for doing so must be a slow and natural one. Many teachers expect more of their students on this point than the students are actually capable of handling, at least initially. The result is frustration for both.

Motivation, personality, and one's ability to converse in English are factors that cannot be readily evaluated by means of an objective written test. Fortunately, classes for adults in Japan are usually small enough that a teacher will in most cases be able to have a private, informal interview with each of the students. Objective factors need not be ignored, but an interview will undoubtedly give the teacher a clearer picture of the student's actual capabilities. In the course of giving the interview, the teacher should check to see just how well the prospective student is able to carry on a conversation. Is his speech rapid and fluid, easy to understand, or is it slow and uncertain? Does he speak in full, grammatically correct phrases (not necessarily complete sentences), or does he speak in seemingly unconnected snatches? Does he make an effort to participate in the conversation, or does he simply let the interviewer ask all of the questions?

On the basis of such an interview a teacher will be able to divide students into three basic categories: (1) those who are unable to answer most of the teacher's questions with grammatically correct and appropriate responses; (2) those who are able to respond correctly and appropriately to most of the questions they are asked, but are unable to generate or sustain a genuine conversation without continual prodding by the teacher; (3) those who are capable of sustaining a balanced conversation without continual prodding, correct speech being used throughout. These categories roughly correspond to how I wish to redefine the beginning, intermediate, and advanced levels.

Classifying students on the basis of their conversational abilities, as in a schema such as this, allows the more subjective factors just discussed to be taken into consideration. Thus, a student with excellent mastery of the language yet lacking the personality, motivation, and conversational abilities to sustain a conversation, should perhaps be placed in an intermediate rather than an advanced class. A student with some grammatical flaws in his speech might perform better in an intermediate rather than a beginning class if his personality is sufficiently open and aggressive and if he has the motivation to drill himself on basic sentence patterns at home or with a tape.

What such a classification does not imply is that the degree to which the student has mastered the technical aspects of the language is unimportant. Conversation is impossible unless these technical skills have been thoroughly assimilated first. But the point that must be emphasized is that students' levels should not be determined solely on the basis of their technical proficiency, as if the only difference between the various levels was one of the degree to which technical proficiency had been reached. In the schema I am proposing, the basic patterns of the English language must be completely learned at what I regard as the beginning level. Only then can one begin working on developing the conversational skills appropriate to the intermediate and advanced levels.

The teacher, again, must not, as is usually done, overestimate his students' abilities. It is only when the teacher has a clear idea of what his students are already actually capable of doing that he will be able to plan his classes in a way that will be appropriate to the students' current abilities and needs. The next section will discuss the specific skills, both technical and social, which can be taught at each of the respective levels. In the course of doing so, the divisions between the three levels themselves will be brought into sharper focus.

Teaching Methods for the Various Levels

Beginning. Situations such as the following are all too common in English classes for adults in Japan. The teacher, having been told that his students have already studied English for a number of years, comes to the classroom eager to enter into what he hopes will be a stimulating conversation. The students are smiling, feeling as if their long years of preparation in English grammar and translation will at last be put to some good use. Still, an uneasy silence pervades the room.

After briefly introducing himself the teacher pauses, giving the students a chance to respond to what he has said or perhaps to ask a question. Silence. He makes another attempt to say something—anything—that will provoke some response from the students. Only more silence. He asks one of the students a question—not an easy one, but not a difficult one either. At first, the student doesn't quite understand so the teacher repeats himself. One can almost see the wheels turning inside the student's head as he first mentally translates the question into Japanese, tries to think of what the teacher might regard as an acceptable answer, scans his mind for the relevant grammatical rules which apply, and then haltingly translates his answer back into English.

The process naturally takes a considerable amount of time, during which the other students may begin to become restless and the teacher must try to hide his sometimes all-too-obvious impatience. Yet for all the effort that has been put into formulating it, the response, when it does finally come, will in most cases be grammatically flawed, often inappropriate, and sometimes simply unintelligible. The student is embarrassed, his confidence is damaged, and he is not exactly enthusiastic about being called on to answer another such question in the future. And the teacher, frustrated and disappointed, is already thinking of looking for employment in some other field besides English "conversation."

A person who had taken an intensive course in music theory but had never sat down in front of a piano to practice would hardly be able to play a composition by Chopin if asked to, even though his understanding of the theory behind the score might exceed that of a practicing musician. Many foreign teachers, however, immediately attempt to have their students perform the most difficult of linguistic symphonies when their students haven't yet fully learned how to play the instruments. All too often the tendency is for conversation instructors to lay all the blame for the poor performances that result from what they perceive to be the students' lack of ability or motivation, or even worse, on the reserved and somewhat passive personalities characteristic of many Japanese students. Teachers who have lived a little longer in Japan may also be able to discourse at length on the inadequacies of English language instruction in the Japanese educational system. However, such criticisms, while often justified, do nothing to improve the adult student's ability to communicate in English. The skills a student lacks must be taught, and if necessary, retaught.

The majority of students one encounters in Japan will not be "true" beginners, but rather "false" beginners. "True" beginners are students who have either never studied English before or who have forgotten virtually everything they had previously learned. "False" beginners have retained some understanding of the grammatical structure of English but they are unable to apply this knowledge to speech. The trick of course, does not lie in applying knowledge about the language to speech, but in being able to say what one wants to say automatically, without any thought or attention being paid to the grammatical rules themselves. Again, all the theory in the world won't help a person learn how to play Chopin; he must rather sit down at the piano and practice. In the same way, all the English grammar a student learns in school won't help him learn how to speak English well; he must rather sit down in the classroom (as well as at home) and practice.

The grammar that Japanese have learned in junior high school and high school very often, in fact, hinders rather than helps a student's oral ability. When asked a question that requires an answer of a particular grammatical form, the imperfectly learned material floating around in the student's mind may come to the surface instead of the answer desired. For example, to the question "Do you like apples?" the student may reply "Yes, I did," even though the past tense has not yet been taught by the conversation teacher. Once the mistake has been explained to the student, he will immediately see where he went wrong, but if a little while later he is asked another question of similar grammatical form he may make exactly the same mistake. To avoid making such mistakes, instead of answering immediately some students will pause for extremely long periods of time while they sift through all of the grammatical rules that could apply to the case at hand.

Problems such as these can be corrected if the pattern is practiced to the point where the student can recall and use it automatically, without reflection. A convenient way to satisfy both the teacher's concern that the basic patterns of the English language be mastered and the students' demand for "conversation" is to use a beginning-level textbook based on the audio-lingual method. Such texts usually have short dialogues that the students practice and memorize, followed by a varity of drills that allow the students to internalize the material being presented. When conducted properly, the students will be able to spend most of the class time actually speaking in English. Teachers' editions to most good textbooks give detailed instructions on how to use the text both inside and outside of the classroom with maximum efficiency.

Audio-lingual textbooks require that each lesson be tightly structured. Only when the students have first had an opportunity to repeat, memorize, and drill the pattern under consideration are they given an opportunity to use it in a conversational situation. In such a situation the students are only permitted to use forms that they have previously drilled and mastered. What are known as "transfer exercises" help to ease the student from the artificial world of the textbook into a real conversational encounter. For example, the text presents the pattern: "I went to _____." A number of drills are then offered in which this pattern is repeated many times with different words being used to fill in the blank. In the transfer exercise the teacher may ask the student to tell him some of the places he went to during the past week, using exactly the same pattern. The student responds: "I went to the store," "I went to the bank," and so on. To extend this into a conversation the students and teacher may, for example, tell each other and ask questions about various trips they have taken, always being careful to keep the sentences employed within the boundaries provided by the material previously learned.

Grammar and translation have their place in the audio-lingual method, but they are used mostly to summarize what has already been assimilated by constant repetition and drillwork. "True" beginners will need a great deal more of such summarizing than "false" beginners. But grammar and translation are never used in the audio-lingual method as a set of *a priori* rules that the students must first learn and then apply. Because the students actually practice speaking the language rather than simply learn about it, the audio-lingual method encourages students to speak rapidly, clearly, and confidently. Practice, and not theory, is where the accent must always be placed.

From the perspective of conducting most beginning language classes, both "true" and "false" beginners can be taught together. This is consistent with the schema for determining students' levels outlined in the first section of this article. Since "false" beginners have only learned about but not actually mastered the language, they will in most cases need to be retaught straight from the beginning, starting with the most basic forms. In effect, the teacher must assume that his students have had no previous training in English, which by the standards this article has been elucidating they indeed have not. While most students, realizing the inadequacies of their previous training, will feel fairly comfortable with such an approach, some "false" beginners may balk at the idea of doing all the drillwork that the audio-lingual method requires and may resent going back to items they were presumably taught in junior high school. They may also feel it is unusual being put into the same class with "true" beginners.

Such feelings are, of course, natural. But again, the real test lies in how well the students are actually capable of using the patterns encountered in a beginning textbook. If they have indeed mastered them and are able to reproduce them freely, then they should by all means be placed in a higher-level class. But if they continually stumble through their sentences, making the same fundamental mistakes, then a course of instruction that starts right from the beginning will be the speediest way to achieve the goal of speaking correctly. If the basic forms have not yet been mastered, jumping ahead to textbooks that are more complex grammatically will probably lead to disappointing results. Some students may be capable of handling more grammatically complex material from the very first lesson, but if the teacher decides to use a higher-level textbook, he must be sure it is indeed appropriate to the students' actual ability.

In explaining these matters to students, care should be taken not to sound condescending. The teacher should simply explain to his students from the start that in learning to speak English they are learning a skill that can only be effectively acquired through repetition and practice. Analogies, such as the one previously mentioned about the difference between being able to understand music theory and being able to play the piano, are also useful. If the drills are kept lively, the pace of the class is kept fast, and, most importantly, the students are given ample opportunity to apply what they have practiced in a "real" conversation, the students will be able to make fairly rapid progress. And the progress the students themselves feel they have made in being able to speak more rapidly and fluidly will dispel any misgivings they may have previously had.

One final note: In the preceding I have concentrated on presenting a method of instruction suitable for Japanese students based on the audio-lingual method. My reasons for doing so are as follows: (1) the audio-lingual method is easily learned by the many teachers in Japan who do not have formal training in TEFL; (2) it meets student expectations as to what should happen in a conversation class; (3) it seems particularly serviceable in correcting the kinds of mistakes most frequently made by Japanese students, particularly false beginners; and (4) it reduces the probability that cultural misunderstandings will arise between teacher and student. There are, of course, many other methods that experienced teachers or teachers with formal training in TEFL may wish to pursue (see especially the books by Earl W. Stevick in the bibliography). These methods, however, usually require one to be thoroughly familiar with the cultural differences that exist between Japanese and Western students; for this reason alone they can only be recommended with reservation to an inexperienced teacher teaching inexperienced students. Some of the cultural differences one may expect to find are presented below.

Intermediate. As I have defined it in the first section of this article, the intermediate level presupposes that the students have thoroughly mastered the basic patterns of the English language. Once those basic patterns have been mastered, students can begin participating in conversations that are less structured than those conducted at the beginning level. Whereas the beginning level is concerned primarily with acquiring basic speaking skills, the intermediate level can concentrate on giving the students greater practice in applying those skills to actual communication. Transfer exercises done at the beginning level are also intended to give the student a chance to engage in real communication, but their highly structured nature limits the student's opportunity for free and unguided expression. Bringing one's students to the point where they can carry on a free and spontaneous conversation, covering a wide range of conversational situations, is the primary goal of the intermediate level.

Students at all levels are extremely fond of "free conversation" periods but usually understand the word "conversation" to mean something different from what a native speaker of English would understand the word "conversation" to mean. To most Japanese students "conversation" refers to one of the following: the teacher asks the students questions that the students take turns trying to answer; or the students ask the teacher questions that require the teacher to launch off into an extended monologue. To the Westerner, of course, "conversation" means a discussion in which all of those present are expected to participate freely, as the spirit moves them.

"Free conversation" at the beginning level should, for the most part, be limited to the transfer exercises mentioned above. At the intermediate level, however, where students have access to the basic tools of the language, they are in a position to begin building something with those tools. Yet, both teacher and student must be fully aware of the cultural differences in how Japanese and Westerners conduct a conversation. Coming to an awareness of these differences is one of the tasks of the intermediate level.

Nancy Sakamoto and Reiko Naotsuka, in their book *Polite Fictions: Why Japanese and Americans Seem Rude to Each Other,* compare Japanese-style conversation to a game of bowling. Each of the participants takes his own turn while the others watch and cheer him on. In the same way that no player is ever expected to complete another player's frame, so too one need not build on what another person has previously said. Each person is given his own separate and distinct opportunity to develop his own theme and approach. Western-style conversation, the authors suggest, is more like a game of volleyball. One player hits the ball over the net and whoever it comes closest to must try to hit it back. Someone makes a statement and expects someone to either agree or disagree with it and give his reasons why. In many intermediate classes the newly-arrived teacher cannot understand why his students let the conversational volleyballs he hits toward them simply fall to the floor. The students meanwhile are wondering why this crazy foreign teacher keeps throwing their conversational bowling balls back up the alley at them! Japanese tend to draw a circle around the topic under consideration and then let each of the participants have an opportunity to describe how what is inside the circle looks to him from his own perspective. Westerners tend to proceed in a more dialectical fashion, starting with a basic idea and then bouncing it back and forth among themselves until all the implications become manifest.

These are not the only differences one will encounter. Westerners are typically taught to express their opinions freely on any topic that comes their way. Japanese, on the other hand, are usually discouraged from expressing their feelings openly. The unspoken communication that takes place between people living together in such a homogenous culture as Japan's makes expressing oneself clearly less necessary than, for example, it is in the United States where people from a variety of different cultural backgrounds must learn to understand and get along with each other. Moreover, Japanese are extremely careful not to criticize someone in public. Contradicting another person's opinion, especially if he is one's superior, may be socially unacceptable. These are factors which definitely influence how a conversation—and a conversation class—are conducted.

For an American, the easiest way to start a conversation is to toss out an idea and let things develop as they may, but if he tries such an approach in the average Japanese classroom it will usually meet with little success. At the intermediate level, then, students can begin learning the rules by which conversations in English are conducted. They can learn the importance Western cultures place on expressing one's opinion forcefully and clearly. Furthermore, they can be given ample time to practice developing these skills.

Some teachers may object that such skills should not be taught in a conversation class. The teacher's job, they argue, is to teach the students a language, not to impose a set of cultural values on them, which is what such training would constitute. There is some justification for concern on this point, because many teachers do indeed approach the matter from the standpoint of zealous cultural missionaries endeavoring to teach the "natives" how to think and speak more "rationally." However, if it is explained to the students beforehand that learning a language involves more than simply learning the mechanics of speaking, but also how to communicate in a way that would be understood by people living in English-speaking countries, most students will look upon such a learning experience as an adventure. The choice as to how much a student will change his thinking or behavior in accordance with the information he is given remains entirely with the student. However, at least when he visits an English-speaking country he will be better prepared to make himself understood and to understand why the people he meets think and act as they do.

Students can, in time, reach the point where they feel comfortable engaging in a Western-style conversation, but the teacher should never proceed by simply sitting down to converse with his students and assume that they will somehow catch on to the intricacies of Western-style conversations. First, perhaps, the teacher should explain to the students what "having a conversation" means to him and the goal he is trying to lead them to. Then he should engage the students in activities that will slowly move them towards that goal. Asking the students simple questions can be expanded into a limited exchange. Students could be requested to formulate opinions on certain non-controversial topics and then share them with the class. The other students could then respond to what has been said. Once the students gain a certain amount of confidence they will begin in a very natural and unforced way to participate more freely and spontaneously in a conversation.

On the cognitive side, students at the intermediate level, having learned and consolidated the basic sentence patterns of English, are in an excellent position to expand the amount of vocabularly they can plug into those patterns. There are many excellent conversation textbooks that combine interesting, vocabulary-rich dialogues, stories, and articles with questions especially designed to generate discussion. Some of the texts available in Japan, however, were written more with Western-thinking foreign-language students in mind, in that they attempt to stimulate discussion by encouraging the students to formulate differing opinions on controversial issues. For reasons already mentioned, such lessons will not be greeted with much enthusiasm. While textbooks at the intermediate level are useful for generating conversation topics, the students themselves should be encouraged to contribute their own topics for discussion as well.

Advanced. The majority of advanced students one will teach in Japan are themselves teachers of English or students who have spent a considerable amount of time living in English-speaking countries. Advanced students are persons for whom the basic sentence patterns are second nature. They also should be fairly comfortable participating in a Western-style conversation. A worthwhile goal for the advanced student would be to reach the point where, if the occasion ever arose, he could function on a linguistic level as normally in an English-speaking country as he does in his own. Students at this level, then, can continue learning as if they themselves were living in an English-speaking country. The materials they learn from would be exactly the same sort of things English speakers use every day. Hearing skills can be improved by listening to radio broadcasts, watching English television programs, attending English plays, and so on. Reading skills can be developed by reading the sorts of things native-speakers of the language read: English newspapers, magazines, and books. Writing skills, if the student desires to learn these (and there are a few students who do) can be practiced by writing letters, essays, articles, poems, even fiction, the best of which the teacher might encourage the students to try to have published. Speaking skills can be sharpened by discussing exactly the same things native speakers of the language would discuss: politics, music, movies, current events, and so on.

It is not difficult to imagine how these separate skills could be combined into a single project. For example, the students could attend an English-speaking movie, read reviews of it in a magazine, write a review of their own, and discuss various aspects of the plot and theme. The possibilities are as endless as culture itself. The teacher will have to be guided by the students' interests—and his own competence in any particular field.

In the course of participating in such activities, the students should be able to reach a level of competence that approaches, and hopefully achieves, fluency. The range of vocabulary available to them will be greatly expanded, and their appreciation for idiomatic nuances of the language greatly enhanced. Students at the advanced level can be encouraged to think and express themselves more abstractly than they have at the previous levels. This, too, may be a new cultural experience for some students, many of whom may be more used to thinking about and discussing problems in terms of particulars. The conversational format can be left completely unstructured.

Conclusion

The conversational skills one learns at each of the three levels correspond to how tightly the teacher must control the students' speech in the classroom. At the beginning level, the teacher must be careful not to let his students wander outside of the patterns they have previously mastered. Classes must be highly structured and the teacher must provide the students with continual leadership and guidance. At the intermediate level, the teacher may withdraw a little, giving the students conversational spaces to be filled in. His role shifts from that of a teacher in the traditional sense to that of a moderator interjecting comments and questions where necessary to keep things moving. At the advanced level, the teacher melts into the conversation group, becoming more an ordinary participant and less a leader. He can make suggestions about which routes to follow, pointing out both things of interest along the way and places where the road is rough, but essentially he must walk beside and not in front of his students. There is some value, however, in letting the students "run wild" for short periods of time at each of the levels. Not only will it help to establish rapport, it will also give the students a chance to accustom themselves to the idea that English is a language people communicate in, and not just a skill students learn in the classroom.

Bibliography

THEORY AND METHODS

DeCecco, John P., (ed). *The Psychology of Language, Thought, and Instruction.* New York: Holt, Rinehart and Winston, Inc., 1967.

Rivers, Wilga. *Teaching Foreign Language Skills.* Chicago: University of Chicago Press, 1968.

Rivers, Wilga, and Mary S. Temperley. *A Practical Guide to the Teaching of English as a Second or Foreign Language.* New York: Oxford University Press, 1978.

Stevick, Earl W. *Memory, Meaning, and Method: Some Psychological Perspectives on Language Learning.* Rowley, Massachusetts: Newbury House Publishers, Inc., 1979.

———. *Teaching Languages: A Way and Ways.* Rowley, Masachusetts: Newbury House Publishers, Inc., 1980.

BEGINNING-LEVEL TEXTS

(Only a partial listing of comprehensive learning programs designed to bring the student up to or through the intermediate level is given.)

Alexander, L. G. *Mainline*. London: Longman Group Limited, 1973. Six volumes: *Beginners A, Beginners B, Progress A, Progress B, Skills A, Skills B*. Can also be integrated with other texts written by Alexander. Includes Teacher's Book, Test Materials, Tapes, and Tapescript.

Castro, Oscar, and Victoria Kimbrough. *In Touch*. Three volumes. New York: Longman, Inc., 1979-80.

Fowler, W. S., J. Pidcock, and R. Rycroft, *Incentive English*. New York, etc.: Thomas Nelson and Sons, Ltd., 1979. Four volumes: *Pleased to Meet You, Let's Go, What Happened?, Themes*.

Hartley, Bernard, and Peter Viney. *Streamline English*. Oxford: Oxford University Press, 1978. Three volumes: *Departures, Connections, Destinations*. Includes tapes and can be accompanied by two additional Workbooks with cassette and *Speechwork*, a book of oral drills with five cassettes or tapes.

O'Neill, Robert. *Kernel Series*. London: Longman Group, Ltd., 1978. Three Volumes: *Kernel One, Kernel Lessons Intermediate, Kernel Lessons Plus*.

INTERMEDIATE-LEVEL TEXTS

Alexander, L. G. *For and Against*. London: Longman Group, Ltd., 1968.

——. *I Think, You Think*. London: Longman Group, Ltd., 1976.

Alexander, L. G., Monica C. Vincent, and John Chapman. *Talk It Over*. New York: Longman, Inc., 1978.

Ockenden, Michael. *Talking Points*. London: Longman Group, Ltd., 1977.

ADVANCED-LEVEL MATERIALS

Four English-language daily newspapers are available in many parts of Japan. *Time* and *Newsweek* are distributed directly in Japan. Other English-language magazines are frequently sold on newstands, covering a variety of interests. Most major cities have at least one foreign bookstore. The Far East Network (FEN), operated by the American Armed Forces Radio and Television Services, broadcasts radio programs daily and is available in most parts of Japan, depending on the quality of one's receiver. Major Japanese television networks frequently broadcast English-speaking programs and movies that can be heard in English on sets equipped for bilingual reception. Nippon Hoso Kyokai (NHK) occasionally broadcasts English-language television programs of merit. The majority of so-called English-conversation programs on Japanese radio and television are not intended for advanced students, however. Many movie theaters show English-speaking movies, though these are almost always presented with Japanese subtitles. The English Clubs of many colleges and universities stage plays in English.

AUXILIARY TEXTS

(A sampling of textbooks that can be used in addition to a regular text with the purpose of consolidating skills at various levels is given.)

Alexander, L. G. *Question and Answer.* London: Longman Group, Ltd., 1977. Contains forty-eight stories with questions, graded for their degree of grammatical complexity.

Dobson, Julia M., and Frank Sedwick. *Conversation in English: Points of Departure.* New York: American Book Company, 1975. Contains fifty pictures with vocabulary lists and questions.

Yamaguchi, Shunji, and Goichi Terachi. *Eikaiwa QR-800.* Tokyo: Gogakushunjusha, no date. Contains 800 general questions on various topics, with model responses, translations, and notes. Tape available.

Teaching English
in Companies

Robert Scott Dawson

A Typical Day

The experiences and opinions in this article are not necessarily universal. Every English teacher in Japan will have a different story about how he got his job and what his job includes. However, what follows does outline the duties and working conditions at Japanese companies.

The majority of in-house language-training programs are found within manufacturing companies. A survey of foreign employees employed by Japanese companies carried out by the Sanno Institute of Business Administration in 1982 showed that about 75% of them were in the manufacturing sector. Furthermore, over 60% of the foreigners employed held jobs classified as Public Relations/Language Resources (42%) or Language Teachers (24%). Language Resources carry out duties such as translation, copywriting, and proofreading for the various divisions of the company.[1] While these are their primary tasks, it not unusual for the language resource personnel to be called upon to teach, and it is common for the in-house instructor to be called upon to do proofreading, editing, and copywriting during the course of a normal day's work. What constitutes a normal day's work? The following account will deal with a "typical" Monday at the company.

The work day starts with the Monday *chorei,* a morning meeting in which all employees of the division participate. All of the employees give presentations at the meeting according to rotation based upon seniority. In some companies, the foreign employees are not required to participate, but making a presentation when your turn comes up does facilitate one's acceptance and does wonders as motivation to continue your study of Japanese. The choice of topics is free; however, the largest number of topics deal with business news gleaned from the weekly magazines or whatever is at the top of the list of "what every good manager should read." Morning meetings will normally last about 15—20 minutes. These meetings serve as a means of disseminating general ideas on management, what is worth reading, and passing information about coming events in the division.

This morning there is a two-hour class. Classes in an in-house program are set up and carried out to meet the specific needs of the students and the needs of the divisions. The level of the course is intermediate and the six students meet twice a week for six months. All of the students usually come from either engineering or administrative sections of the company. This segregation facilitates the selection of textbooks and materials for use in the classroom. As the classes are held during working hours, the subject matter of the course is supposed to be relevant to the tasks the student might be called upon to carry out in English on the job. The administrative-section members of the course do not need the ability or vocabulary to explain a highly sophisticated production machine and the engineers fail to see the relevance of learning about how to sell in English.

After lunch there is another class, a writing class. As was the case with the morning class, the students and their bosses expect the students to learn skills that will be directly applicable to the job. By dividing the class into two components, a rather traditional lecture/activity component and a proofreading component, the course seems to meet the expectations of both the instructor and the students. This writing class meets once a week for one hour on the first and third Monday as a class, and for three hours on the second and fourth Monday of the month as a tutorial/proofreading session. The materials for this tutorial session are brought by each student and consist of correspondence and documents from the student's section, preferably documents written by the student. The instructor must teach what he regards to be needed by the students, and the students must carry something tangible back to the office from the class. If the student is not satisfied with what is offered by the instructor, he will simply forget about the class and not attend.

Upon returning to the office one sorts through the mail and announcements that have accumulated during the morning. One files away the catalogues and begins to plow through the announcements. The announcements are all in Japanese, so one who cannot read Japanese finds himself dependent upon the kindness of his neighbors to determine what is relevant to carrying out his duties. However, one is responsible for everything that comes across his desk and must stamp each announcement as acknowledgement of receiving it. One has to be careful because what may seem to be of absolutely no concern at the moment may prove important later.

There will be several ongoing projects that will usually take up the rest of the time. One of the reasons companies start up in-house programs is to produce supplementary materials that meet the linguistic and lexical requirements of the company and are, in effect, English tailored to meet the specific needs of the company. It would not be economical for publishers to produce texts for any but the largest industries. Manufacturing companies tend to view all activities as productive activities; therefore, something tangible, such as supplementary materials and texts, must be produced. Since the average instructor is familiar with neither the technology upon which the industry in question is based, the production processes, nor the managerial operations of the company, a substantial amount of time is spent learning what makes the company tick in order to produce English training materials that will meet with the approval of the management. In the same vein, companies are also very interested in producing and administering tests to measure the ability of their employees to function professionally in English and measure the efficiency of the in-house program. Accordingly, researching the commercially available tests and counter-balancing the costs of administering a test in-house is another matter that is of concern to companies.

If the company has a language laboratory, one must also be ready to prepare taped materials to supplement other class materials, as well as prepare classes that are held in the L.L. Once a company purchases an expensive L.L. for the relatively small audience of those students involved in its English or other foreign languages classes, it expects learners to make as much use of the L.L. as possible.

Other duties include preparing materials to be used by managers for self-study, writing reports on topics related to the English-language program, purchasing materials for use in the various classes, and proofreading and editing correspondence and documents that may be subject to public scrutiny.

The classroom instruction needs are far too great for one person to take

Distribution of Work Hours in a Typical Forty-hour Week

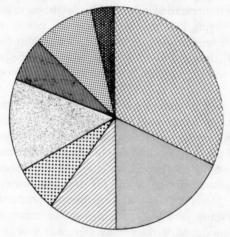

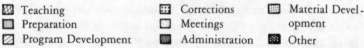

▨ Teaching	⊞ Corrections	▦ Material Devel-
▢ Preparation	▢ Meetings	opment
▨ Program Development	▥ Administration	▧ Other

The pie-chart shows the content of a typical forty-hour work week in an in-house program. While the sample was small, only eight employees, and the chart is actually an average of all the responses, the results shown above were found to be in general agreement with with experiences of those who replied (all eight were members of in-house programs in the Kansai region). Below are the minimum and maximum percentages of the work week dedicated to the various activities as compiled from the individual replies.

	% of Time Minimum	% of Time Maximum	Average
Teaching	20	65	34
Preparation for Classes	15	30	19
Program Development	5	30	13
Corrections/			
Proofreading	3	10	6
Meetings	2	7	15
Administrative Duties	2	24	6
Material Development	7	15	10
Other	4	10	5

care of; thus another duty of the in-house program instructor will probably be the management of the part-timers that are hired by the company to instruct classes. The part-timers will usually arrive around 5:00 P.M. Once they have checked in and communicated any problems they might have with their classes or schedules to you, they proceed to their classrooms to get them in order before the students arrive. As the in-house full-time instructor, one must oversee and report on the quality of the instruction provided by the part-timers. This involves observing classes, discussing class procedures with the teacher if need be, and providing a report to the management on the class.

During the course of a month, class schedules will remain the same, but everything else is quite flexible. One might be called upon to interview potential students, participate in various divisional or sectional meetings, teach at four-day intensive English camps, and always be ready for surprises. If time is available, you may participate in training programs offered by the company and take part in seminars that the company feels will lead to your further professional development as an asset to the company.

Getting a Job

A Japanese company has several options when considering how to introduce language training and improve the English competence of those employees whose jobs require it. The first option is not to provide training. A widely held point of view is that employees should pursue skills such as English as part of one's own self-improvement program. To this end, companies encourage participation in classes at nearby language schools and correspondence courses arranged by company training sections.

A second option is to make a contract with a school or outside agency to provide a language-training program to be taught on the company premises. From the company's point of view, this is probably the easiest way to provide English language training. The school or agency provides curriculum, texts, and instructors, and works hard to develop a close working relationship with the company training section to anticipate as well as meet the needs of the company.[2] Since almost all of the problems of organization and administration are met by the school, the company is spared the inconvenience of introducing foreign instructors into the company. The school/agency serves as a buffer between the foreigner and the company, and is responsible for all personnel matters: pay, tax, health insurance (if available), sponsorship, etc. However, from the company's point of view the cost is expensive, ¥8,000—¥10,000 per hour depending on the proximity of the school to the company, and the return on the investment is often difficult to measure. Since the time the student spends in class is usually the only time during the week he will use English, progress seems painfully slow and expensive.

Some larger companies give the responsibility of teaching English to a subsidiary within the company "group." This approach eliminates the school/agency by forming a similar organization that finds teachers and schedules courses. At the outset, the performance of this organization may be a bit irregular, but if the company perseveres, the savings will justify the effort. Several years ago a large electronics company in Tokyo that contracted its language services from a large school set up a language training program in one of its subsidiaries after the school was the subject of a teacher's strike and classes were brought to a halt. The program there has grown and matured to the point that it is now offering language-training services to other companies. For the large companies, the creation of a buffer within the "group" to insulate the company from the problems of hiring a foreigner is possible. However, for most companies that have recently recognized a need for improved language ability among their employees, this option is not practical.

An increasing number of companies, under the vague and ill-defined label of "internationalization," are taking a different tack; they are hiring foreigners and integrating them into their organizations. Companies are taking the unsettling step of bringing a foreign instructor into their homogeneous operations to reduce costs, reduce time delays related to language difficulties, customize their existing language training, and foster "internationalization" within their organizations.

How does one find a job in one of these in-house programs? What sort of interview process is involved? And what sort of contract should the successful job hunter expect? The answers are not easily given because of the wide variety of programs and personnel policies in different companies. However, some guidelines are possible.

While a few larger companies are recruiting overseas, one of the most important factors in finding a job is being in Japan. The fact that you are in Japan tells the employer several things about you. First, your presence shows that your interest in the country is great enough that you made the sizable investment of coming to Japan. Second, they realize that you have been in Japan for a while, long enough to overcome those first pangs of homesickness. Third, it indicates you have already had some experience working with a Japanese organization and have learned how to deal with it. Another factor is that the company does not have to add the costs of transportation to the starting costs of a full-time position in the company.

Assuming you are in Japan and have a proper visa, you already are employed. However, the fact that you are employed does not mean you are satisfied with your present position. A perusal of the daily English language press, the *Japan Times* for the Kanto region (Tokyo and its environs) and the *Mainichi Daily News* for the Kansai (Kyoto, Osaka, and Kobe), will educate you to the extent of the demand for qualified instructors and the most critical factor with regard to employment, the proper visa. The classified ads are valuable to one who has not been in Japan or acquired the most important key to finding a good job, contacts.

Prior to my present position neither of my previous jobs were the result of an advertisement. My first job was the result of a letter of introduction from my university economics professor to a friend at a university in Tokyo who provided an introduction to another friend and so on. The result was a job with a reputable school within their company class program. Two years later when I changed employers, the new position as an instructor in the in-house program at a major electronics company was the result of an introduction that led to instruction of a part-time class and finally employment as a full-time instructor. Companies and schools as well often try to avoid the cost of advertising and the uncertainty of choosing from among candidates whose culture and values are different from their own. For the most part, the candidates do not speak Japanese, a factor that further complicates the process—the people doing the interviewing are often less than secure in their command of English. An introduction by a friend or current employee is seen as a statement of the trustworthiness of the job applicant. This sometimes leads to an interview that is more of a confirmation rather than a selection process. Being introduced by a friend also gives you the advantage of screening the employer (checking the working conditions, administrative practices, pay, etc.) before the interview.

Before discussing the interview, a few comments on what to have ready for the interview for a position in a company in-house program are in order. Some of the following suggestions may seem condescending on my part, but having worked from both sides of table, I am constantly surprised by the number of people who do not take the most basic steps to insure a good interview. As you have taken care to make sure your resume is in good order prior to the interview, make sure you are in good order and represent what you feel the employer wants, that is, dress naturally but conservatively. The interviewers will view you as a potential employee of the company—whether the job opening is for a part-time class or a full-time position in the company training program, and company employees usually wear a suit to work. Next, be prepared to provide documentation concerning your academic and professional background: transcripts, diplomas, letters of recommendation, work experience (teaching and other; the fact that you spent your summers working in a factory might weigh in your favor), and anything else that you think might improve your chances. And last but not least, don't forget a photograph: the photograph provides the people who must make a decision with a quick and easy way of remembering who you are.

Now that you have got an interview, what should you expect? The company will have two primary concerns. How well will you integrate into a Japanese environment and how long will you remain with the company? Whether you are answering questions about your professional background, teaching methodology, professional goals, or lifestyle, the people on the other side of the table are evaluating you on the basis of how well you can accomodate yourself and function within their office with the least amount of disruption in the office's daily routine.

The second concern is your professional background. The normal hiring pattern among Japanese companies is to hire a "generalist" and train him to meet the needs of the company. A "generalist" is normally a young man fresh out of college. Upon entering the company he goes through an intensive period of indoctrination into the company culture and operations. As time passes the stature and skill level of the employee grow, and he moves up the ladder of advancement.[3] The fact that you are a professional, and applying for a job that in theory is quite specific within the organization, means that the company is considering an action that is new to them. This raises two questions. Should they hire a "generalist," someone possibly without academic training or professional background, but someone who will be willing to adapt himself to

238

the needs of the company? Or should they choose a "professional," a person who will bring specific skills to the job and put them into action? The key word is "expectations," on the part of both the company and the employee. Can they function together in harmony when the going gets rough, or will the ground rules set by the company totally frustrate a person whose professional goals are at variance with theirs? This does not mean you must compromise your ideas of what constitutes good language training, but it does mean that you must clarify—during the interview—what the company wants from you.

During the interview, be prepared to answer many questions that are designed to determine your sincerity as well as your competence. Think about why you came to Japan, what you think about the Japanese culture, what the word "internationalization" means. These are questions that are important to the interviewers and thus important to you if you want the job. Have a firm idea of what your professional and lifetime goals are.

Although there is some debate within personnel sections as to whether to hire a "generalist" or a "professional," an M.A. in TESOL (or the acronym of your choice), teaching experience, or both will weigh in one's favor. Some companies are going to great expense to recruit highly qualified individuals from overseas. But the critical question remains: "How well will the foreigner fit into our company?"

Assuming that you make it through the interviews, what should you expect from the contract? Most contracts are quite simple documents. For tax purposes, the contracts between schools or companies and their part-time instructors treat the instructor as a *jigyoosha,* a self-employed person. Thus, the spirit of the agreement is the same as in one between two organizations: the instructor is a subcontractor providing a specified service to the company. This means that the articles of the contract are exclusively concerned with the obligations of the instructor. The document will normally be short, one or two pages, and contain articles that cover the following points:

1. A statement of the duties and responsibilities of the employee are given. (The heart of this article is usually a simple statement that "your job is to provide instruction.")

2. The hours you are to work are specified. (A part-timer who shows up early for work may not be welcome if the employer has no space except at the assigned hours.)

3. The duration of the agreement will be specified, usually three months, six months, or a year.
4. A statement is [usually] made that transportation costs to and from work will be borne by the company.
5. The means of terminating the contract will be stated. This normally requires written notification of the employer thirty days prior to terminating the job.

The above has specifically dealt with the conditions with which a part-timer might have to contend. If one is being considered for employment in a full-time in-house program, the contract articles above will constitute the basic framework of the document. However, the contract will, depending upon the personnel policy of the company, be far more detailed. In some cases, the company may choose to use the contract to reassure the prospective foreign employee of the sincerity of the company. In this case, the final contract becomes a fairly complex document, as many as twenty pages, covering everything from a detailed job description, to formulas for calculating overtime, to the details of home leave. On the other hand, the company may choose to go the route it follows with its Japanese employees, a brief, vague general document that confirms the obligations of the employee to the company and vice versa. Personnel divisions have a tendency to press for what they are most comfortable with, a short contract. Since your only choice in the matter is to sign or not to sign, you must make the final choice based upon the merits of the document placed in front of you.

Having said this about contracts, I would like you to take to heart the words of a Japanese manager given to a foreign employee concerning a change of companies and contracts: "If you are not happy with the contents of the contract, don't sign it. If you are happy with the contract and feel the change of jobs is in your best interests, sign it and forget it." In a very large company, foreigners tend to be assigned specific tasks and are placed in a niche to carry out their given job for as long as they are happy. Within smaller "large" companies that will only require a few foreigners, the scope of the work expected to be carried out by the foreigner is likely to be far wider than could be explained in any contract. The key words are flexibility and initiative because you will be expected, like a new Japanese employee, to make your job and grow within the organization. While this advice in itself may seem vague, it is good to keep it in mind as one approaches his first weeks of employment.

Until now, the focus of this article has been on the foreign instructor's daily activities and getting a job, but it is also useful to examine why he is in the company in the first place and what the company expects from him.

Company Teaching as a Career

The first reason a company will give you for the creation of an in-house program is "internationalization." Unfortunately, no one is able to give an adequate definition of the term. When brought down to a company level, it means doing your job in English. As English has become the de facto language of international trade, to do business outside of Japan it is essential for the sales staff and a substantial number of the technical staff to be competent in a foreign language, usually English. "Internationalization" has become a catch phrase in companies who want to sell and be recognized as leaders in the world market.

Ten years ago, English-language training was generally an off-time activity encouraged by companies but given little support. In the mid-70s companies began to revise their training programs and add foreign languages to skill-development programs. In most cases, the employee had to bear part of the expense of instruction and learning materials, with the company paying 50% or slightly more. As the costs of contracting with outside organizations increased, the incentive to form in-house teaching organs grew, and recently the number of companies hiring or planning to hire foreign instructors has increased.[4]

The purpose of these in-house programs is to improve the communicative skills of the Japanese staff, but what skills does the staff feel that it needs? A study published in the *JALT Newsletter* (February 1983) asked students from the in-house training program of Mobil Oil in Tokyo how they use their English in business; the results were as follows:

	Reading	Writing	Face to Face	Phone
Never	1.7%	7.0%	47.9%	68.0%
Occasionally	7.3%	40.8%	45.4%	29.2%
Sometimes	52.4%	49.1%	6.3%	2.5%
Often	38.5%	3.1%	0.3%	0.3%

When asked what kinds of English were most important to them, they answered as follows:

Technical	50.2%	Business	39.8%	Negotiating	25.8%
Social	21.8%	General	64.4%	Other	11.0%

One of the significant findings of this survey was how important students considered English to their careers: essential, 74.7%; useful, 23.5; unnecessary, 1.8%.[5] Students of English would naturally tend to value their course work, but even so, a 74.7% "essential" response is impressive. The international nature of the oil business means employees need a command of English to advance within the managment. However, executives at many smaller companies are encouraging their employees to improve their language skills. Within the ranks of the growing number of smaller companies with international aspirations, a substantial number of in-house programs are now being developed.

The working conditions in large Japanese offices seem to be extensions of the production line: large impersonal operations where documents move from one desk to another until all required actions have been taken. The image is deceiving. Actually the office is a beehive of occupational and personal relationships. Duties within the employee's own section take up almost all of his time; but within the division and the company as a whole, the young Japanese employee maintains a support network based upon the year he entered the company. New employees usually join the company on April 1 and single employees usually reside in an inexpensive company dormitory. Since they all join the company on the same day, they share the same company indoctrination program, and experience the same insecurities, frustrations, and joys. Thus, a strong bond of friendship develops between these young men as they grow within the company and share their personal lives in the dormitory.

Within this framework of relationships you, the foreign instructor, may seem an interloper. The regular workers wonder, are you an employee, or do you provide a specific service as a subcontractor? In your own section, there should be no problems to speak of, depending upon your command of the Japanese language. Your fellow workers know you have been brought into the organization to carry out a specific task, and they will assist you in any way they can. They are interested—curious might be a better world—in you, and look forward to a long and harmonious relationship. Harmony in the office is a by-product of people knowing one another, and group activities, such as going out for drinks after work, are frequent. Such activities enable you to establish communication with people that you would otherwise only deal with from afar.

Outside of your office you are still an outsider, a curiosity rather than a member of the team. There are barriers that can only be broken down by time, for in the land of life-time employment you are considered to be a short-timer. If you are only going to be around for a short time, company employees outside your immediate area will see little reason to establish contact with you.

The most persistent and discouraging problem you will have is the seeming indifference in the other divisions and sections with regard to class attendance. Training, whether it be technical in nature or language training, competes with work time. The training section is competing with the student's section for his time. A section manager's primary concern is the completion of the tasks in his section, and when the completion of the job comes into conflict with class time, there is no doubt about priorities: the student does not come to class. This will result in sporadic attendance and create many class management problems. A characteristic of in-house training is small classes of six to ten members. But when class attendance runs at about 50% (and the 50% that came to this class will more than likely be the 50% that will be absent the next), following one's syllabus and achieving course goals becomes serious problems. There is some compensation since the motivation of the students is quite high, as indicated by the previous figures on the career-value students place upon English, but it can be discouraging to have a job teaching people that are not allowed to come to class.

A by-product of this conflict of interests concerning the utilization of the student's time is the foreign employee's concern about the company's commitment to the in-house program, that is, his job security. The western tradition of labor vs. management, as opposed to the Japanese idea of labor and management working together, is a source of concern regardless of how many times the boss tells you not to worry about it. Life-time employment is frequently touted as one of the keys to Japan's economic miracle, but the extent to which it applies to foreign employees is uncertain. About 21% of those included in the Sanno Business Institute's survey of foreign employees considered themselves to be lifetime employees while the remainder were contract employees.[6] And, as mentioned before, all contracts provide an escape clause for both the employee and the company. The classification of a foreigner as a life-time employee boils down to the wording of the contract and the personal relationship between the foreign employee and the management.

The greatest barrier to the acceptance and advance of the foreign employee is competence in the Japanese language. How far could a foreign employee in an American, British, or any western company be accepted as a productive member of the team or hope to advance if he could not speak English or whatever the language of daily operation was? The foreign instructor is hired to provide instruction in his native tongue, but that does not mean the people working around and with him will all be able to use English.

Having competence in Japanese is not a prerequisite for surviving in a Japanese company, but some proficiency goes a long way to overcoming problems you will encounter as an employee and resident in Japan, which include everything from knowing which Saturdays are working days to knowing how and where to keep your visa up to date. During company time you will find that most of the people you have dealt with in classes will try to work with you in English, but when work is over they do not want to play in English. Developing the close personal ties that make you a true member of the company team will ultimately depend upon your Japanese ability. Unfortunately, most companies do not consider teaching you Japanese as part of their foreign employee development program. Learning the language is your duty as part of your self-development program. The company may provide funds for the study of Japanese, but you will be hard pressed to find the time and energy to make use of these funds.

Conclusion

Throughout this article I have referred to the employer or prospective employee as ''he.'' A combination of sexual bias and work rules causes companies to think twice before hiring a woman. The rules are laid down by the Ministry of Labor and determine the number of hours a woman may work per day and the number of overtime hours allowed per week. The outside activity most important in developing good working relations, drinking with the guys, becomes a problem. A single foreigner might be asked to live in the company dormitory, but most companies do not provide such accomodations for their female workers. The length of service of a female employee would also be expected to be shorter than that of a male because the normal pattern is for the female worker to leave upon marrying. Thus, although some women are being hired, employers are much more comfortable with a male worker. Women, even if they have excellent credentials, may anticipate prejudice in hiring and promotions.

Since length of service is of great importance to Japanese employers, foreigners who are married to Japanese nationals, usually a Japanese wife, also have an advantage over other applicants. The rationale is that Japanese family ties will tend to make the foreigner more reliable. Upon marrying, most couples soon make a decision to return to the husband's homeland or reside in Japan. Since the Japanese social security system still depends upon children's support of parents in their old age, there is often considerable pressure on a daughter to remain in Japan, especially an oldest daughter. To the company looking for a long-term employee, this situation suggests that the foreigner will be in Japan for quite some time.

After all is said and done, is it worth the effort? The answer depends upon the personality of the individual. If you are ambitious and thinking of moving on to bigger and better things, working in a Japanese company is probably not for you, and the company would probably not choose you in the first place. If you are a patient team worker who gets satisfaction from completion of a job well done, and if you have a positive interest in Japan, employment in a company will be secure and satisfying. Once you develop a sense of loyalty and prove your value to the company, you will find that the company will bend over backwards to make you a member of the team.

Notes

1. Takeshi Ooishi, Allan Bird, Katsunaga Yamazaki, and Hidehiro Aritomo, *Survey of Foreign Nationals Employed in Japanese Enterprises in Japan* (Odawara, Japan: Sanno Institute of Business Administration, 1982), p. 2. This study deals with all foreigners working in Japanese organizations in Japan. It con-

tains a wealth of statistical data and insight on how companies deal with foreign nationals.

2.   Kenji Kitao, "The Second In-Company Language Program Seminar (Part I)," *JALT Newsletter* 8:1 (January 1984), p. 9. This short article provides some information on in-house programs from the point of view of schools and agencies providing services to companies and company management.

3.   Ronald Dore, *British Factory—Japanese Factory: The Origins of National Diversity in Industrial Relations* (Berkeley: University of California Press, 1973), pp. 46-54. If you are interested in learning about Japanese companies, there is no better place to start.

4.   Kitao, *JALT Newsletter* 8:1, p. 9.

5.   Gaynor Sekimori, "Preliminary Report on an Analysis of the English Needs of Business People," *JALT Newsletter* 7:2 (February 1, 1983), p. 2. This brief article is full of valuable information about student expectations.

6.   Ooishi, et al., *Survey,* p. 16.

Teaching English at Japanese Companies: Professionalizing Methods and Materials

Richard Berwick and Janet Heyneman

UNTIL A FEW YEARS AGO English teaching at Japanese companies could have been characterized in a word: *part-time*. Teachers would have been assigned by the English-conversation school, or by an agent specializing in contracts at large companies, to teach between two and four hours a week at a particular company. Now the most exciting development in English instruction at Japanese companies is full-time instructional services offered *in-house* by language teachers with solid professional backgrounds.

We begin this chapter by examining the effects of this gradual trend of greater professionalization on methods and materials used in English programs at Japanese companies. We also want to survey the great variety of techniques, methods, and approaches to English instruction at Japanese companies. In order to offer the reader up-to-date information of use in selecting among prospective teaching positions, we have asked a group of our colleagues to document the teaching situation at five companies in addition to our own, Kobe Steel, Ltd. As far as we know, our report on this methodological survey is the first of its kind to be published in English in Japan. Finally, we intend to put things into perspective by offering the reader a capsule description of what it is like to work for a Japanese company as an English teacher.

Professionalization in English Programs at Japan Companies

When we say "professionalization" we mean, basically, three things: 1) the academic and experiential qualifications of those applying for full-time work at large Japanese organizations have improved; 2) newly hired teaching staff are increasingly knowledgeable about the latest approaches to and materials for EFL (English as a Foreign Language) instruction; 3) active membership in such professional organizations as JALT (Japan Association of Language Teachers) is encouraged by the company and exercised by the foreign teaching staff. All of these trends have important implications for the ways in which English is taught in company settings.

Qualifications. We have no statistics on the matter, but it is our impression that people "just drifting through" Japan on their way to some other place are less likely to be asked to teach company classes than was formerly the case. Large companies with in-house programs—such as Kobe Steel, Ltd. and Sumitomo Metal Industries, Ltd.—are now very unlikely to even consider offering a year's teaching contract to someone who cannot document a strong teaching background or graduate preparation in .ESL (English as a Second Language) or EFL.

There are, of course, plenty of exceptions to this trend. Individuals with eager and enthusiastic personalities or company connections will probably always have an advantage over most others who must be willing to compete for teaching positions at companies largely on the basis of their qualifications to teach. This is particularly true among companies that hire entirely on a part-time basis (the majority, at the moment) and whose hiring practices have not been much influenced by standards of professional teaching practice. In general, however, there is a growing demand for well-trained foreign staff, and this means that foreigners who want to teach but who don't have the background are eventually going to be at a disadvantage in Japan.

Now that we have indicated, roughly, where the cutting edge for company employment is likely to fall, what can we say about the backgrounds of those who are employed? One way of looking at this question is to imagine that a given company wants to employ a particular kind of person to teach English on a full-time basis, and has to specify qualifications in the form of an advertisement. Kobe Steel placed just such an ad in the nationally circulated *Mainichi Daily News* (January 17 and 23, 1984) "seeking teachers with an M.A. in TESOL or three years of ESL experience to work full time. An engineering/technical or business background is helpful." Other things being equal, we think most companies would advertise similarly (if they were to advertise at all), although it is probably safe to say that no hiring guidelines are carved in stone; a well-intentioned manager may suddenly drop all interest in academic qualifications if he believes a job candidate will work wonders for the company.

It is also probably safe to say that if people are hired on the basis of their high qualifications they will be expected to reflect them in their work performance. This "if" is a big one and the fact that we mention it here should indicate that managers in charge of hiring foreign teachers do not always know or care about teaching qualifications. In a professional in-house company teaching program, however, colleagues, if not managers, will expect the holder of an M.A. in applied linguistics to know, for example, the differences among *contrastive analysis, error analysis,* and *needs analysis*—and the implications each of them have for "syllabus" design. Those who hold an advanced degree and those who have accumulated at least several years of teaching experience will be expected to know how to create rapport with students, start and manage classes smoothly, have students do most of the talking, and so on. In short, the qualified teacher can be relied on to negotiate most of the basics of teaching English without having to be told what to do.

Approaches and Materials. Beyond competence in the basics, however, professionalization entails either knowledge of or willingness to be exposed to specializations current in the field of foreign language instruction. In this respect, company language teaching at a professional level in Japan shares the same values as professional language teaching in other contexts, such as at a university or language school.

One example may help to illustrate this point. The ways company employees use (or will use) English for their work can be researched. The fruits of this research can be considered a part of the English-language needs-assessment process and can be employed to design content for courses devoted to helping employees accomplish their specific purposes through English. ESP (English for Specific Purposes) is, in fact, a major branch of second- and foreign-language instruction with obvious applications in company language teaching situations and in any language learning situation for which purposes can be specified. Unfortunately, untrained or inexperienced teachers cannot be expected to know how to plan or conduct ESP courses; nor can managers who know nothing about specific-purpose instruction be expected to support it without a bit of re-education. The results of our survey of methods and materials in use in company-based programs (discussed more fully below) indicate that full-time, in-house programs are more likely than part-time programs staffed by itinerant teachers to offer ESP courses—telex writing or technical proposal writing, for example. But the survey also indicates that ESP still takes second place to general courses supported by English-for-everybody-in-general materials.

Although we might like to have more ESP in company programs, we recognize that a gap exists between the real and ideal methodological worlds. This gap suggests an important professional function for well-trained teaching colleagues either in the company setting or at regional and national conferences: the introduction of new or important methods and materials—ESP methods and materials as a case in point—to teachers who are unfamiliar with them. Again, professionalization of English teaching at Japanese companies is not an accomplished fact; it is, rather, a trend which has to be nurtured before it is going to have an impact on the quality of English used by company employees.

One area in which professionalization of company English teaching has received a great deal of support is the breadth and depth of high quality published materials increasingly available in bookstores and at publishers' conference displays. Over the last decade, there has been a gradual shift from purely structural, grammar-based materials to mixed or language function-based materials. Publishers now cater to company language-training needs by offering an extensive variety of specific-purpose texts and tape series, keeping in frequent touch with teachers and administrators of company programs and closely following the main trends (and bandwagons) constantly evolving in applied linguistics.

A brief word of caution here. There is so much material of potential use to teachers in company programs that judicious selection has to occur constantly. Although a well-intentioned manager might order everything on a publisher's shelf (we know of one case when this did happen), appropriateness of level, content, and approach to language learning must be considered when selecting texts. This requires a reasonably clear sense of instructional values and a serious desire to fit materials to students' purposes. In company language teaching, professionalism is clearly indicated by this approach to materials selection. A related issue—use of materials especially designed by the teacher to fit the needs of a particular group of employees—will be examined in the next section. For the moment we want to emphasize the importance of choices that are based on a commitment toward improving the quality of instruction.

Organizations that Support Company Language Teaching. The two organizations that offer the highest degree of professional support for company language teachers are JALT and TESOL (Teachers of English to Speakers of Other Languages). The 2,700-member JALT is perhaps the more relevent source, since the large majority of its members share a concern for improving the quality of instruction offered to Japanese learners of English. A significant fraction of the sessions operated at the JALT annual conference deal with English instruction in business environments. In addition, monthly local JALT chapter meetings, periodic business special interest group (SIG) sessions, and occasional seminars on in-company language programs (there have been three so far) are excellent sources of background and ideas for anyone involved in company language teaching.

We don't want to leave the impression that business topics per se are the only ones worth pursuing in the professional organizations. To the contrary, the ordinary monthly meetings of local JALT chapters provide introductions to techniques and materials with no direct bearing on company language teaching but with a high utility value for teachers willing to adapt them to local company circumstances. A few of the more recently presented topics have included, for example, the use of simulations in ESP, magazine pictures for small group activities, daily newspapers, and the chalkboard. The monthly JALT newsletter, now called *The Language Teacher,* has initiated "My Share," a column offering "a forum for teachers willing to share an idea, game, technique, or classroom activity" (January, 1984). The column should prove of particular value to teachers who are unable to attend their local meetings.

TESOL, a 10,000-member organization of English teachers scattered around the globe, cannot compete with the local appeal of JALT, its affiliate in Japan. It can, however, offer a number of resources to company language teachers, including TESOL publications at members' discounts and a comprehensive monthly newsletter containing articles from the borderline theoretical to the eminently practical. (TESOL's "It Works" is the counterpart of JALT's "My Share.")

The professional support for company language teachers offered by JALT and TESOL is now being recognized by managers of the in-house programs. Membership dues are viewed as a kind of inexpensive capital investment in the teaching program; expenses related to attendance at the annual JALT conference are borne by the company under the category of "business trip." Attendance at the annual overseas TESOL convention is still not regularly financed by the companies (the expense would be enormous), although Kobe Steel generally manages to send one or two of its teaching staff to TESCO each year. Since this level of support (for attendance at international conventions) is still exceptional, it would be inaccurate to characterize it as a trend. On the other hand, the fact that financial support is available at all suggests that Japanese companies have begun to perceive the link between quality English teaching and professional activity.

We next want to examine the way teaching is handled in a variety of company settings by presenting the results of a materials-and-methodology survey. Our main goal here is to offer the reader a broad, reasonably representative view of instruction at Japanese companies.

A Survey of Techniques, Methods, and Approaches in Company Language Teaching

In-company language programs with full-time foreign staff are still relatively rare in Japan, but several of the larger companies have programs that have been in operation for as long as ten years, and others have new programs that are in the process of development. In order to get an idea of what is going on outside of our own company (Kobe Steel), we have gathered information from five other company programs using a questionnaire addressing these areas:
- overall goals of the teaching program
- student expectations regarding the program
- communicative proficiency of the students
- job categories/job functions of students
- applications of English by company employees

- ways of establishing and maintaining rapport with students
- texts and materials in use (including teacher-made)
- favored methods and techniques
- courses: types offered, length, intensity
- suggestions for the first class
- suggestions for daily/weekly lesson plans
- special problems to be expected and how to deal with them
- other comments

Our summary of the data begins with a brief profile of the companies surveyed, and then organizes information into the following combined categories: goals and expectations; student characteristics and program types; rapport; materials, methods, and techniques; and attitudes toward learning and course planning. (Please see Appendix A for an outline of the types and lengths of courses offered at the companies surveyed.)

1. *Kobe Steel, Ltd.* is a company of 33,000 employees. The company program employs 13 teachers in two language centers: Kobe and Tokyo. All of those teachers are employed full-time. The company also contracts a large number of classes with outside teaching agencies. The program has been in operation for about eight years, gradually increasing in size over that time. The program is included within the Personnel Department.

2. *Nippon Steel, Ltd.* is the largest steel company in the world. Although the company's language program has been in operation for a number of years, it employs teachers only on a part-time basis. Like Kobe Steel and Mitsui and Co., Nippon Steel has its English program under the supervision of the Personnel Department.

3. *Mitsui and Co., Ltd.* is a giant trading house with domestic, import, export, and offshore operations. The range of its trading includes such products as autos, inorganic chemicals, and petrochemicals. Mainly part-time teachers conduct the language program. The company, through its Personnel Development program, contracts with several outside schools for a variety of additional English-language instructional services.

4. *Chiyoda Chemical Engineering and Construction Co., Ltd.* is an integrated engineering firm providing worldwide engineering, procurement, construction, and project-management services. Three full-

time coordinators (who also teach) are supplemented by language school teachers giving English instruction at four different locations in the Kanto region. The English Program is part of the Education and Training Department.

5. *Matsushita Electic Co., Ltd.* is one of the largest companies in Japan, with factories and subsidiaries all over the world. It has a very large program (with students numbering in the thousands) which employs part-time teachers supervised by a full-time coordinator).

6. *Sumitomo Metal Industries* employs 20 teachers in 9 different sites all over Japan. Its teachers are mainly employed full-time (there are now 11 full-timers) although nine part-timers also work in the program. The company's program is organized within the Personnel Development and Education Department.

Survey Results

In some cases, English classes are offered during company time, with employees being given time off to attend. Other company programs offer classes after hours, with students either volunteering or being volunteered to attend. The size of the full-time teaching staffs varies from one to fourteen; some companies employ a coordinator full-time, with teaching done by a combination of full- and part-time staff. One can guess that the amount of coordination required increases with the number of part-time teachers. In most cases, the in-house program is supplemented by classes taught by outside teaching agencies under contract. The number and variety of courses taught increases with the size of the full-time staff. This is usually due to the full-timers' greater access to company information, knowledge of students' jobs, and sufficient preparation time to develop original materials and courses.

Goals and Expectations. From the companies' point of view, the most commonly stated goal is to increase the "pool" of employees who will be able to use English for their work. This and the goal of "internationalization" indicate a fairly typical lack of specific goals on the part of the companies; other somewhat less comprehensive goals mentioned are the elimination of the fear of foreigners, preparation for overseas assignments, and the improvement of technical language skills.

The language teaching staff listed their programs' goals in more specific terms: review and "activation" of past learning was often mentioned, as well as the "un-learning" of fossilized forms and "Japanese English." Speaking and listening are given more emphasis than reading or writing, with a communicative emphasis overall. Culture-study and "exposure to foreigners" were cited as important, as well as the development of such specific skills in technical and business English as description of machines and processes, negotiation, and correspondence.

The most commonly cited learner expectation, as seen by the teachers, was the increase in their understanding of people of other cultures. They also hoped to be able to see improvement and apply their study to their jobs.

Student Characteristics and Program Types. Most of the company programs deal with students from a wide range of levels (from, roughly, 0-4 on the Foreign Service Institute Scale) one company required a level "5" on its own company test (a relatively high score) for admission to the program.

Some of the programs deal entirely with white-collar workers, mainly engineers, while others serve the whole range of employees from factory workers to top executives. Women, on the other hand, generally do not hold positions of responsibility in Japanese companies and are viewed by management as relatively cheap and temporary sources of labor—regardless of their educational backgrounds. Given these circumstances it is very unusual to find companies allowing women to study during company time even though many company women have to use English, at varying levels of sophistication, to do their work.

Some of the applications of English by company employees are listed on the following page.

Rapport. Four companies offered suggestions for establishing rapport with students. We can summarize their comments in the following way: It is important to establish personal contact by "shedding the teacher mask" and participating in recreational activities with students outside of class. Several companies have intensive "retreat"—type programs as part of their regular language programs. Further, the teacher's own status as a company employee can create a bond with students if they see that the teacher takes it seriously, since Japanese tend to feel a bond with fellow.

Table 1
Some Typical Applications of English
by Japanese Company Employees

Technical	Business	Technical/Business
reading and writing technical articles	use of English on overseas trips for sales, negotiations, presentations	hosting foreign guests
reading and writing technical specifications	correspondence	correspondence
technology transfer projects	meetings with customers and suppliers	telex writing
technical instruction	contract and other legal writing	study abroad
technical discussions, negotiations	orientation to overseas projects through English	communicating with foreigners working in the company
technical presentations at international conferences	—	—

company members. Trust and confidence in the teacher increase as s/he shows an interest in and knowledge of company activities and concerns. This is perhaps the most important difference between in-house and outside-contract teachers: In-house people have the opportunity, over a period of time, to be able to respond knowledgeably to specific student needs. If students come to recognize the teacher's need to know about their jobs, they in turn begin to make an effort to help educate the teacher as a future language resource-person.

Material, Methods, and Techniques. The teaching materials in use in company programs vary widely. At Kobe Steel we use almost entirely teacher-made and teacher-gathered materials, an extreme example being a simulation of an overseas engineering project, where students must research and discuss alternatives, and negotiate contracts. In this case, we provide real and made-up technical reference materials, and the students come up with the rest. Coordinators at another program have drawn up a syllabus of notions and functions to be covered and recycled at each level, and then provide teachers with a list of materials suited for each level. Some of these are commercial materials, and others have been made by teachers using in-company research and information. An in-house-designed textbook series is used at one company for all of its classes, and another company program serving only high-level students uses entirely commercially-produced video materials. A bibliography of some of the published materials used in company programs is provided in Appendix B.

The companies surveyed differ as to their leanings toward general English or English for specific purposes. This naturally influences their choice of materials. About half of the companies use some sort of business or technical English material. We might hazard a guess that programs with a large number of the teaching staff employed full-time would have more time to analyze students' needs more specifically and choose materials based on that analysis. Another factor might be the variety of jobs students come from. In some cases, engineers, businessmen, and factory and clerical staff may all be in the same class. This makes it more difficult to address each student's job-related language needs. Yet another factor is the staff's teaching orientation: some company teachers prefer to structure courses around published texts, while others like to develop their own materials.

Companies also vary in the methods and techniques they favor. Two companies prescribe pattern-practice based on a main structural text, but leave the choice of activities up to the teacher as long as the text material is covered. Most companies do not prescribe any particular method, but the orientation of classroom activities seems to be communicative overall. Some favorite techniques mentioned are: fluency squares (please see Appendix B for details), role-playing and simulations, pair and small-group work, conversation management exercises, adaptations from the Silent Way and Total Physical Response, use of pictures, speeches and presentations, and problem-solving activities.

One of the questions we asked our colleagues at the other companies was, "What would you suggest for the first class?" The responses were similar. The teacher should give the students an opportunity to get to know each other, perhaps by pair interviews or round-table self-introductions. The outline, goals, and main materials of the course should be described, as well as the expectations for attendance, homework, etc. One company suggested that students not be asked to "perform," but that the teacher should choose non-threatening ice-breaking activities to help the students get used to each other and the teacher. Another company suggested that the teacher take a survey of how the students use or come into contact with English in their jobs—a sort of mini needs analysis.

When we asked teachers to describe their classes from the perspective of daily or weekly planning, it was suggested that one identify the major focus of each class, make sure the activities chosen suit that focus, provide for a clear sense of continuity from one class to the next, and review periodically. As with any class, of course, lesson planning depends on the time allotted to each class. For example, in a three-hour block of time it seems clear that one would divide the time between several different activities. In such a course for low-level construction machinery engineers at Kobe Steel, we usually spent one hour on a structural accuracy activity, one hour on "survival" or "activation" activities, and then one hour on an activity somehow related to the students' particular field, which in that case was construction machinery.

Attitudes Toward Learning and Course Planning. Teaching in a Japanese company involves some special problems that one might not encounter in other teaching situations. Some are related to the character of the Japanese businessman as a learner. Since most of these people have a genuine need to use English on the job, they may express some anxiety about the time it takes to raise their level of English, or about not being offered spectacularly effective short-cuts to the exact sort of language required in their specific situations. Also, Japanese students in general tend to be reticent, and the teacher must think carefully about how to draw them out. Pair and small-group work are helpful, as well as activities that provide an opportunity for students to use their own personal and job information in language practice.

Other problems relate to the administration of a language program within the structure of the Japanese company. Some companies, like Japanese universities, hesitate to have students separated by language level, preferring to keep "freshmen" or same-department people together to foster good group relations. When this is the case, it is sometimes possible to form sub-groups by level within the class, or to set up a situation where students can take responsibilities appropriate to their language level. (See *JALT Newsletter*, now *The Language Teacher*, November–December 1983.)

Motivation varies from unbelievably high to quite low. This depends partly on whose idea it was for the student to study English. (Students generally cannot or will not refuse a manager's assignment.) Another factor in motivation is how the student feels about why he needs English. If he is studying because he will be sent to work on a construction site in the Middle East for two years without his family, his attitude toward English may not be enthusiastic.

Lateness and absence are recurrent problems in company classes. Students tend to be extremely busy, and their work generally takes priority over English study. Experienced teachers usually go into class with several alternative plans in mind, in the event that key students are not there. It is important that the program administration retain the right to drop persistently absent students from the program. One reason for poor attendance is that some managers tend not to take English study seriously. Working toward language proficiency is a long-term proposition, and short-term deadlines take priority. In the long term, we might say that company language programs have the additional task of changing managerial attitudes toward the process and requirements of language learning. This would involve making clear the difference between language training and other types of training where performance objectives and testing might be more clear-cut and where progress can be measured more directly.

A Day in the Life of a Company Language Teacher

We would next like to offer an impression of the in-house teacher's day from a personal point of view. Since presenting this point of view will necessarily be an exercise in generalization, the "fact-like" details should not be taken as universals. What we hope to do here is give the reader an example of the sort of schedule an in-house teacher might have on one particular day and propose interpretations for activities on the schedule.

TIME	SCHEDULE/COMMENTS
8:30	Enters office, a large room with over forty desks belonging to department members. The foreign teaching staff sit together in one island of desks. Says "Good Morning" to teaching colleagues and "Ohayo gozaimasu" to Japanese staff. Gets coffee and sits down to look over lesson plans for the 9:00 class, Basic English 2. [It may seem odd to recommend "unwinding" at the beginning of the day, but rushing in to take on a class with no time to relax is a poor way to begin the lesson and greet colleagues. A half hour before classes is a reasonable head start.]
9:00	Goes to classroom to meet BE 2 students for the first time, as this is the beginning of a new term. Smiles, sits down at the table with the students, introduces self, and checks to be sure everyone is in the correct room for BE 2. [Meanies with bull-whips get lots of silence and discipline, but probably little responsive talk from the students. A pleasant disposition and somewhat subdued enthusiasm for teaching the group will help make future classes work more easily.] Starts a warm-up activity: puts the students in pairs for interviews, from which the students may get to know each other a bit. Hands out a simple interview form to guide the students in their questioning. About 30 minutes on this activity, after which the partners introduce each other to the class and open the questioning to other class members. Introduces self, giving basic information: length of time in the company, in Japan, native country, etc. Then opens the floor to the students for questions. [Plenty of time spent over introductions is an essential way to begin a new class. This need not be terribly formal; in fact, an informal and humorous introductory activity is especially useful in putting the students at ease.] Then goes over the basic goals, materials and requirements of the course, making sure the students understand each point.
9:55	(10-minute break) Sets the students up in small groups for an activity with

TIME	SCHEDULE/COMMENTS

Cuisinaire rods and blocks, where they will take turns giving and receiving instructions for placing the rods in various arrangements. This is meant to diagnose their skills in the language of shape, location, and spatial relations, which will be one of the first language areas in the course.

10:20 Reviews some of the words and expressions of location written on the board as the students worked. Then asks the students to look over the first unit in their main text before the next class, thanks the students for coming, and ends the class. Then spends a few minutes making notes on the students, the language they seem to know and not to know. Makes notes on areas to cover in future classes.
[Diagnosis should be repeated from time to time during the course. The results of diagnosis, an error analysis for individual students, for example, should help the teacher tailor future lessons to students' needs.]

10:45 Goes back to the office, gets coffee, sits down to make a final go-over on an editing assignment for an employee who will come at 11:00. It is a letter responding to a request for technical specifications on a company product, written by a Mr. Tanaka from the Engineering Dept.

11:00 The writer of the letter arrives. He and the teacher have some difficulty communicating, but Mr. Tanaka manages to get his intentions across using a diagram.
[Editing technical or business documents seems to be an inescapable part of the job, particularly if the teacher is an in-house employee, and thus is expected to do more than teach. Communication difficulties should not be allowed to frustrate. Can be extremely rewarding work given patience on both sides.]

12:00 Lunchtime. Everyone eats the company boxed lunch while sitting at their desks. After eating, the teacher reads the *Japan Times,* while other department members chat in the kitchen,

TIME   SCHEDULE/COMMENTS

play cards in a continuing tournament; some managers are playing Go.
[Lunchtime is the wrong time to finish off last minute tasks, particularly if they involve making requests of other people in the office. Ditto for use of the phone.]

12:45   End of lunch. Teacher goes over lesson plans for 1:30 class, Technical English.

1:30   Goes to classroom for continuing Technical English; students have already gotten into their groups to work on an ongoing project: imaginary Rube Goldberg-type machines that they are designing, and will describe in written technical reports and then in oral presentations. One group is working on a "Wake-up Machine." As the students work in their groups, the teacher circulates among the groups, offering help with language when necessary, often referring back to sections of the text *Nucleus: Engineering* on description of structure, function, and process, which the class covered earlier in the course.

2:15   Class breaks for ten minutes. During the break, a student approaches the teacher with 10 pages of technical specifications which he would like checked by tomorrow. The teacher asks whether next week would be all right, and the student reluctantly agrees.
[Well-intentioned people can take advantage of the teacher; new teachers, in particular, have a tendency to do anything asked of them. A rule of thumb for anyone who does not intend to put in overtime regularly: take on extra work that can be scheduled comfortably within a normal work day.]
The students return; as they go on with their small-group discussion, the teacher goes around to each group and asks for a brief, oral progress report. At the end of the class, the teacher reminds the students of their design schedule and deadlines for preparation of their written and oral reports.

3:00   Class ends, teacher makes notes on some of the areas the

TIME   SCHEDULE/COMMENTS

students have had difficulty with, and then returns to desk. His/her section manager comes over and starts a conversation about the coming holiday. This goes on for about thirty minutes.

[Managers often talk with their people informally, socially, in the office and for fairly long periods. Although some teachers may find it strange to deal with topics that seem to have no relation to work, managers often feel that maintaining good human relations in the office requires them to know something about the personal lives of workers for whom they are responsible.]

Plans classes for next day, and continues work on an ongoing materials-gathering project: looking through company documents, pamphlets, and other publications for diagrams of plants to be used in classes for practicing description of spatial relations, and manufacturing process flow charts to be used in future Technical English classes. Telephones a former student to ask for help in finding such diagrams, and the student invites the teacher to go drinking on Friday night. The teacher agrees.

4:30   Meeting with a teaching colleague for brainstorming ideas in a business simulation course to be taught next term.

5:30   Teacher leaves the office.

Conclusion

For people interested in teaching English in Japan, in-company programs offer some special attractions: a chance to see one's students actually go out and use what one has tried to teach, a possibility of developing a feeling for students as colleagues as well as students, and, in some cases, access to company information that can help the teacher narrow and refine teaching goals more than is possible when working from outside the company system. The professional quality of in-company teachers is increasing, and at the same time there has been an increase in the resources available to teachers for professional development. We hope that we have been able to paint a reasonably clear and accurate picture of what it is like to teach in a Japanese company, and offer some ideas as to where one might begin.

Appendix A

A Summary of Courses and Terms at Selected Company Language Programs

COMPANY	COURSE	TERMS
Sumitomo Metals	General English (7 levels)	2 hrs, twice a week, 20 weeks
	Technical Writing	2-3 day intensive residential course
	Legal English	series of 1-2 day seminars
	Managers' Courses (general English)	2 hrs/wk, once a week, 20 weeks
	Special Courses and private lessons	vary
Nippon Steel	General Conversation	2 hrs, three times a week plus 2 weekend seminars per month, 5-month terms
	Freshman Intensive	9 days, residential
	Intensive (not for freshmen)	2 weeks, residential
	Business Letter Writing	2 hrs, once a week

COMPANY METHODS AND MATERIALS

COMPANY	COURSE	TERMS
	Technical Writing	2 hrs, once a week
	Others	vary
Mitsui and Company	BBC Video Courses	13 weeks (13 episodes)
	CBS News-based Course	5-week segments, renewable
	Special Courses arranged by depts. with language schools (ILC, ELEC, etc.) and freelance teachers:	20 weeks (generally) leading to courses indicated above
	pre-employment intensives	
	freshmen intensives	
	general and business English	
Chiyoda Chemical	General Conversation Intensive	7.5 hrs/day for 15 days, then 4-5 days residency
	Evening Prgm. (all levels)	2 hrs, twice a week, generally 90-hr. terms
	Technical Writing (by Japanese Staff)	2 hrs/week, 90-hr. terms
	Business Writing (by Japanese Staff)	,,
	Freshman Extensive (Business Communication)	7.5 hrs/day for 2 months, incl. 2 residencies

COMPANY	COURSE	TERMS
Matsushita Electric	General Conversation	five hours/week, 5-month terms
	Pre-TOEFL	open-ended, 5-6 hrs.
	TOEFL Preparation	open-ended, 20 hrs/week, 4-6 hrs/day
	Overseas Prep. (intensive)	6-7 hrs/day, 4 wks.
	Overseas Prep. (trainees)	6-7 hrs/day, 6 months
Kobe Steel (Tokyo Language Center)	General English	1 hr 15 min, 3 times a week, two 13-week terms
	Early Intermediate Business English	,,
	Intermediate Business English	1 hr 15 min, 2 or 3 times a week, two terms
	Advanced Business English Seminar	1 hr 15 min, twice a week for one term, plus a 3-day Management Game seminar
Kobe Steel (Nada Language Center)	Basic English 1-4	1 hr 30 min, twice a week, 11-week term
	Improving Writing	2 hrs, twice a week, one term
	International Area Studies	1 hr 30 min, twice a week, one term
	Speech/Debate	2 hrs, twice a week, one term

COURSE	TERMS
Engineers' Course	2 hrs, twice a week, one term
Technical Communication	2 hrs, twice a week, one term
Jabal Project 1 (simulation)	2 hrs, twice a week, one term
Jabal Project 2	2 hrs, twice a week, one term
Bid for Power (BBC video course)	1 hr 30 min, twice a week, two terms
Business Communication	2 hrs, twice a week, one term

Appendix B

Selected Texts and Teaching Materials for
Use in Company Language Programs

(We have limited these references to materials with a business or technology slant. Many general materials are also used in company programs.)

ITEM/AUTHOR·	SOURCE/ PUBLISHER	COMMENTS
1. *Fluency Squares for Business and Technology* (Phillip Knowles and Ruth A. Sasaki)	Regents	Controlled fluency practice with concepts common to business and technology

ITEM/AUTHOR	SOURCE/ PUBLISHER	COMMENTS
2. *Bid for Power*	BBC English for Television	Elegantly produced serial drama based on a technology development project in a fictional country
3. *The Sadrina Project*	,,	Serial video drama of a travel-business intrigue
4. *The Bellcrest Story*	BBC/Oxford U. Press	Video drama in a corporate setting
5. CBS News tapes	available on a rental-subscription basis:	Selections from the CBS (American television network) evening news
	Rentacolor Japan, Ltd. 1-21-4 Hamamatsu-cho, Minato-ku, Tokyo 105	
6. *Nucleus: General Science* (Martin Bates, Tony Dudley-Evans)	Longman	A good introduction to common language uses in science and technology (structure, function, process, etc.)
7. *Nucleus: Engineering* (as above)	,,	Same format as above, but within context of engineering
8. *Basic English for*	Oxford U.	Numbers, shapes,

ITEM/AUTHOR	SOURCE/PUBLISHER	COMMENTS
Science (Peter Donovan)	Press	motion, plus structure, function, etc. as in *Nucleus*. Good visuals.
9. *English for Science and Technology: A Handbook for Non-Native Speakers* (Thomas Huckin, Leslie Olsen)	McGraw/Hill	First half an introduction to formats and principles of technical communication, second half a usage and style review for non-native speakers
10. *Handbook of Technical Writing* (Chas. Brusaw, Gerald Alred, Walter Oliu)	St. Martins	A good, quick reference on usage, format, and style in technical documents
11. *English in Focus* series (eds. J.P.B. Allen, H.G. Widdowson)	Oxford U. Press	Titles on electrical engineering, mechanical engineering, etc. A good teacher reference for technical language
12. *English for Careers* (Eugene J. Hall)	Regents	Same as above
13. *Manage with English* (P.L. Sandler, C.L. Scott)	Oxford U. Press	A high-intermediate text for business English and business concepts
14. *Yoshi Goes to New York* (John Battaglia	Pergamon	Authentic listening materials on the theme

ITEM/AUTHOR	SOURCE/ PUBLISHER	COMMENTS
and Marilyn Fisher)		of a Japanese businessmen's trip to New York
15. *Business Talk* (Gareth Hughes, Adrian Pilbeam, Christine West)	Longman	Authentic listening passenges and dialogues on business topics
16. *Eight Simulations* (Leo Jones)	Cambridge U. Press	General content; simulations well thought out, fairly well supported with documentation
17. *Simulations in Language Teaching* (Ken Jones)	,,	Background reading for those intrested in using or writing simulations
18. *Language Training* (periodical)	Language Training Services, 21 Wigmore St. London W1H 9LA	A slim quarterly devoted entirely to language training in industry

Private Lesson Teaching

William Albert McBean

The Situation in Japan

Private lessons are an important area of teaching in Japan. They can be effective, enjoyable, and lucrative. Usually considered supplementary work, there are teachers who support themselves on private tutoring alone. Private lessons take place everywhere—in apartments, tea rooms, hotel lobbies—and at all hours. Many students who don't have the time or inclination to attend regular classes benefit from such instruction. Several language schools I am familiar with usually instruct ten percent of their students on a private basis. I have long enjoyed teaching English conversation through private lessons. Indications are that the demand for this type of instruction will continue to grow.

Although native-speaker private tutoring is common wherever English as a second or foreign language is taught, little has been written about it as a separate area of the English language teaching field. A study by this author researched tutoring to determine its scope and nature, with particular reference to Japan ("Tutoring in ESL," 1978 University of Hawaii M.A. thesis). The information here is based on that research, over twelve years of active private lesson teaching experience, and conversations with colleagues.

Getting Started

In Japan it takes time and connections to get things done. This holds true for private lesson teaching, expecially in setting up an ideal teaching situation. There are thousands of potential students who would love to have the chance to study English with a native speaker on a private basis. The demand is much greater than the supply of native-speaker teachers. Most who want to study privately can't afford the lesson fee, yet for many others a fee of up to ¥8,000 (about U.S.$32.00) per hour is a reasonable expense. I once had a company president say to me, "I'll pay whatever you desire." To him, the cost was irrelevant; finding someone who could teach him in his office during the day was his problem. He had been unable to "find" a teacher until he heard about me through a business acquaintance. This problem of student finding teacher and teacher finding student is complicated. Almost all of those thousands of potential students have one thing in common: they won't agree to study with a total stranger, that is, someone who has not been introduced to them, at least indirectly. The company president who needs a private tutor to prepare for a trip abroad would rather go to the trouble of signing up for a private lesson at a language school than attempt to find an in-office teacher on his own. The school, as the middleman, introduces him to a teacher and saves him the anxiety of dealing directly with an unknown foreigner. This Japanese trait of avoiding business dealings with strangers is a strong one. Unlike some Western countries, Japan is not a country of quick, easy relationships. To Japanese, "getting to know someone," involves observation and communication over a period of months or years. Still, some teachers find being a "friend of a friend" is sufficient to gain the approval of prospective students.

There are some ways, however, of attracting private lesson students, even if you are a stranger. To begin with, start thinking positively and creatively. Ask yourself, "First, how can I begin, and then, how can I expand my circle of acquaintances?" You then might consider doing things like 1) going to nearby universities and posting notices; 2) handing out flyers to students—college students have great interest but limited budgets so you would want to encourage small group study; 3) putting advertisements (in Japanese) in the local neighborhood paper. Due to population density, your neighborhood can be a good source of lessons; the convenience factor of living near your home is attractive to students as is a lower lesson fee that results from teaching at home. One close friend returned to the Kansai area of Japan without guaranteed employment. His visa was approved because of his marriage to a Japanese. After securing lodging, he went around his neighborhood and put flyers in the mailboxes of residents. Within a few weeks, he was happily working and earning a living wage. And, as usually happens, the word never stopped spreading.

For advertising, the national English and Japanese dailies are less effective, but a couple of the papers offer low-cost rates for non-commercial advertisers. Another idea is an advertising supplement that your local newspaper distributor will insert in any of the Japanese dailies that cover your locality. Japanese "juku" (cram schools) rely heavily on this insert advertising. An enterprising teacher I know once stood at his train station exit during rush hour and passed out flyers for a few weeks. His idea paid off in a number of private lessons.

The list of measures the newcomer to Japan could take to find private lessons is limited only by one's imagination and time. I've mentioned just a few ideas that have proven effective. Whether you have come to Japan with a job contract or are completely on your own will naturally affect how active you need to be in this regard.

I cannot overstress the importance of introductions in locating good lessons. It is a source that will expand in time if you extend yourself. For example, you should socialize within the foreign community at every opportunity. Let your teacher friends know you have time and want students. Many a good lesson has been passed from a departing to a newly arrived teacher at a party. Teachers too busy to take on more work are happy to pass lesson requests to newcomers provided they have the opportunity to do so. Join professional organizations such as The Japan Association of Language Teachers (JALT). To increase your teaching opportunities in these ways, two things are essential: a telephone or the use of one, and a name card that you will want to circulate freely. Another word of advice in this regard is to dress and act in a professional manner at all times. Too many new English teachers underestimate the importance Japanese place on appearance. Often, appearance is all prospective employers have to judge you by.

In discussing how to get started, I've mentioned some ways of "finding" students. Further advice would be to make yourself available to be "found." Most teachers queried on this point in a survey connected with my 1978 research stated that students sought them out. It's first a matter of visibility—getting to know people, then patience and availability. One thing is certain, the longer you stay in the country the busier you'll get.

Private Lessons vs. Classroom Instruction

When you begin teaching you will want to know some of the differences between private lessons and classroom instruction. Foremost, studies have shown that tutoring is more effective than classroom instruction. The reason is the quality of the time spent between student and teacher. Given a good interpersonal relationship, a private lesson teacher can, through immediate feedback and attention, guide the student's progress to a degree unobtainable in the classroom. This close, dynamic interaction between student and teacher is the characteristic that gives the private lesson its value. On the other hand, some tutors reported in the survey they did not enjoy private lessons because of the constant pressure of intimate contact. They felt insecure in the one-on-one situation, indicating a preference for classroom teaching because of the psychological and physical "distance" factor. A classroom teacher can give himself a rest by assigning written work or activities; the private lesson teacher is "on stage," so to speak, throughout the lesson. The private lesson offers no podium, no invisible barriers. Personal learning atmosphere and rapport take on added meaning: they determine not only how much the student learns, but how long he stays with you. Similarly, your personal obligation to the student increases because there is no school support structure.

If you're a professional English teacher, your training has prepared you for classroom situations. Likewise, the texts you use are usually written for classroom use. This is not a serious problem because most of the teaching and learning principles you know, and most of the texts on the market, are applicable to private lesson teaching. The key word here is adaptation. Nearly all teachers surveyed reported that they had to alter their teaching approaches and adapt their texts considerably to succeed in private lesson teaching. A break from classroom doctrine and routine was necessary.

Teachers in Japan are entertainers of sorts, in some cases merely on account of their foreignness. The feeling of being a novelty, the object of curiosity and scrutiny, will be more apparent in the private lesson. Whereas in the classroom the student has to share his fascinating foreign teacher with many others, in the individual situation you're his alone and he has more questions about you and your culture than he knows how to ask. You will want to capitalize on such interest because you have the freedom to create a natural syllabus of spontaneous topics and activities. This one point makes private lesson teaching more enjoyable than classroom teaching for many instructors.

Japanese students generally hope for the development of a close relationship with their teacher. They often want to have a foreign friend, and this may well be one of the private student's objectives. Japanese take their friendships seriously. Indeed, tour guides, babysitters, sponsors—even spouses—have been found by native speakers among their Japanese students of English. Some teachers have reported a psychoanalyst-couch aspect to private lesson teaching; some students (especially women) are looking only for a listener who stands outside their culture to whom they can spill out their sad marriage tales, loneliness, and so on. Understanding motivation is important. In the survey, a few female private lesson teachers reported that male student interest in the teacher occasionally went far beyond what would be expected in a normal student-teacher relationship. This was probably the result of the sexual fascination that many Japanese men have toward foreign women. Young, single teachers, in particular, would want to be on guard against such ulterior motives.

Although I have tried to point out some of the general differences between the two types of teaching, many of the differences are matters of emphasis. The same qualities required for success in the classroom apply to tutoring: patience, flexibility, understanding of the student, and knowledge of the subject matter.

Choosing Materials

Choosing materials (books, activities, ideas) for the private lesson is a joy. There are no constraints such as an administrator dictating what materials to use and how to use them. You simply do what best suits both parties. Thus, a lesson can be tailored to meet the ability, needs, and interests of one student. Proper evaluation is important. Learn why the student is studying English. Is it because of a business trip to the U.S.A. in a few weeks? Does the student need to pass a TOEFL test? Or, do you have two housewives who are studying out of interest rather than necessity? Unlike in the classroom, the motivation for study can be discerned; therefore, the student's objectives can be put into clear focus and met with the proper combination of materials.

A few private lesson students will let you know just what kind of lesson they desire. Most will leave it entirely up to you. A good general approach is to base half the lesson on a suitable text, with the other half strictly oral in the form of discussion, questions and answers, or other techniques. A text is basically what the teacher makes of it. Any text, any piece of learning material, can be good in the hands of a good teacher. Some teachers refuse to use a text, believing it hampers true communication; others wouldn't teach without one. In the survey, a middle stance prevailed, with most teachers believing in the judicious use of a textbook.

To the student, a textbook in hand gives a sense (sometimes inaccurate) of security and continuity. It can serve as a measure of progress and achievement as lessons are completed. More important, a text (especially one with tapes) serves as a continuous learning source since your guidance and stimulation is usually limited to once a week. Don't expect students to study much on their own—they generally don't. They seem to expect miracles from that one or two hours a week they spend with you. You'll need to encourage them to study on their own, and a textbook gives them something to study. One teacher I know asks her students to telephone her mid-week between lessons for a 5 to 10 minute chat. While some might consider this an infringement of privacy or unpaid teaching, she got good results.

There are two general groups of books available in Japan from which to choose for the lessons. One group consists of texts of basic English as a second or foreign language. These texts are graded by level, provide a logical grammatical progression, and are written for general classroom use. They normally include a combination of dialogues, listening practice, drills, role-playing, activities, and reading and writing. A related type is the English for Specific Purposes (ESP) text, which focuses on a specific profession such as engineering, medicine, or business. The texts are available at bookstores such as Kinokuniya and Maruzen.

For the new teacher, a textbook-based lesson is a safe and sure way to get started. The teacher's guides that accompany the texts give step-by-step instructions for using them. The guides also expose you to the methodology recommended by the writer. In a sense, they teach you how to teach. As you gain experience, you will naturally adapt the text to your teaching style, and, of course, to the needs and abilities of your student. As long as you consider a textbook as a starting point for a lesson and are not a slave to it, you'll do well.

The other group of books includes all useful volumes that aren't intended for use as basic texts. They range from picture books to conversational topics based on Japanese culture. Although it's impossible to list many of this latter type, I would like to mention a few that teachers here have found suitable.

Points of Departure. (J. Dobson and F. Sedwick. American Book Co., 1981, 112 pp.) Widely used by teachers here, it contains 51 unordered scenes with vocabulary and questions. The student can choose those topics that interest him. Lessons are meant to be a point of departure for a more personalized focus on the topic.

Explain Yourself. (P. Nicholson and R. Sakuno. Maruzen Publishing Service, 1982, 63 pp.) Twenty-nine Japanese topics with oversized pictures and questions. Interest is spontaneous since students are talking about their own culture. .

Let's Talk About Japan. (S. McCabe and I. McMicking. Macmillian, 1981, 81 pp.) Twelve chapters based on natural conversations as they might occur between native speakers on topics dealing with aspects of Japanese culture.

Talking About Japan. (P. McLean. Asahi Press, 1979, 145 pp.) Thirty-three lessons designed to enable a Japanese to talk about himself, his family, and his culture.

Incredible Japan. (Charles E. Tuttle, 1975, 119 pp.) Although written for the foreign observer of Japanese culture, this paperback has a broad range of topics that easily lend themselves to discussion. Facing pages have explanations and appealing cartoons that cover customs, legends.

Caring and Sharing In The Foreign Language Class. (G. Moskowitz. Newbury House, 1978, 343 pp.) One hundred and twenty strategies known as humanistic, affective, or awareness exercises that attempt to bring out what students feel, think, and know about themselves and others. Best for small groups, but the book has many good communication starters for individual talking.

Play Games With English. (C. Granger. Heinemann Educational, 1980, 74 pp.) Humorously illustrated games, puzzles, and quizzes that are fun for both teacher and student.

Survival English. (J.F. de Fretias. Macmillian, 1978, 101 pp.) A handbook for notional language practice. All the ways a student can express 50 different feelings, e.g., sympathy, ignorance, loss for words, etc.

English For A Changing World (Cue book 1). (Scott, Foresman & Co., 1976, 30 pp.) Appealing color pictures that can easily get a conversation going. The booklet is a pull-out supplement to the main text and can be ordered separately for less than ¥200.

Between East and West—Cultural Barriers Q & A. (T. Iwabuchi and M. Okada. Central Press Ltd., 1983, 86 pp.) From a newspaper column in the *Daily Yomiuri,* this booklet answers interesting questions sent in by foreigners about customs and behavior that have affected them in a personal way.

Cultural Encounters: What to Do and Say in Social Situations in English. (C. Ford, A. Silverman, and D. Haines. Pergamon Institute of English, 1983, 94 pp.) A booklet with illustrations, 50 problem situations, and possible reactions. The topics stimulate discussion about manners and conduct acceptable in the U.S.A., U.K., Japan, and the "Ideal World."

The Guinness Book of World Records, The World Almanac and Book of Facts, and other titles of this nature also contain plenty of discussion-stimulating material.

The above list is intended to give you an idea of the type of general books that can be used effectively in a private lesson. Although lacking in pedagogical principles, they provide motivation for open-ended discussion on a variety of topics naturally interesting to the student. You should be able to find these and others in the larger bookstores. For a more complete selection, you can write the publishers' representatives and request a catalogue. Also upon request, you can usually get a free examination copy of almost any textbook that need not be returned. It is best to make these requests on your school letterhead paper, if available, using the business address.

When considering a book for adoption, be mindful of:

1. Student age, ability, interests, background, and purpose for studying English.
2. Length of the course and hours per week.
3. Structural grading, vocabulary, and appropriateness of the English.
4. Reading passages, dialogues, and story line (they should be realistic and of interest to the student).
5. Suitability of the visual format, spacing, and illustrations.
6. Emphasis on oral or conversational English.
7. Opportunities offered for student identification, expression, and follow-up.
8. Suitability to your teaching approach/style.

Nearly all books contain a mass of material that can seldom be completed given the time limits of private lessons and the tendency toward free talking. Plodding through a single book's lessons, in order, can be discouraging. Select and adapt materials for optimal interest and pedagogical efficiency; this includes copying (check copyright particulars) from several sources to make your own syllabus.

A word of caution is in order here on something I call the "free-conversation syndrome." Some students come to a lesson with the idea that they want only free talking without the use of materials or an organized plan of study. For the advanced student who can converse on a broad range of subjects, this may be no problem. For the majority, however, the pitfalls of only free talking can result in a deterioration of the lesson and subsequent loss of interest. To whatever extent you encourage it, free conversation is not truly free anyway—the teacher must guide it.

Although I have discussed only written materials in this section, the most effective teaching aids are what is termed "realia": real things that can be seen, felt (personal feelings, too), heard, and even smelled that elicit genuine, spontaneous, and purposeful communication. Some examples: a walk in a park discussing what is observed; listening to a record while using the jacket to discuss meanings; following a recipe and making cookies. Obviously, for "realia," the possibilities are limitless.

In choosing materials for your private lesson, the only problem should be one of time limitation. If you take a flexible, creative attitude in planning, you will find there is so much that you can and will want to do that it is frustrating not to have the time to do it all.

The Lesson

Being a good private lesson teacher means being a good conversationalist. Private lessons are generally exercises in guided free conversation with the impetus provided by the teacher in the form of materials, questions, and activities. Furthermore, most private students are at least low-intermediate level or above and have a strong interest in, or need for, conversational English. Making conversation with a student sounds easy. But, like teaching in general, to do the job properly requires work. More than just conversing, you're instructing, and this necessitates organization and preparation. Also, lessons are often taught outside a teacher's regular schedule. The odd hours, plus commuting that may be necessary, can be taxing.

In beginning a series of private lessons, the first few sessions are quite important. Based on those initial meetings, the evaluation regarding ability, needs, materials, and objectives will be made; and rapport, teaching/learning standards, and expectations will be established. Concerning rapport, teachers stated in the survey that creating a good rapport with the student was the most important factor affecting the success of their lessons. Evaluation should concern the student's general conversational ability. How well can he communicate now, and how well will he be required to communicate? From the beginning, think seriously about how you can best help him learn English—not what you can do to help yourself get through the lessons.

You'll soon note that the average student begins with a poor self-image as a speaker of English. Actually, most students have a knowledge of grammar and vocabulary sufficient to communicate on an elementary level. However, the typical student has had no opportunity to use English in its spoken form and therefore lacks confidence. Confidence-building through positive reinforcement and encouragement will be an important aspect of your work. Until confidence is gained, students are often frustratingly reticent. The student is there by choice, so he is motivated to learn English for one reason or another. Capitalize on that motivation and establish a personal relationship with your student by getting to know his interests, background, and why he decided to study. Allow the student to talk about himself and the things he is interested in. Take advantage of his natural curiosity about you by encouraging him to ask

questions. Establish a friendly, relaxed atomosphere. Except for the occasional special-need student, most want to enjoy their lessons much as they
would enjoy a flower-arranging or a dance lesson. It's best to approach
the lesson from this point of view.

You might consider beginning by covering basic, immediately useful
expressions such as greetings, apologies and responses, requests, introductions, etc. A good notional-functional text that covers situational
language will be useful for this. As I mentioned in my discussion of
"realia," the more useful the language—the closer it comes to real
life—the more interesting it will be to the student. Avoid getting bogged
down too much in written English; rather, relate the contents of your
written materials to the student's life, to his real world, as much as possible. Let the materials be a means to an end, not the end itself. For example, suppose you're on a textbook lesson dealing with clothes. After the
material has been presented, you would naturally want to ask the student
about his clothes. "What color is your shirt?" is not the most realistic
(would he ever ask such a question?) or stimulating of exchanges.
However, if followed by "What's your favorite color shirt? Why?" feelings and reality come into play. People instinctively react with greater involvement to feelings than to abstractions. The expression of attitudes
and feelings may sometimes be difficult in the classroom; in a private
lesson such activities consume a large portion of the lesson time.

Be mindful of the pace and tempo of your lesson. Experiment with different tempos, but make the lesson progress as rapidly as possible. Ideally, the pace should be based on the student's ability, not the teacher's
lesson plan. If you push the lesson too fast, both you and the student will
end up feeling impatient and frustrated. The student needs to feel that
he's going along at a comfortable pace. Expect plenty of pauses. The student needs time to put into words what is going through his head. While
periods of silence make many Westerners uncomfortable, this is not the
case with Japanese. Foreign language teachers, especially, need a great
deal of patience. In teaching something as natural as one's native
language, it's difficult to empathize with the learner, let alone understand the linguistic proesses and problems he has to cope with. That is
why studying Japanese can make you a more understanding teacher.

Besides controlling the speed and the tempo of a lesson, remember to
maintain variety. Thus, you can avoid the monotony that causes lack of
interest. In a ninety-minute lesson, three to four different activities

should provide ample variety. Although you may be tempted to stick with an established formula, try new ideas or techniques even if they don't appeal to you at first. I've been surprised so many times by students' loving an activity that I thought they wouldn't take to (because it didn't appeal to me) that I've learned not to rule out anything. Yet, what works for student A may not work for student B, so be flexible. Creative variety can make your students look forward to their lessons and be sorry when they are over.

What about repetition and drills in the private lesson? Some repetition is good for students at all levels as it enables them to imitate the sound system correctly. For a low-level student who might benefit from a thorough textbook lesson, some drilling may be in order. In general, keep both to a minimum. Students can drill and repeat at home if textbook or teacher-made tapes are available. Make your goal the realistic use of English, not manipulation or analysis of it. Japanese students have a tendency to be overly concerned with small grammatical points. The lesson time is too precious for more than an occasional explanation of an important grammar point.

Be conscious of how much you talk and how you use the language. Obviously, the more you talk, the less opportunity the student has. From fear of lessons "dragging," most teachers overtalk. Be a stimulator, get your students to talk, and strike a balance between speaking and listening. As a general rule, be yourself and speak normally. With low-level students you will find a careful choice of sentence structure, vocabulary, and speed imperative for making yourself understood. The language introduced should follow a logical progression from listening to speaking, from simple to complex, and from a low to high level of abstraction. Personal "yes-no" questions can be handled by the most basic of students. More complex "or" questions in which part of the answer is modeled for the student can follow. Still more challenging would be the five "Wh" (Who? When? What? Where? Why?) information questions because the student has to give the whole answer. Finally, opinion-type questions call for original thought and language. These are simple examples of language gradation that a teacher should be conscious of.

Language consciousness is important, but I must caution that there is a fine line between deliberate, simplified speech and "teacher speak." "Teacher speak" might be called a linguistic "disease" that can creep up on teachers in time. It is a manner of "talking down" to a student by speaking abnormally slow, over-pronouncing, and using only vocabulary and syntax that you know from experience the student can understand. When used regularly, "teacher speak" distorts the student's impression of the language and robs him of learning opportunities. This is why many students complain that, while they can understand their English teacher, they can't make sense of anything that is said when they meet a tourist on the street or go abroad. To simplify this complex problem of proper language choice you first need to understand well the student's capability. Then, try to adjust your word choice and usage to a level slightly above his. (But don't be misled by reading ability which is several steps higher than listening/speaking ability.) Doing this challenges the student to reach out in an attempt to understand, thus enabling him to absorb new vocabulary and structures.

Classroom teachers sometimes teach all four skills—listening, speaking, reading, and writing. With few exceptions, private students desire to keep reading and writing to a minimum. Except for low-level students, reading should be used primarily to stimulate spoken language. Writing, such as in a workbook, can be good reinforcement outside of the lesson for younger students. All students should be encouraged to prepare for lessons in advance and to listen to English on their own. To this end, you'll need to give out your materials (including tapes if you make them) a week in advance and be clear about any homework you want done. Don't forget review. Review is often neglected in the teacher's zeal to move ahead. Pedagogically, it is very important.

A serious teacher will keep a notebook for lesson plans and notes on the student. It's extra work, but lesson planning does pay off in better teaching. This is a must for the new teacher. The lesson plan should list overall objectives, the main points to be taught, and detailed information about materials, activities, and procedures. Keep it flexible to allow for deviations that inevitably occur. Don't neglect this universal teaching aid. Rather than going to a lesson with guilt feelings from walking in cold, go with the confidence and security that good lesson planning provides. Students can discern whether you have made thoughtful preparation or whether you're just giving an impromptu performance. For the teacher who can speak Japanese, what about using it during the lesson? I believe that limited use, at the right time and in the right way, is beneficial. A little joking is great for helping the student to relax and maintaining a friendly atmosphere. If a few words of Japanese can clarify a communication block and enhance the flow of English conversation, don't hesitate to use them. Do avoid the tendency to translate every time the student can't understand. Instead, use paraphrases, gestures, synonyms, drawings, or other strategies to get the meaning across. No matter how much of a struggle it may be for both parties, the student should leave the lesson with the satisfaction of having used English at least 90 percent of the time.

Where do private lessons generally take place? Teachers reported they most often taught in their residences and secondly in the pupil's residence. Tea rooms and hotel lobbies are also used—frequently lessons must accommodate two busy schedules. One teacher I know gave lessons in the back seat of a chauffeured limousine driving between Osaka and Nagoya. A certain company president traveled from headquarters in Osaka to the company's branch office in Nagoya at the same time each week. The busy executive wanted to spend those hours brushing up on his English with a native speaker. (The teacher was provided return transportation, of course.) A teacher in Kobe taught a doctor who preferred to practice speaking English while dining and drinking. Every Saturday night the teacher was treated to dinner and drinks at the Kansai area's most expensive restaurants. Teaching privately in Japan certainly has its interesting twists. Usually the teacher's convenience determines where the lesson will be held. Money is also a consideration, since teachers tend to charge more for a lesson away from home.

One often hears about the merits and demerits of various teaching methods. They range from the older audio-lingual method with its drills and pattern practice to the communicative methods that are popular nowadays. I believe most good teachers develop a mixture of techniques from the various methods into what becomes their own personal method. Again, experimentation, refinement, and adaption are the keys to this. If I were asked to recommend the best teaching method for private lessons, I would have to coin a phrase and endorse the "conversational method" because this kind of teaching permits the use of real conversation that supplants the use of a particular method.

I have deliberately avoided recommending specific teaching ideas because the interests and requirements of individual students are bound to be different. When considering ideas to use, bear in mind that the majority of students prefer a happy, non-academic atmosphere. Therefore, if what you do is enjoyable, educational, and gets them talking at the same time, you can't go wrong.

It's a Business

In recent years, Japan has become one of the most popular countries for English-language teachers. There are several reasons for this: an interesting culture, respectful students, modern living, and money. The wonderful experiences the country offers for personal and professional growth far outweigh that of making money. However, notwithstanding the high cost of living, the potential for getting ahead financially as a teacher is not as limited as in one's home country. In fact, teachers surveyed said their primary motivation for taking on private lessons was to make extra money. Moonlighting can easily mean the difference between basic economic survival and a comfortable lifestyle. Income is limited only by a teacher's time and energy—such is the demand for native English teachers. While this demand in the university and language-school sectors has been declining due to teacher influx, the private lesson sector is virtually unaffected. As we have seen, private lessons are not a matter of supply and demand; they are a matter of one teacher being personally introduced to someone who wants private tutoring.

Given the "self-employed" nature of this kind of work, the teacher can dictate how much money he will teach for, who he will teach, and when he will teach. The student, on his part, expects to pay much more for a private lesson than for a group lesson. Teachers generally consider time spent teaching privately to be worth just as much as an equivalent amount of time in the classroom. In other words, an hour of teaching is an hour of teaching—whether the lesson fee comes from one or ten students. This fact may be useful when explaining costs to prospective students.

Lesson fees paid to private lesson teachers range from approximately ¥3,000 (about U.S.$12.00) to ¥10,000 (about U.S.$40.00) per hour, plus transportation. Language schools offering private lessons charge students similarly. Those fees may not be so attractive as they seem. You cannot earn that kind of money eight hours a day. There is a strong demand for teachers from 5 to 9 p.m. when almost all students want to study. Conversely, it's difficult to find private lessons during the day. The average instructor teaches from 2 to 4 hours a day, primarily in the hours mentioned (except high school and university teachers, of course). Traveling time lost affects lesson fees negatively. It is common to spend an hour one way, in crowded commuter trains and buses getting to an outside lesson. Thus, a two-hour lesson becomes four hours out of one's time. Teaching requires preparation time and this is considered in the lesson fee. Finally, any private lesson teacher who is academically trained and/or experienced provides a personalized professional service. All things considered, you'll find a lot of teachers making a good living while at the same time having the free time necessary to study and enjoy the culture. But, I must hasten to add, few of them are getting rich.

Most of us don't mind talking about money to the business manager of a school. But it can be discomforting to broach the subject with that single student who earnestly wants you to teach him, because lesson fees tend to be expensive for most people. It is much easier to discuss payment through a third party, and in the Japanese fashion, this is often done. When discussing fees directly, remember that while Westerners like to get to the point and put money matters first, the Japanese way is to save such uncomfortable topics until the end of a conversation. (In fact, at lesson-fee time, students usually place their payments in an envelope and apologetically set it at the teacher's elbow rather than put money directly into the teacher's hand.)

Teachers base their lesson fees on these considerations: 1) what language schools and colleagues are charging; 2) the financial situation of the student; 3) the time and financial situation of the teacher (busier teachers being more particular); 4) whether it's prime time (5—9 P.M.) or in the daytime; 5) whether the lesson is at the teacher's home or outside (usually 25 to 50 percent more for an outside lesson).

Whether you wish to charge high or low fees, I believe it's sensible to take a businesslike approach. This can eliminate subsequent misunderstandings. For example, put down in writing the terms of the lesson. Be clear about what happens in the case of holidays, cancellations, etc. As all schools do, request payment in advance on a monthly basis. You then gurantee X number of lessons (usually 4) per month. Allowing payment at the end of the month, depending on the number of times a student studied, increases the possibility of cancelled lessons. It is likely that the student will pay less for your lesson than he would at a language school, and save himself the cost of a non-refundable "entrance fee." In addition, your lesson offers the chance for a personal, friendly relationship, unlike the commercial situation in a language school.

Some teachers feel it makes more business and educational sense to teach small groups of 2-3 students. The teacher can earn more than if he were teaching one student, yet at less cost per student. The small group gives shy, low-level students peer support; it also allows students on limited budgets a chance to study. For the teacher, it eliminates some teaching pressure because of pair-work and group dynamics that are missing in the one-on-one situation.

Last, you must know that all who are legally employed are required to pay taxes. English teachers generally pay about 10 percent. Tax payment receipts are necessary for visa extensions. For further advice about how to handle your taxes and other financial matters, it would be best to consult with experienced teachers.

The Problem with Private Lessons

An introduction to private lesson teaching in Japan would be incomplete without discussion of the one serious problem you'll run into—students' giving up on their lessons, often abruptly, before much of anything is accomplished. That private lessons lack a sustaining nature was borne out by the teacher survey. If you have a private that continues for over a year, consider yourself fortunate. Teachers reported that the majority of their students stopped studying after just 4 to 6 months. There are cases where students commit themselves to study for a limited period, such as for one month before a business trip abroad. In general, though, study commitments are open-ended.

Frankly speaking, this quitting problem discourages teachers, causes scheduling problems, and, to be sure, is not conducive to maintaining a steady income. New students eventually turn up to replace those that quit, but knowing that the cycle will most likely repeat can be demoralizing. You may take consolation in knowing that the problem is widespread throughout all areas of teaching. Language schools, for example, usually consider a dropout rate of 50 percent to be normal. That is, in any given language school class, only about half of the originally registered students can be expected to still be attending classes at the end of the term. Moreover, these are students who have paid their term fees in advance. The percentage of all enrolled students that continue for more than one year seems to be correspondingly low. Schools accept the high turnover in enrollment as the nature of the business. This perfectly normal situation, however, acutely affects the private lesson teacher because of the direct, personal relationship.

Why do students quit so easily? The answer is complex. One reason seems to be that too many students study on a whim without considering that learning a language requires considerable effort. After that realization is made, and the student is faced with the two to three years of serious study required for progress, the temptation to give up is great. Unrealistic expectations about what a private lesson can do also leave students discouraged. For others, English conversation is viewed as a hobby, to be dropped as soon as interest wanes. For still another group, I suppose, the novelty of studying with a foreigner is the attraction. Simple curiosity is soon satisfied and apathy sets in. A student that is unhappy with a teacher's methods may find it easier to stop than to express his desires. A problem with children is that they are sometimes dumped off by mothers who are as desperate for a few hours away from their kids as the fathers are to have their children experience a flesh and blood foreigner. One woman who teaches children often has to tell mothers the child is not making progress. They frankly respond that that's not the point; it's important that the child interact with a foreigner. This thinking probably applies to some adult situations as well. To be sure, these types of motivations are not conducive to long-term study.

The fact that the length of study is felt to be open-ended (and therefore not discussed) may be part of the problem. I wonder how many teachers ask their students; "How long do you want to study?" Although you can't expect a student to truthfully answer, "Until I lose interest," raising the issue gives it significance. I know a few teachers, who, having seen many private lessons come and quickly go, treat commitment seriously. These teachers ask the student to promise to study for a minimum period of, say, six months, at which time the student has the option of continuing or stopping. Since you're not a business entity, you can't demand three to six months advance payment as language schools do. Generally, though, Japanese will not break a spoken promise unless it is unavoidable. The intention is to give the teacher an idea of the length of the lesson for professional and personal planning and to try and eliminate abrupt quitting. Quitting is the last thing on a new student's mind; they're positive and exuberant. Broaching the subject can dampen goodwill and cause the student to doubt the teacher's good intentions. Therefore, most teachers avoid the subject and just hope for the best.

Understand that there are students who want and need breaks from time to time. They are unlikely to state such a desire, however. Housewives may not want to study during the busy months of August and December/January. A student may want to stop for two months before a university entrance exam. Talk these things over in the beginning. Don't make the student feel obligated to continue steadily without exception. Actually, this obligation problem is one reason why many students and companies prefer to contract lessons through language schools or agencies. Contracting avoids the issue of an open-ended commitment to one individual, which, in turn, avoids hurting the feelings of that person should the employer suspend or terminate the lessons. I've known cases of company lessons (direct hire) where class size has declined from 20 to just 1 or 2. Out of a feeling of obligation to the teacher, management let the class limp along until the teacher finally left—to the company's relief. Going through a "middle man" (language school or agency) also gives the employer the advantage of working with a variety of teachers, getting rid of a teacher that is not liked, and contracting for a set length of time depending on student demand.

For whatever reasons students stop studying English conversation, the private lesson teacher has to cope with and counteract it on a personal level. Motivation is the key—not only how motivated the students are, but how effectively teachers are able to motivate them to continue. If, through your creativity and earnestness, the student is enjoying himself and has a feeling of progress, chances for a long-lived lesson are good. The only answer to the quitting problem is a preventative one: give 100 percent effort each and every lesson.

Conclusion

As you teach in Japan, you'll gradually learn to evaluate the private lesson field from your own perspective. I've given my views and suggestions in the hope that your start will be a smooth one. Remember that it takes time and patience to be successful here in any endeavor. Learn to appreciate private lessons for what they are: a unique aspect of English-language teaching with separate pedagogical ramifications. This extends to materials selection and the lessons themselves with the emphasis on conversation based on stimulating materials and "realia." Approach your work as a professional educator but with one eye to the business aspects. You want to help students to the best of your ability while providing a secure, livable income for yourself. Appreciate the students that continue your lessons, and don't fret over the ones that stop. Remember, too, that quitting is partially preventable through a proper combination of approach, materials, rapport, and sincere effort. Finally, enjoy it all—the country, the financial and cultural opportunities, your work, and each and every student.

Total Physical Response:
From Simple Actions
to Classroom Drama

Dale T. Griffee

for H.P.

> *The sea is wordless*
> *but it tries to talk to us.*
> *We carpenters are also translators.*
> *We build with sounds, with whispers & with wind.*
> *We try to speak the language of the sea.*

Erica Jong

THIS ARTICLE DESCRIBES a listening technique that could be called learning through action, but in professional language circles today it is referred to as Total Physical Response (TPR). In this article, TPR will be referred to as Listen and Act in order to emphasise the use of this technique as a basis for mini-dramas that any teacher can use in a classroom.

A good context in which to begin is the school environment, by which is meant classrooms and students. Classrooms vary in size. In most commercial language schools they are small, while in colleges or universities they can be big or even cavernous. Classrooms in newly built buildings generally have a smooth and polished look to them, and often have electronic equipment such as tape recorders, videos, and overhead projectors. The older rooms are often bare with a grimy look. There is a prison-like sparseness about them. Most classrooms don't have any pictures, maps, graphs, or decoration on the wall.

In most schools, the administration doesn't seem to give the teachers—especially the native speaker teachers—many guidelines. They escort you to the door, give you a textbook and say *"onegaishimasu."* The textbook can be anything from a new series with lots of color pictures and communicative exercises to a hopelessly out-of-date, repeat-after-me text. The new teachers usually follow the text faithfully for a while (what else can they do?), then gradually become dissatisfied. Then follows a search for the right text, which never seems to end.

What about the students? They tend to be university students of fairly uniform age or young businessmen or women. One senses that their main goal is travel, but some seem to have taken up the English language as a hobby.

Either way, it has always been hard for many teachers to determine correctly the students' motivation or sometimes even their level. Often students give the impression of being at a primitive level only to reveal their sophistication later in the course. Most school administrations either will not or cannot help in evaluation of students. School administrators are native Japanese speakers who communicate with the students in their own language—which gives them few clues as to their ability in English. In general, Japanese are trained to be passive in expressing themselves. This has a certain charm, but it tends to make communication difficult.

In real life, Japanese ride motorcycles, go to discos, climb mountains, play tennis, and chat incessantly in coffee shops. In language classrooms, they sit mutely around a table or in rows, waiting for their teacher to give them some particle of information. And if called upon, even for their opinion, they may reply or they may have a conference before offering a "correct" answer. Thus, most schools form classes made up of passive students at varied levels of English ability.

There are many options a teacher has in this situation. In this article one such option, learning through actions, will be explored.

Acquiring Language: Say It Again, Sam

How do we learn language? How can we teach language? How does action assist both learning and teaching? These are intriguing questions. But I would rephrase the first question, changing *learn* to *acquire*. How do we acquire language? The word *learn* is closely associated with the activity of the rational analytical mode of the brain, for example, sequential, verbal, logical, one-thing-at-a-time thinking (Markley 1982). I would prefer to use the word *acquire,* which is associated with the activity of the visionary, intuitive mode of the brain, for example, spacial, visual, and sensory perception. We *learn* rules, vocabulary, and patterns. Learning is conscious. But the knowledge of a language that enables us to speak is subconscious. It is acquired, not learned (Krashen 1982).

Research over the last several years points increasingly to listening as the key activity in acquiring language (Winitz 1981). Drills and rote memory can actually produce a situation in which the students are speaking but not understanding what they are saying. H. Douglas Brown, in a summary of issues in first-language acquisition, states: "Too many language classes are filled with rote practice that centers on surface forms. If Ausbel is correct in his theory of learning, the frequency of stimuli and the number of times spent practicing a form are not highly important in learning an item. What is important is meaningfulness. Contextualized, appropriate, meaningful communication in the second language seems to be the best possible practice the second-language learner could engage in" (Brown 1980). In other words, we learn (in the sense of acquire) by acting in a meaningful context in which the language input is understandable. Let me give two examples of a meaningful context provided by real life in which language was acquired:

A ten-year-old boy was sitting on the third-base-line bleachers in a baseball park near his home. It was a small ballpark and he had been there many times. Behind the third-base bleachers was a building at which were sold soft drinks, candy bars, and hamburgers. It was the only building behind the third-base bleachers. The Public Address announced that the concession stand was open and was now selling soft drinks, candy bars, and hamburgers. The boy had never before heard the word "concession." He decided it must refer to the building behind him and its activity.

Or take the case of the foreign teacher in Japan who was leaving his school building with several students after his class. It was a very dark night as it had been raining. Instead of walking to the corner and crossing with the light, the teacher and several students ran across the street. One of the young woman students cried out *abunai.*[1] Several years have passed but the teacher still remembers the word, the woman student, the darkness of the night, the cool feeling after the rain.

Do these two stories tend to prove that all vocabulary can be learned by means of meaningful context? In the case of a speaker's native language (L1), I think it does. Karl Diller devised a test to determine an adult native speaker's vocabulary and concluded that by the time we are seven years old our recognition vocabulary is more than 50,000 words. Especially remarkable, Diller noted, was that junior high-school students increased their vocabulary by an average of 75 words per day with no special effort (Diller 1978). All native speakers of any language know thousands of words that they don't remember how, when, or where they learned. Occasionally they used a dictionary, but very occasionally. These thousands of words were learned in context—sometimes by guessing and sometimes through explicit instruction, such as a lecture.

What are the implications for learning a language in a classroom? While it may not be possible to learn all vocabulary items in context, it does seem that the more a teacher can create a meaningful context, the more language will be acquired, simply because we acquire language when a context is created in which we hear and understand.

But what is it we understand? Do we understand rules? words? structures? No. What we understand is the meaning. A context is necessary for acquisition because it is the context that gives us both linguistic help (*abunai, concession*) and extra-linguistic help (the dark night, the building behind the third-base bleachers) which cement and hold the meaning.

This is the role of action in language acquisition and language teaching. Using action is one way for a teacher to create a meaningful context in which students can promote the subconscious acquisition of L2. Action forces students to focus on meaning rather than rules and their use.

From a pedagogical or teaching point of view, there are several contributions actions can make:
1. The students make few, if any, mistakes.
2. Actions focus the attention of the students where it belongs—not on sounds, stress, cadence, or grammar, but on meaning.
3. Often students who can read, write, and even speak English are unable to understand normal spoken English. Listening and acting corrects this situation (Palmer 1925).[2]
4. Actions give the teacher something to talk about. Actions provide

subject matter that is presented to the entire class and that can be observed by everybody.

5. Actions help language comprehension. If the teacher picks up a blue car while at the same time saying, "pick up the blue car," the meaning is clear.

6. Action provides feedback. The teacher does not have to ask if the student understands. The teacher can see.

7. Action helps memory. If you drive a car to a certain place once, you can usually find the place again. This is because your muscles and eyes remind the brain where you turned left and where you did not.

8. Last, actions that would not be interesting when stated in your native language (e.g., go to the person standing by the door and take her to the board) become interesting when they are stated in a foreign language and then understood by the student. And as Asher has noted, almost any school program can produce fluency if the students stay in the program long enough (Asher 1977). The trick is keeping the students interested enough to stay.

Active Listening: See How They Run

Having presented a case for using listening combined with actions, let us examine the technique. Suppose you are teaching low-level students that could be classified as low or false beginners. In other words, your students have studied grammar, they seem to know many words including some rather difficult low-frequency words, and they know some set phrases. But they speak haltingly or not at all. This would be good class to begin with.

On a card that is easy to hold, write some simple actions such as stand up, walk, and sit down. Then add some locations. Your commands might sound like "Walk to the table; pick up a pencil; give the pencil to me; sit down." Now try combining some of the phrases. "Go to the table and pick up the red pencil and then sit down." Short connectives such as "and" or "and then" do not have to be explicitly taught. The sample cards below could be used to elicit actions from a class of false beginners.

The method of using the cards is rather simple. After making out the cards, assemble the necessary props (here you need pencils, a chair, string, a book, money, a box). In class, display the props on a table where they will be visible to all students. Then, reading verbatim from the cards, perform several—never more than three—of the actions commanded. On the sample cards, sequences are headed with instructions to the teacher. After you have repeated the sequence you wish to introduce, ask a student or maybe a group of three students to perform with you as you read the commands and go through the actions again. The other students generally absorb the language material, and you can ask any member of the group to perform the sequence, usually without your assistance. This phenomenon, in fact, is what makes seemingly passive learning possible: the students who watch imagine themselves acting out the same sequence, as they may well be called upon to do. Those students who perform the task have the double reinforcement of observation followed by performance.

Lesson 2 (1)

Teacher: First put several objects on the table, e.g. pencils.

Point to that one.
Now point to that one.
Now point to that (blue) one.

Give me that one.
Now give me that one.
Now give me that one.

Put this one on a chair.
Put this one in front of the door.
Put this one near a window.
Put this one on the board.
Put this one in front of a window.

Teacher: Point to the door, etc.

What's the name of that?
What do you call that?
What's that?
What's the name of that?

Teacher: Hold up a piece of string.

Take this string.
Tie the string around a pencil
OK. Now untie it.

Sample Listen-and-Act Card for Classroom Use (Part 1)

TOTAL PHYSICAL RESPONSE

Lesson   2 (2)
Here, take this string.
Tie the string around your
  book.
Give me the book.

*Teacher: Give the book to
  someone else.*

Here, take this book.
Untie the string.
Give me the string.

*Teacher: Put the string
  somewhere.*

Everyone, close your eyes.
Wait.
Now open your eyes.
Where's the string?
Look for the string.
Find the string.
Give me the string.

*Teacher: Put some money
  on the table.*

Look at the money.
Point to the money.
Point to the (dollar, quarter).
Give me _____.
Put the _____ (here / there).

Pick up all the money.
Put it into the box.
Put the box here.
Thank you.
Sit down.
Open your books to page 15.

Sample Listen-and-Act Card for Classroom Use (Part 2)

Now perhaps you might want to incorporate a classroom task that is real in the sense that it actually needs to be done, for instance, erasing the board. A good rule to follow is that the teacher should never do anything in the classroom that a student can do. The teacher should make every such task a listen-and-act exercise. You could write on your card this series of commands, for instance: "Go to the board. Pick up an eraser and erase the board. Thank you. Now put the eraser on the tray and sit down, please." As before, the teacher should perform all these commands while saying them. Then the teacher can ask a student to perform the commands while the teacher and the student do them together. Finally, the teacher can read the commands, and another student should be able to perform them. If the student has any problem, the teacher should not hesitate to demonstrate again.

Later you can condense this orally to something like "erase the board, please," or "Yumi, would you erase the board?" In the latter case the polite expression *would you* will be acquired unconsciously in the same way as the connectives were acquired—which is a very natural way to learn a language. Now you have several cards ready for class. For reference, let us call these cards "listen-and-act cards." On these cards you have written the basic actions and commands for a given lesson. Here are some rough guidelines for writing your own listen-and-act cards:

I.   First review. Begin with easy material, for example, some actions previously practiced, or a simple exercise.

II.   Next new actions, that is, new vocabulary. Don't forget, the teacher demonstrates all new actions before asking the students to do them. The teacher must think up ways to present both verbs as well as nouns. Usually the more simply they are presented the better. You might collect a bag of props to help you in this phase. Your students will soon become familiar with the names of these props,, so the same props can help you demonstrate new actions. Don't overlook pictures and maps that can be brought into the room or even mounted permanently.

III.   Tasks. In addition to erasing the board, tasks could include moving the tables and chairs to make additional space for your action lessons, folding chairs, dividing students into groups, physical exercises, playing with objects such as coins, and working at the board.

IV.   Long sentences for the conclusion. Several commands can be combined to form one rather long command. It is also possible to create a unique form of a command. For example, if you had students point to their heads and you had them put a book on the table, you can ask them to put a book on their heads. They might be surprised at such an unusual command, but they will be able to understand.

In this way, anywhere from several minutes to an entire class period can be devoted to listening, and a variety of actual tasks can be incorporated into your lesson.

From Actions to Mini-Dramas:
The Play's The Thing.

A mini-drama is a short drama, initially presented in the command form, that includes a story or plot. It is easy to present in a typical classroom setting because it is written for that purpose. Here is a sample mini-drama from my book *Listen and Act:*

2:1 🔲 Scene
Script

1. **This is a cake shop.** You are a customer and you're a clerk.
2. Customer, **open the door to the cake shop, put your head in the door** and ask, "Are you open?"
3. Clerk, look up and say, "Yes."
4. Customer, walk to the show case and look at the cakes. **Point to a cake in the show case** and ask, "What do you call that?"
5. Clerk, look at the cake the customer is pointing to and say, "Banana cream."
6. Customer, point to another cake and ask, "What do you call that?"
7. Clerk, look down at the cake and say, "Strawberry delight."
8. Customer, say, "Give me three cakes please." Then **Point** and say, "I want that one and that one and that one."
9. Clerk, pick up the three cakes, then **put the three cakes into a box,** close the box, and **tie a string around the box.**
10. Customer, **give the clerk some money.**
11. Clerk, take the money and say, "Thank you." Give the box to the customer.
12. Customer, **take the box and walk out of the shop.**

🔲 Listening
Check

Look at the pictures on pages 16 and 17. **Listen. Which picture?**

1. Point to the cakes.
2. Tie a string around the box.
3. Say, "Are you open?"
4. Walk out of the shop.
5. Give the clerk some money.

For Exercises. Use Workbook 2:1

© 1982, Lingual House

There are at least two compelling reasons to expand the use of listen-and-act cards into these more involved mini-dramas. The first is that you will soon run out of classroom-centered actions and tasks. The second is that isolated actions have no continuity and little meaning in and of themselves. To put it another way, you will soon run out of things to do and will get bored. Classroom dramas, or what I am calling mini-dramas, extend the educational value of acting in response to commands by incorporating a story line, and can at the same time provide a bridge to role-playing and unstructured conversations.

Following are some thoughts to be kept in mind when writing a mini-drama:

1. Any situation of interest to the students can be used.
2. The commands constitute the listening aspect, which should be longer than the dialogue aspect.
3. The command form is used throughout.
4. Ideally, for every spoken line there is an action.
5. Mini-dramas can range from very simple to complex in the terms of grammar, vocabulary, actions, or plot.
6. Props found in the classroom can be used, for example, chalk, or a book, or props can be brought into the classroom for use in the mini-dramas, for example, a toy pistol or money.

To present your mini-drama, first use related listen-and-act cards to warm up your class, and to introduce them to some of the actions and objects they will encounter in the mini-drama. It is not necessary, however, to introduce all new vocabulary words. In fact, some items are best introduced in the context of the drama itself. Actions such as ''get in'' are difficult to introduce. What could a student get into? But in a mini-drama, a student can easily get into a car represented by a chair.

Next, gather your props and have the students watch as you demonstrate every role of the mini-drama. A tape is convenient because it not only saves your voice, it also leaves your hands free of the script. After the demonstration, pass out scripts and read together. When you are satisfied, call for some students to come forward. Designate one student to be the ''reader.'' Only that student will have a script. The reader will direct the others both to act and speak. If this goes well, break the entire class into groups and have them perform simultaneously. Have the students rotate within groups so every student does every part, including the reading part. This process can be done in one class period or extended over several periods. If the mini-drama is to be done again in a later class you will not need to repeat this process. The second time, scripts can be quickly passed out: the students will do the performance in a fraction of the time.

Some reflections on the mini-drama are in order. One obvious point is that the mini-drama facilitates small group work in large classes. The mini-drama is one way to utilize every member of the class. A second point concerns teacher dynamics. You, the teacher, will be very busy at the beginning of a mini-drama presentation. Then you will gradually move from the center of the classroom action to the sidelines as you watch your students perform. A third point concerns student dynamics. You will notice the students in a group working together to help each other. The reader will repeat a line several times if necessary, for example. You will not have to instruct the class to do this. By removing yourself to the edge of the action, you allow the students to move to the center and to act as teachers for each other. This can never occur in a traditional classroom, but occurs automatically when students perform mini-dramas.

After your students have completed a mini-drama, you have several options. One is to stop and do something else. Another is class performance. Another is to arrange with a fellow teacher to have his class become an audience for a performance. By this time the reader will not be necessary. The students will be surprised that they have memorized not only the actions, but also each and every word of the dialogue. Yet another option is role-playing.

In role-playing, the teacher gives the students an open-ended situation and asks them to solve a problem. In typical role-playing, for example, student A is assigned to be a waiter and student B is assigned to be a customer. Student B is told he has lost all his money, something he discovers only after he has eaten an expensive meal. Neither the students nor the teacher know what the solution will be. Role playing gives the students a chance to practice a possible real-life situation. Sometimes, this situation is from the student's own point of view and sometimes from a different point of view: for example, the student plays a character different from himself.

Role playing usually consists of three parts: (1) a situation and character assignment and (2) a problem (3) with many possible endings, although society does provide some conventional solutions for common problems.

The purpose of role playing is not to teach or give the students new data. Rather, the purpose is to practice the language ability the students already have even though it many not have been mastered. It forces the students to apply what they know and in some cases to innovate on their feet. One of the issues involved in role playing is student confidence, and this is where the use of mini-dramas can be helpful.

Whereas role playing is unstructured conversation and action, a mini-drama is highly structured conversation and specified action. Therefore, participating in a mini-drama gives the students a framework of confidence and prepares them for the freedom of role playing. If all else fails, the students have at least a minimum of language and action from the mini-drama to get them through the role playing. While some teachers may feel their classes are not ready for unstructured conversation, others find their classes are far enough along in English-language study to benefit from and enjoy this adventure.

To use the mini-drama to set up a role-playing situation, first practice a mini-drama until the students can do it without a reader. The teacher might, at this point, supplement the mini-drama with additional language such as objects to buy, prices, types of hotel rooms, etc. Now, several mini-dramas can be linked. For example, after practicing mini-dramas that involve getting a room in a hotel, buying pastries in a cake shop, and withdrawing money from a bank at which a robbery occurs, students can be requested to do them in a sequence, in other words, one after the other. Or they can be requested to pull aspects of these dramas together in a new form. The instructions might be to arrange for a room in a hotel, then go into the hotel cake shop and buy something. While this is going on the teacher might hand a toy pistol to another student and encourage a robbery, leaving it up to the student whether to steal money or cakes. Another twist is to specify the location. Simply locating the cake shop in Waikiki in Hawaii energizes students. Some may have actually been there, but even if not, all of the students seem to have a very clear image of what Hawaii is like. Finally, the teacher might also stipulate a reason for being there, such as a honeymoon.

In Conclusion: Good News and Bad

1. Students at all levels need listening practice, but it is more important for the lower-level students.
2. Listening can be considered the first step in learning a language. "One canot say what one does not know"(Gary 1978). Listening is the way a language moves from being somewhere out there to being inside our heads.
3. Speaking a foreign language, especially when one doesn't know it well, takes a lot of psychic energy. But listening reduces the energy level required, which reduces tension and anxiety. When tension and anxiety go down, receptivity and enjoyment go up.
4. The teacher has a way of communicating with the students. All classroom instruction can be done in L2.
5. The teacher can speak at a normal rate of speed. You—don't—have—to—speak—like—this. Students listen not to individual words, but to meaning, a skill that is required in the real world. In the sentence "Go to the door," probably most students would hear only the words *go* and *door* on a conscious level. Unconsciously they hear the words *to* and *the*, but they probably hear them together as one unit.
6. The teacher has a strategy for teaching vocabulary in L2. Since many native English speakers are not fluent in Japanese, one of the common problems is how to teach vocabulary. They can try for an approximate word in Japanese, but this is risky business. Usually if they can't explain the meaning, they have to give up and have the students go to their English-Japanese dictionaries. Students learn the meanings of words in many ways, and there is no single best teaching method I know of. Teachers use gestures, pictures, translation, dictionaries, other teachers who are conversant in both languages: in fact, anything that works. But by using an active listening technique, the teacher can introduce not only basic words but also key explanatory words such as the words *same* and *different*. For example, most Japanese students are familiar with the English word *difficult* because it is the accepted translation of the Japanese word *muzukashi*, which is a very common word in the

vocabulary of a Japanese student. But they are usually not familiar with the English word *hard*. One of the common meanings of the word *hard* is "difficult." Having taught the key explanatory words *same* and *different*, the teacher can more easily explain that "hard" means the same as "difficult."

Can everything be taught using listening and acting? Those of us who use the listen-and-act technique are frequently asked how we would teach the meaning of words such as *democracy* and other abstract words. Those who ask this question never explain exactly why they would want to teach these words to a class, especially a low-level class. James Asher, the educational psychologist most associated with learning through actions—he coined the term Total Physical Response or TPR—suggests teaching abstract words by writing the words on cards. The teacher would then give such commands as "Louise, give democracy to Bud; Pauline, pick up justice from the table and give it to Ken." This strikes me as pushing a technique beyond its capability. Asher is more realistic when he cautions against introducing abstract words too early.

The answer is, of course, don't teach abstract words to low-level students. There is no reason to; the teacher would be jumping too far ahead. Before trying to teach abstractions, work on the concrete action verbs and nouns. After learning several hundred basic words, students can be taught the meanings of more abstract vocabulary items by means of these simpler words.

There is, however, another group of words that is difficult to teach using learning through actions. This is the group that is used to indicate personal desires or interior feelings and includes words such as *should*, *like*, and *want*. False beginners usually know the lexical meaning of these words. Their main problem is recognizing such words when they hear them. For these students the teacher does not have to "teach" the words so much as practice them. The words will not be appropriate in the commands you write on your listen-and-act cards. However, they can be used in your mini-dramas because the context will carry the meaning. And for true beginners, you might have to use some of the more traditional methods of conveying meaning—even translation.

Learning through action is a dynamic tool in the hands of a prepared teacher, and mini-dramas extend and amplify that dynamic. But my last words are of caution. No technique, no textbook, can carry you through a class, much less a career. Variety is still the spice of life. Our fate as language teachers is always to be adapting new techniques and to supplement any texts we use, even those we have written ourselves. We are like carpenters, always building. We try the impossible. We try to translate the language of the sea.

Notes

1. *Abunai* is usually translated as "dangerous." In this case, an native English speaker might have said, "Be careful!" or "Watch out!"
2. The first three of these insights come from Palmer (1925), whose contribution to learning through action is generally ignored. This is unfortunate, because his book is the first to treat the subject in a comprehensive manner from a pedagogical point of view, that is, from a viewpoint helpful to a classroom teacher. It is still useful today.

Acknowledgment

Thanks are due to Steve Brown for helpful comments on an earlier draft.

Bibliography

Asher, James F. (1977). *Learning Another Language Through Actions*. Sky Oaks Production, p. 2.

Brown, H. Douglas (1980). *Principles of Language Learning and Teaching*. Englewood Cliffs, N.J.: Prentice-Hall, p. 61.

Diller, Karl Conrad (1978). *The Language Teaching Controversy*. Rowley, Mass: Newbury House, pp. 128-31.

Gary, Judith Olmsted (1978). "Why Speak If You Don't Need To? The case for a listening approach to beginning foreign-language learning." In H. Whitaker, ed., *Perspectives in Neurolinguistic and Psycholinguistic: A Series of Monographs and Treaties*. New York: Academic Press.

Griffee, Dale T. (1981) "A New Look at Total Physical Response." *Cross Currents* 7(2): 43-49.

———(1982). *Listen and Act: Scenes for Language Learning*. Tokyo: Lingual House, p. 18.

Krakowian, Bogdan (1981). "Techniques of Teaching in the 'Pre-speaking' Period." *System* 9(2): 133-39.

Krashen, Stephen D. (1982). "Acquiring a Second Language." *World Language English* 1(2): 97-101.

Markley, O.W. (1982). "Exploring the Future with Both Sides of the Brain." Paper presented at the 4th General Assembly of the World Future Society, Washington, D.C., July 28, 1982.

Palmer, Harold E., and Dorothee Palmer (1925). *English Through Action.* Tokyo: Kaitakusha (1955), pp. 43-44.

Winitz, Harris (1981). "The Comprehension Approach: An Introduction." In H. Winitz, ed., *The Comprehension Approach to Foreign Language Instruction.* Rowley, Mass.: Newbury House, p. ix.

Contest Conversation: A Shortcut to English Fluency in Japan

Richard E. Freeman

Contest Conversation

You are all familiar, no doubt, with speech contests. Have you ever heard of or observed a conversation contest? As far as I know, no such contest exists, at least on an organized basis. The only one I have seen or heard of was conducted informally by me a few years ago in one of my English classes. And it was not carried through to a single winner.

But I am sure you can imagine a conversation contest. The closest thing to it would be a debate with two people. Rather than engaging in a debate, however, the contestants would be having a discussion—an ordinary conversation. There would be one or more judges, and the best speaker would be the winner.

As in debates and speech contests, there would be certain standards for judging, such as content, delivery, and mastery of English. In a conversation contest, the criteria for winning would be mastery of English and conversational ability.

In the classroom, it may or may not be desirable to hold a contest, as such. One reason I did not pursue to completion the contest previously mentioned was the realization that it was of no particular benefit to the class to determine who was the best or worst speaker of English. The purpose of the class was to try to improve the English ability of all the students.

Thus, rather than refer to this classroom activity as a conversation contest, I prefer to reverse the words and call it Contest Conversation. Contest Conversation, then, can be thought of as the classroom practice for a hypothetical conversation contest, or as the classroom counterpart of such a contest. It is my hope that someday there will be conversation contests throughout Japan, to augment speech contests and debates. Then the classroom practice could be for other than a hypothetical contest.

In the meantime, the purpose of Contest Conversation is to provide practice in oral English to improve fluency. This is done, first of all, by teaching students to monitor and correct themselves. They learn this by first learning to monitor and correct their classmates, in the areas of both English and conversational ability.

ConCon in a Nutshell

Briefly stated, Contest Conversation, or ConCon, is a classroom technique that motivates students to speak, teaches them the art of conversation, and instructs them in peer-tutoring and self-monitoring of their English. In as little as nine minutes of class time, it permits all of the students in even large classes to have two guided "free conversations" with two others in a game-like atmosphere.

The class is divided into groups of three, four, or five. The students take turns having a conversation and serving as listener-advisor or "judge." The key to the success of the method lies in the criteria for judging that serve both to guide the judges and to teach the speakers. Moreover, the teacher may add, or substitute, other criteria that he or she may want the students to concentrate on concerning grammar, vocabulary, or any other aspect of English.

The method can be used by either Japanese or native English teachers in almost any sort of English class. The teacher can elect to be merely master of ceremonies and time-keeper, or can circulate among the groups to advise the judges, encourage or correct the speakers, or even grade the students on their performance.

Moreover, the teacher need not change his or her present method of teaching or use any additional teaching material. The only requirement is to provide about nine minutes at the end of the regular class to practice the activity. If even that much time cannot be spared, ConCon can be carried out in six minutes (three two-minute speeches). ConCon can serve as a kind of dessert for the lesson, a verbal reinforcement of the material studied, and provide a motivation for learning more powerful than the desire for a grade.

English Conversation

The first step in introducing Contest Conversation to the students is to make them aware of the dual nature of English conversation: English ability plus conversational ability. They tend to think of it as simply speaking English. We have to remind them that there are even native speakers of the language who have difficulty holding up their end of a conversation.

As a concrete example, I relate an incident that happened to me at the English-speaking church I attend in Tokyo. During the coffee hour afterwards, I happened to be standing next to an Englishman. Unable to think of anything else to say to get the conversation started, I took a sip of coffee and said, "The coffee is tasty, isn't in?" He merely replied, "Yes, it is."

I tried again with an even more inane comment: "Nice day, isn't it?" He merely agreed, "Yes, it is." In desperation I excused myself to say hello to a friend across the room.

When I tell this story, I act it out in front of the room with an imaginary cup of coffee in my hand and an imaginary Englishman beside me. I pretend to be speaking to him, and then I move into his position and pretend he is speaking to me. The students, laugh, of course, and I point out to them that the problem obviously is not a matter of English ability, but of conversational ability.

The Art of Conversation.   The little drama I act out, in fact, unveils two key rules in conversation technique:

1.   Avoid answering only yes or no. Volunteer additional information. The Englishman could have agreed that the coffee was tasty, for example, and then added that he was from England and he preferred tea. This would have opened two avenues for me to pursue the conversation. Even to the question, "Nice, day, isn't it?"

he could have added that the weather forecast was predicting rain, or that it was warmer (or colder) than in England.

2. Avoid inane questions or comments. Give your partner a meaty question. "How do the English make coffee?" would have been better than my question. "How does the weather in London compare to that of Tokyo?" may have inspired more of a response than "Nice day, isn't it?"

The students are quick to grasp these rules, especially the first one. another rule that they immediately take to heart is one I call "Cooperation." This is extremely important in Japan where students in the same class are apt to range in English ability from abject beginner to advanced.

The need for this rule became apparent after listening in on a conversation between two students of disparate English ability. The superior one asked the other, "What kind of music do you like?" Struggling to find words to express himself, the other could say no more than, "I like, uh, I like, uh, uh. . . ." Meantime, the inquirer was tapping his finger in boredom, glancing at his watch, and getting angry at me because I had paired him with someone of such inferior ability.

Instantly, "Helps Partner" became one of the key rules of Contest Conversation. It became the duty of both parties, especially the one of superior ability, to help the other to carry on the conversation. With one stroke this rule solved the problem of differing levels of ability. Instead of being bored, the one of superior ability found himself challenged to find ways to converse with a partner of minimal ability.

Again, I act out scenarios to show them; first, the "horrible example" of the uncooperative partner, as just described and an example of how he could have helped:

Mr. Fluent:	What kind of music do you like?
Mr. Broken:	I like, uh, I like, uh . . .
Mr. Fluent:	Classical music?
Mr. Broken:	No, I like, uh . . .
Mr. Fluent:	Country and western?
Mr. Broken:	No, I like, uh . . .
Mr. Fluent:	Rock and roll?
Mr. Broken:	Yes! I like rock and roll!

The point is that "Mr. Broken" cannot handle the who, what, when, where, why, and how questions too well, but he is able to answer yes or no. So the challenge for "Mr. Fluent" is to create the yes-or-no type questions necessary to extract from "Mr. Broken" such information as he could get from a partner of greater ability with a simple what, why, or how.

Conversation Criteria. In this way, keys to the art of conversation are presented to the students. Altogether five keys are introduced, although each has two or more parts. These are as follows:

1. Initiative. As evidence by the aborted conversation with the Englishman, if no one took the initiative, there would be no conversation at all. Therefore, credit is given to the one who gets the conversation started and tries to keep it going. Most conversations start with a question and the more stimulating the question, the better. But the students are reminded that many conversations begin with a comment or statement, rather than a question. A brief selection makes the point:

> I think I'm coming down with a cold.
> There's a good drama on television tonight.
> I broke up with my girl friend last week.
> I wish I could quit my club.
> You look as if you've seen a ghost.

Such comments, of course, should be of a sort that would elicit a response that could get a conversation going.

2. Response. As mentioned earlier, the students are quick to learn that a simple yes-or-no answer is a demerit. One should give the other party more information than his question requires. Moreover, the information should be as interesting as possible so as to keep the conversation going.

3. Follow-up. This is a response to the response. It mainly indicates that the one who initiated the conversation is really listening, and it is at this point that the importance of listening is stressed. I have a repertoire of imaginary and actual dialogues that I act out to illustrate this point. The following may seem a ridiculous exaggeration, but there will still be students in the class who will not comprehend it:

> Student A: What did you yesterday?
> Student B: I killed my neighbor's cat.
> Student A: Oh. I went to the movies.

Of course, Student A should have responded with an excited "What! When? Where? Why? and How!"

With that introduction, many students will understand the failure of the student in this actual interview to follow up:

> Student: What difficulties have you experienced living in Japan?
>
> Foreigner: Difficulties? I don't have any difficulties. But I used to have many difficulties.
>
> Student: Do you like o-sushi?

4. Cooperation. In addition to helping one's partner, the students must remember that they are involved in a conversational dialogue, not a monologue. they should not monopolize the conversation, even if they should be the better speaker. To do so will earn them demerits, not credits.

It is also well to point out at this point that helping one's partner to say what he's thinking is not limited to classroom situations in which unequals are matched. It takes place everyday in conversations between native speakers of perhaps any language, as in the following example:

> Englishman: Did you see that comedy on TV last night? I forgot the name of it.
>
> American: With Woody Allen?
>
> Englishman: No, with Dustin Hoffman.
>
> American: Do you mean "Midnight Cowboy"?
>
> Englishman: Yes, that's it. What a great film.
>
> American: Do you call that a comedy?

5. Knowledge. In simple conversations in the classroom, knowledge is not of particular significance. Topics of general knowledge are usually discussed. But as the students improve in conversational ability the teacher may assign more difficult topics to be researched at home for discussion at the next meeting of the class. In a reading class, the subject for discussion could be the material in the textbook. The better-prepared student, then, would get more points.

Sometimes, rather than "Knowledge," I call the fifth criterion "Personality" and treat it as a kind of catch-all for such qualities as enthusiasm, show of interest, friendliness, and even wit and humor. Sometimes, as in speech contests, I include manner and bearing. The art of conversation, after all, is truly an art, and as such cannot be categorized precisely. This gives us leeway to define it as we see fit under varying circumstances.

Conversation Summarized. The art of conversation, in essence, is the ability to help get a conversation started and to keep it going. Everything one does to promote this is good and whatever one does to hinder it is bad. To a large extent this can be learned and practiced. The five general aspects of conversation technique can be summarized as follows:

1. Initiative: Gets conversation started with stimulating questions or comments.
2. Response: Answers more than yes or no; volunteers information.
3. Follow-up: Listens well; responds appropriately.
4. Cooperation: Helps partner; does not monopolize conversation.
5. Knowledge: Informative, interested, enthusiastic, personable.

With this list as a guideline, the students learn both to judge their peers and to improve their own conversational techniques.

English Criteria

There are five criteria for evaluation of English ability in Contest Conversation, nicely balancing the five keys to conversation technique. For the most part these are the commonly agreed oral and listening skills, with preference given to those considered suitable for students to judge.

Criterion Number 3, for example, is Pronunciation, but the students are not expected to be able to judge the whole range of English sounds, only the most important ones, and only when they feel competent to do so. It so happens that two or three of the most common English pronunciation difficulties for Japanese are at the same time among the most important sounds in English and the easiest to observe and correct. These are th, f, and v.

These are important for the very reason that they are easy to observe and correct. If one mispronounces th, f, or v, it not only sounds bad, but looks bad. But the very fact that the error is visible means one can correct it by looking in a mirror, for example. And a student judge can presumably see the error even if he cannot hear it.

The five criteria are as follows:

1. Fluency (Speaking smoothly and easily)
2. Grammar (Using correct, not "broken" English)
3. Pronunciation (Especially th, f, and v)
4. Vocabulary (Knowing many words and how to use them)
5. Comprehension (Hearing and understanding ability)

Again it is important to make clear to the students the meaning of some of the criteria. The difference between Fluency and Grammar, for instance, can be demonstrated by speaking fluently an ungrammatical sentence such as "Yesterday I go Yokohama to visit wife's mother on car," in contrast to the grammatically correct but nonfluent "Yesterday I . . . uh . . . I . . . went to Yokohama . . . by car . . . to visit . . . my . . . uh . . . mother-in-law."

Incidentally, it should be remembered that the criteria given here for conversation and English are not immutable. The teacher can feel free to alter them in any way he or she sees fit. The number of items could be reduced, for instance. The English criteria could be limited to Fluency, Grammar, and Prouniciation. Other criteria could be added or substituted, such as Enunciation and Intonation. Grammar could be limited to one particular point, each week, such as noun-verb agreement; Pronunciation could concentrate on "th" until all students mastered it.

Conversation Grouping

Basically, the class is divided into groups of three. In each triad, the students take turns being a speaker and listener. Let's say there is a triad composed of Tom, Dick, and Jane. First, Tom and Dick have a conversation and Jane listens. Then, Jane and Tom have a conversation while Dick listens. Finally, Dick and Jane have a conversation and Tom listens. If we called them A, B, and C, it would look like this:

		Speakers	Listener
1st	Conversation	A & B	C
2nd	,,	C & A	B

3rd	Conversation	B & C	A

You will notice that each member of the triad is a speaker twice and a listener once. If we allow three minutes for each conversation, as I usually do, it means that in ten minutes or less, every student in the class can have two conversations with a different partner. This is regardless of class size.

Of course, the class will not always divide equally into triads. Sometimes there will be one or two students extra. If so, you can make one or two groups of fours. There are two ways to do it.

1. Two and two: Two speakers and two listeners. This is ideal if you want to hold a class conversation contest, in which case you should divide the whole class into quads, rather than triads, as follows:

		Speakers	Judges
1st	Conversation	A & B	C & D
2nd	,,	C & D	A & B
3rd	,,	A & D	B & C
4th	,,	B & C	A & D

Note that each member speaks twice and judges twice, but it requires four conversations. When practicing Contest Conversation with both quads and triads, you may wish to drop the 4th conversation so that the quads will finish at the same time as the triads.

2. Three and one: You might like to try three speakers and one listener. In real life, there are often three people engaged in conversation, so it is good practice. For contests, you may have two judges, making a group of five. Be aware, however, that with three speakers there is a tendency for the participants simply to take turns speaking, as if they are engaged in a mini-speech contest, rather than a conversation. The grouping would be as follows:

		Speakers	Listener
1st	Conversation	A, B & C	D
2nd	,,	D, A & B	C
3rd	,,	C, D & A	B
4th	,,	B, C & D	A

Note that each participant speaks three times and is a listener once.

The Listener. What is the purpose of the listener, you might ask. Why not pair him up with someone so that everyone can have three conversations instead of two.

The listener serves a very important function. Actually, rather than "listener," I prefer to call him an "LAJ" for "Listener-Advisor-Judge." As a listener, he serves to motivate the others to speak. If we simply paired up everyone in the class, we could never be sure that they would speak. With the listener there, they are obliged to speak.

Furthermore, it is the listener's duty to really listen and advise the speakers of any mistakes he notices. Often we don't notice our own mistakes, but others do, or can if they try. The partners in the conversation are too busy talking to worry about each other's mistakes. This is the job of the "Listener-Advisor."

Sometimes, instead of practicing contest conversations, the teacher or students may wish to have a real conversation contest. In that case, the "Listener-Advisor" then becomes a contest judge. Thus we call him an "LAJ," or "Listener-Advisor-Judge."

Incidentally, in a class conversation contest, the ideal number of students would be multiples of eight. In a class of 16, for example, there would be four quads, each of which would choose one winner. The four winners would then have another contest to choose the best speaker in the class. Or the entire class could listen and take part in the final selection, with everyone voting.

In a class of 32, there would be two finalists who could then have a conversation contest with the class as judge.

Advising and Judging. Usually I ask the LAJ simply to monitor the conversations and advise the speakers of any shortcomings he may have noticed: "Dick, your follow-up was not so good. You often changed the subject instead of commenting on what Tom said." "Jane, try to remember to pronounce your "th." (Almost everyone can pronounce the "th" sound. It is more a matter of remembering to do it.)

But sometimes to keep the students on their toes I give the LAJ's a scorecard and ask them to actually rate the speakers. Also, when we have a class contest the LAJ's must really judge the winner.

In those cases, English ability should be rated 5 points and Conversation ability 5 points, for a maximum of 10 points. A zero could be added to put it on a scale of 100. In other words, each of the five skills under English would be worth one point (or 10) and likewise the five skills under Conversation ability.

CONTEST CONVERSATION

Judging is difficult, however, and in a short conversation the LAJ usually has neither the time nor opportunity to evaluate all ten skills. It is helpful if each skills is considered on a scale of 1 to 5, as is usually done in Japanese schools. Thus:

> 5 = Excellent (like a native speaker)
> 4 = Good
> 3 = Average
> 2 = Fair
> 1 = Help!

Sometimes for laughs I include a zero, which I say stands for SOS or the Sound of Silence.

The LAJ tries to judge each skill, but if he does not have time or cannot make a judgment, he should give the person a 3 (for average). With 3 as a starting point, he should add or subtract one or two points, depending on whether he noticed something positive ($+$) or negative ($-$) on the part of the speaker.

Using this system, a scorecard for a conversation between Dick and Jane might look like this:

	Dick	Jane
ENGLISH (25 points)		
1. Fluency	+4	−2
2. Grammar	3	+4
3. Pronunciation	−2	+4
4. Vocabulary	3	3
5. Comprehension	3	+4
CONVERSATION (25 points)		
1. Initiative	++5	−1
2. Response	+4	−2
3. Follow-up	+4	3
4. Cooperation	−2	3
5. Knowledge	−2	−2
Total	32	28

Multiply by two to put it on a scale of 100. Thus, Dick scored 64 and Jane scored 56.

It seems complicated, but if you study it briefly it will be clear and rather simple. Each plus means the judge noticed something favorable and each minus something unfavorable. Starting with a 3 for each skill, he added one for each plus and subtracted one for each minus. Thus he gave Dick a 2 for Pronunciation and Jane a 4. He gave both a 3 for Vocabulary, which means he probably could not judge that category. He gave Dick two pluses for Initiative and Jane two minuses. Thus, he added 2 to 3 for Dick, giving him 5, and subtracted 2 from 3 for Jane, giving her 1.

Of course, such calculating takes extra time, and if it is not available, or the teacher feels that such detailed judging is unnecessary, he or she may ask the students to judge simply by their general impression of the two speakers. I call it intuitive judging. The LAJ should still keep in mind the ten criteria while listening but he need not give points for the individual criteria. He could merely give an overall score, such as 8 points for A and 6 for B, on a scale of 10.

Topics for Discussion. One final matter is how to choose topics for discussion. One good way is to ask the students to list two or three subjects which they would like to discuss. Usually they list such topics as sports, movies, books, hobbies, and music. You can choose one of those and have all the groups discussing the same topic, or you can let the speakers take turns choosing a subject from their own list. Or the teacher can decide the subject. Some good general subjects are:

Your school	People and Machines
Men and Women	People and Nature
Husbands and Wives	A Person and his Friend
Children and Parents	The Young and the Old
Cars and Bicycles	Hot and Cold

As mentioned earlier, as the students improve in their ability to converse, subjects which require study or preparation can be introduced, assigning them for the following week. Or, if it is a reading class, the material covered that day in class could be the topic for discussion.

The Role of the Teacher. You may ask, just what does the teacher do during Contest Conversation? The answer is that the teacher is free to do whatever he or she likes. That is the wonderful thing about it. If he likes, he can merely be timekeeper. He can wander around and listen in on the groups. He can take part as a speaker. He can help the judges. He can even be chief judge and give grades. He can have some of the conversations recorded to be analyzed later in order to teach the entire class the fine points of speaking and judging. He can, if he gets hungry, even go out to lunch. The students will carry on happily without him.

Conclusion

Contest Conversation is a classroom activity that motivates students to speak, teaches them the art of conversation, instructs them in peer-tutoring and self-monitoring of their English, and in as little as nine minutes permits all the students in even large classes to have two guided "free conversations" with two others in a game-like atmosphere.

If Contest Conversation could be instituted in the secondary schools from the time students began studying English, it would have the following advantages as a solution to the English fluency difficulties in Japan:

1. It could be started simply and easily without any fanfare in every classroom in Japan.
2. It would take only five or ten minutes of class time.
3. The teachers would not have to be fluent in English themselves and thus would not have to be sent abroad to improve their English (although this would be good for them, of course).
4. The teachers would not have to change their teaching method. They could continue using the translation method, if they liked, or any other method.
5. We would not have to wait interminably for universities to include hearing and speaking tests in their entrance examinations.

Finally, with all students practicing Contest Conversation for a few minutes a day, this would surely end the phenomenon of Japanese people having to apologize for not being able to speak English after studying it so long. In a very few years, there would not be any students of English in Japan who could not speak English.

Readers in Council:
Letters to the Editor About
English Teaching in Japan

W HILE THE *Japan Times* often carries articles and commentaries on English teaching in Japan, from time to time readers express opinions on this topic in the form of letters to the editor. This selection of letters, begun in February 1983, continued for two months and finally had to be called to a halt by the editor on April 19: "With this letter," he wrote, "we wish to close the correspondence on the subject of teaching English."

When I asked the eighteen writers if I could reprint their pieces, I promised that I would make no comments about individual letters, and let the authors speak for themselves. Some of the contributors, however, speak more from conviction than knowledge or experience. This is not a count against their letters, though, because strong opinions, even incorrect ones, are strong shaping forces in any environment. My advice to readers of this section is that they enjoy the extremes to which some of the letters go, but also that they accept that the strangest of these opinions has its loyal adherents.

Thanks again to the writers for their personal kindness in allowing me to reprint their letters. Two of the contributors could not be reached, so their letters have been summarized. The final letter, though not from the *Japan Times,* also deals with teaching English in Japan—in 1859. We leave it to the reader to decide how much things have changed since then.

Teaching English

To the Editor:

It seems to me that many unqualified *gaijin kyoshi* (foreign teachers) are working for English-conversation schools all over Japan. Some of them aren't even native speakers of English. Obviously, very few of the *gaijin kyoshi* appear to have had special training for teaching English as a foreign language or as a second language (EFL or ESL). The owners of English-conversation schools are apt to hire Caucasians so they can advertise that they have *gaijin kyoshi* — many of them. This is because, in Japanese, the word *"gaijin"* has the same connotations as *"Caucasian."*

As a result, some *gaijin kyoshi* tend to talk too much in class and often ask questions for their own sake without knowing how the students are bored by their stupid inquiries like the following:

"What time did you get up this morning?"

"What did you have for breakfast?"

"Where did you go yesterday?"

"For what?"

"Why?"

This is hardly person-to-person communication. It is far from being real-life communication, at least. Conversation, however, is not merely a technique but human communication. So, even in a free conversation class, questions should be authentic. Otherwise, your classroom dialogue will end up as "pseudo-communication." Students do not like make-believe, playhouse type of questions — even as a means of teaching EFL.

The role of native speakers in a conversation class is, in my belief, to do more listening than speaking. Most of the students are eager to speak in English rather than to listen to their teacher. In other words, they want to see how much they can make themselves understood in English. They want to try out their English with foreigners.

Of course, you may ask whatever you really want to know about the student. But you shouldn't ask what you don't want to know. Your students are aware whether or not you are eager to communicate with them.

I do hope you foreign teachers of English will treat each of your students as a human being and enjoy getting to know them through English.

TSUNEO KIMURA
Tokyo, February 26

*　　*　　*

Having taught English for over two years in America, Taiwan, and Japan, I felt it necessary to respond to Mr. Tsuneo Kimura's letter (Feb. 26) regarding English-conversation teachers in Japan.

Mr. Kimura complains that most of the conversation teachers here have no training in teaching English as a second language and are hired merely because they are Caucasian.

So what? English conversation teachers are not hired to teach English. They are hired to give students the opportunity to put their English to use. It is foolish to think that a trained teacher is any better in this capacity than an untrained one.

In an English-conversation class, the ability to communicate and engage in conversation is more important than the ability to explain the difference between a gerund and a participle. Teachers are hired accordingly. Being a trained teacher does not make one a natural conversationalist. In fact, many trained teachers find teaching grammar much easier than engaging in conversation. Mr. Kimura must learn to separate the two facets of language acquisition.

Mr. Kimura goes on to cite lack of formal training as the reason foreign teachers do most of the talking in class. Any teacher would much rather listen to a student than listen to himself talk about his own trip to Bali eight times a day, six days a week. Unfortunately, most students come to class with absolutely nothing to say.

Teachers try their best to generate conversation by bringing up topics in the news or asking about Japanese customs, institutions, and cultural peculiarities. The students, however, show little interest in these matters or any others. Japanese students in general show a deplorable reluctance to discuss any matter of consequence. They avoid any form of opinion, feeling, or commitment. Given these conversational taboos, the teacher is left with only weather, breakfast, travel, and work as topics.

"This is far from person-to-person communication." True. But whose fault is that? Mr. Kimura ignores the fact that it takes two people to have a conversation. The student always has the option of changing the topic if he finds the teacher's boring or trite. Regrettably, most Japanese students go into class with an "Entertain me!" attitude.

This attitude is further enhanced by the Japanese school owners and staff, who lead the students to believe that just by sitting in a room for 40 to 50 minutes with a *"gaijin"* they will be able to develop some sort of fluency as if by osmosis.

Most of these students do no studying or preparation outside of class. Like an English textbook gathering dust on the shelf, coming to class without making the slightest attempt to say anything is a waste. Like texts, conversation classes are mere tools. It is up to the student to use them wisely. If the student is not prepared to use this resource, then he'd be better off spending his money at the local "snack."

Contrary to Mr. Kimura's contention, most teachers are interested in their students. Most of the teachers are here because they are interested in Japan, and that includes its people. Regrettably, many students have no interest in conversing with their teachers. Mr. Kimura and others who share his view had better realize that if they themselves have nothing interesting to say, they doom themselves to listening to things in which they are not interested. Before you can reap a harvest, you must first sow the seed.

RICKFORD GRANT
Osaka, March 12

*   *   *

Mr. Kimura accurately points out that not many *gaijin kyoshi* in language schools in Japan have had special training in the teaching of English as a second language. He goes on to say that, as a consequence, language classes can become mind-numbingly dull, as the questions asked of the students by the teacher revolve round such mundane areas as waking-up times, breakfast foods, and the like. Mr. Kimura suggests [that] for real communication to take place there has to be greater authenticity in the language used by teacher and students alike.

He states a problem, in fact, which has been brought up countless times in these columns and elsewhere—how can the teacher's desire to foster genuine communication in the classroom (and this in not a factor depending solely on "training") be combined with the basic ingredients for language learning which the students themselves bring to the classroom (motivation, a sound fundamental knowledge, a willingness to experiment with the language, etc.) to produce a coalescence in harmonious discourse in the classroom, and, ultimately, outside in the real world?

One possible feature of this problem, and I only add this to the pile of similar theories propounded over the course of time, is that both students and teacher are unaware, in their own separate ways, of what "communication" actually means to the other. The word has, after all, become a rather glib catchall in recent years, a convenient umbrella term which covers almost any kind of involvement between two or more human beings; almost synonymous at times with the Japanese term *haragei,* where language as such can be more of a hindrance than a help.

Would it perhaps not be easier for all concerned to return to the teaching/learning of the arts of conversation—without the superficial attraction of "communication" but certainly more identifiable? Would Mr. Kimura and others faced with the same problem accept that communication, whatever that might actually be, follows as a consequence of successful *conversation* and that for a conversation to be successful, certain linguistic and social skills have to be learned and practiced and that these skills are classifiable, at least up to a point that "communication" is not?

To say that teaching people to converse is easier than teaching people to communicate is putting it too simply perhaps, but it takes some of the quasi-psycho-humanist mumbo-jumbo out of what should be the relatively straightfoward business of encouraging speech between people of differing linguistic and cultural backgrounds. Bring back conversation! Leave communication to group therapy, where it belongs!

JAMES DUKE
Tokyo, March 12

[Mr. Shintaro Saito of Tokyo, who contributed a letter printed on March 24, could not be contacted to request permission to reprint. A summary of his 200-word letter follows.]

Mr. Saito comments that the responses to Mr. Kimura's letter place blame for poor pronunication upon the teachers. Saito believes that native Japanese can never achieve "an American accent." Japanese learners need not worry, however: "I was told by Professor Hutton of Trinity College in England and Professor Schlesinger in the U.S. that I should always try to assert my individuality and never imitate another nationality." Furthermore, "both professors added that my physical constitution is different from that of Occidentals and that when I try to imitate their intonation it looks and sounds very funny, no matter how correct I am."

Teachers should not ask Japanese students to imitate their own speech patterns. Saito knows "many foreigners who speak fluent Japanese," but when he challenges their intonation they force him to admit that he heard and understood all they said.

*   *   *

English teachers nationwide must be all eyes over the latest epistolary donnybrook ignited by Mr. Kimura and taken up by Mr. Grant. This reader couldn't resist adding his ¥20, jumping into the fray.

To begin with, much of Mr. Kimura's argument is, indeed, as Mr. Grant implies, fatuous, simply stating the question in a one-sided way. Unfortunately, Mr. Grant weakens his otherwise articulate and well-written riposte with a glittering generalization like "Japanese students show a deplorable reluctance to discuss. . . ."

Still, having taught for 14 years (three of which were spent here), I have found many Japanese students alive, sincerely interested, and intent on making a significant contribution to most any class I have taught.

Nonetheless, this doesn't negate the merits of Mr. Grant's observations. Truly, many Japanese choose to be inert, uninvolved, demonstrating a "laid back" attitude toward class participation. Many contribute next to nothing. And most don't study.

But this doesn't mean the teacher need not, as Mr. Grant suggests, possess academic credentials proper for or relating to teaching. If such is the case then might we not ask the ineluctable and intriguing question: Why couldn't *any* marginally educated Caucasian (check the unemployment rolls back home, Mr. Grant, you'll find many) teach English, while at the same time being unable to correct infelicities of grammar, pronunciation, etc., *as these arise in class?* Many will not because many cannot.

Why is this so? What is the answer? Or maybe, as Gertrude Stein is supposed to have said—what is the question? Why does this situation prevail? Let me attempt one guess. Could it be that the language schools (agencies) who hire unqualified "teachers" do so for simple pecuniary reasons? Could it be that it's far more expedient to hire those who are willing to work for a minimum wage, those who couldn't otherwise be so engaged at more reputable institutions, thus creating a substratum in an otherwise honorable profession, detracting from the job many of us here are trying to do? Dare one even ask it?

This seems to be part of the question that the two extreme positions fail to address.

DAVID WEINBERG
Tokyo, March 24

*   *   *

Does Tsuneo Kimura realize how much a foreigner is paid for a lesson?

A foreigner told me that he was hired by a conversation school with an internationally well-known name, and this school gets ¥7,000 from a student for a lesson, whereas a foreign teacher gets only ¥1,200 [of that] from the school. How can a qualified teacher accept such unreasonable terms?

I must say that both teachers and students are the victims of a big business named education.

TAKAHIRO ISHIGOOKA
Tokyo, March 24

*   *   *

This is in response to Mr. Rickford Grant's letter (March 14) regarding the role of English-conversation teachers in Japan, and Mr. James Duke's letter (March 14) suggesting "the teaching of the arts of conversation."

Mr. Grant complains that Japanese students in general are reluctant to discuss any matter of consequence, and that most students do no studying or preparation outside of class.

A teacher should encourage the students to speak out in a foreign language by choosing appropriate and relevant topics to discuss in class, and giving feasible assignments so that the students can prepare at home.

That's why the English-conversation teachers should have qualifications for teaching English, at least a B.A. Teaching English as a foreign language. TEFL is a highly technical strategy requiring linguistic and cultural backgrounds of the target language as well as the linguistic and cultural backgrounds of the students. Just sitting and conversing with the students in class is not adquate.

Mr. Grant asserts that "English-conversation teachers are not hired to teach English." Teaching English conversation, however, is an integral part of TEFL. I disagree with Mr. Grant's idea of a trained teacher. Being a trained TEFL teacher does not mean that he/she has "the ability to explain the difference between a gerund and a participle." Teaching grammar is not required of foreign teachers because it is the domain of Japanese teachers who mostly know it much better than native speakers of English.

Mr. Duke suggests that we should "bring back conversation" rather than stick to the "superficial attraction of *communication.*" Communication, however, involves verbal and non-verbal communications. Verbal communication is divided into oral and written phases. Conversation being only part of oral communication, it should be taught in this context. Teaching the "arts of conversation," which Mr. Duke suggests, is not sufficient for teaching conversation in TEFL. TEFL teachers should zero in on teaching English as a means of communication for international understanding.

TSUNEO KIMURA
Tokyo, March 26

*   *   *

As a foreign language teacher, I would like to give my full support to Mr. Grant's letter of March 14 on the subject of "teaching English" in Japan.

I do agree with Mr. Grant that Japanese students come to class with an "Entertain me!" attitude and that they "show a deplorable reluctance to discuss any matter of consequence." I honestly believe that even Shakespeare would be a failure as an English teacher in Japan due to the poor attitude of the students who, as Mr. Grant says in his letter, "do no studying or preparation outside of class."

Taking this into consideration, it really does not matter if the conversation is about breakfast or any other trivial topic. The background of Japanese students on themes such as religion, politics, sex, or any other common subject is so shallow that it would be madness to ask for their opinion on such topics in a foreign tongue.

Learning a second language is difficult and it is even more difficult when the students believe that the teacher will make them speak the language. The teacher's role is to guide the student and the rest of the job is up to the student who has to work harder.

I have had private students for free conversation classes who constantly came to me with nothing to say. It is ridiculous! I do agree with Mr. Kimura that many teachers are not qualified, but at the same time, the caliber of most students is so poor that it would be a waste to give them an excellent teacher.

I give you an "A" for your letter, Mr. Grant!

LUIS CANALES
Kyoto, March 26

*　　　*　　　*

I think Mr. Shintaro Saito's letter (March 24) opened many English learners' eyes and surely encouraged them. I myself am one such earnest student whose chief worry is why our pronunciation and accent cannot be as good as those of native speakers despite constant effort. Mr. Saito confirmed a well-known fact, referring to the difference in physical constitution between Occidentals and Japanese, that we cannot perfectly imitate the speech of native English speakers.

The opinions of two native-speaker professors, as Mr. Saito quoted in his letter, that non-native English speakers should rather assert their individuality in their English speaking, is a thought shared by Professor Suzuki of Keio University who has long advocated "Englec." As long as

English is the international language most widely used the world over, there surely exist variants, and such variety rather attaches a "taste" to communication through the language. Imagine what it would be like if every representative spoke perfect American or British English at the United Nations. It certainly would bore the audience.

So, I believe the most important thing in studying English, for students and teachers alike, is an honest aspiration to communicate with other nationals and make friends with them by understanding their cultures. With such a pure desire, minor defects in pronunication or accent would not be an obstacle in communication. On the contrary, if English learners lack this attitude, they will come across as hollow and unappealing however fluently they may speak like a native speaker.

A reader also suggested in this column that the age limit for studying English be lowered to the fourth grade or so. But, I fear this involves the danger of losing a "Japanese" personality. Without first well learning one's own language, traditions, and culture, a man can never be a good English speaker in the international arena because people will naturally expect him to speak of things Japanese.

TAKAHITO MIYAZAWA
Odawara, Kanagawa, April 4

*　　　　*　　　　*

Now you have done it. I read Mr. Kimura's letter (Feb. 26) and had some views at the time, but didn't think them important enough to advance. However, we now have on March 24 the opinions of Mr. Saito, Mr. Weinberg, and Mr. Ishigooka, and I now feel the subject is begging for my opinion.

I started the business of teaching English in Vietnam in 1964 because someone had to make it possible for us to communicate with the people, and it didn't require a college degree to teach someone to say "This is a hammer." The problem then, as now, was the American who couldn't or wouldn't learn the Vietnamese language.

It was at this time in my life that I experienced the joy associated with teaching anything that was well-received by students. While teaching English to crafts and trades workers I found that most of them could not read or write their own language, and here I was about to teach them a new one. Fortunately, I could teach them both languages at the same time. I taught them to read and write things like "Where is the hammer?" in two languages, and I never had better students to work with.

Teaching in Japan off and on since 1977 has not been as thrilling an experience, but it is still somewhat of a satisfying thing to hear a Japanese say "Thank you very much" in English no matter what kind of accent they may have picked up from a former teacher. Mr. Saito, just be yourself. I have Japanese friends with Cambridge accents and to me it really sounds funny, but I understand what they are saying. I can't always say the same for some Americans and other Westerners I listen to from time to time.

Mr. Weinberg, your credentials are showing. Granted, people who study the language should get what they are paying for, but a simple conversation course doesn't tax the three college degrees I hold. In fact, big words used by a dummy are still just big words, and a dummy is still a dummy. The key to teaching English isn't a college degree, unless the learner must pursue the study under formal circumstances.

I don't know as much as Mr. Ishigooka does, such as who pays what or who gets paid. I do know there are many levels of language that need teaching for many reasons. Some time ago a Japanese lady, who came to me for enough instruction so she could travel outside of Japan, came back from her trip saying: "I wasn't afraid. I could actually order a meal and ask a question that I could get an answer to that I understood."

While the *Japan Times* may continue to publish articles on this subject, and it is important to do so if only to get teachers to deliver just what has been paid for by a person, and for students to stop wasting their money, I believe we need to cut off the self-centered, self-important tutor at the pass. We need to recognize that there are as many communication needs satisfied as there are people who try to help another person to learn to express himself or herself and to learn to undestand others.

Peace to you no matter what your mother tongue happens to be.

FRANK L. KAHREN
Iwakuni, Yamaguchi, April 4

*   *   *

I myself was once a student of English and am now a teacher of the subject, and I felt a little disgust after reading the comment by Luis Canales (March 26).

First of all, foreign teachers are not aware of the Japanese mentality of "not hurting the other person's feelings face to face." I have lived overseas for quite a long time and feel that you foreigners go to extraordinary lengths in insisting on your own opinion in any trifling matter, not to mention politics, religion, sex, etc. Often you will not even listen to others.

In conversation class, English-speaking teachers are apt to correct the way of thinking, not speaking, of the students or, in short, to insist on their own opinions, which might have derived from your national trait of saying clearly "yes" or "no." This attitude of correction is the best way to discourage students from speaking. Students generally do not like to argue with their foreign teachers.

Secondly, if somebody can discuss freely and deeply on any subject in a foreign language, the person does not need to be your student anymore. For Japanese, it is far more difficult to think in English that for you English speakers to think in other European languages. I wonder if you know of the difference and difficulties of the Japanese language.

Please do not forget that when somebody speaks a foreign language imperfectly, he looks silly. The same thing would happen to you, Luis Canales, if you were a student attending a Japanese course. Be careful that your unqualified Japanese teacher does not say, "It is a waste to give them an excellent teacher!!"

Very luckily I always had excellent professors in my college days and had active English conversation classes.

KATSUKO HIRUMA
Tokyo, April 4

*   *   *

The difficulty in teaching English in Japan arises when the teacher begins to realize that *many* Japanese students are like people who practice Zen, i.e., they are passive, reticent, uninvolved, etc. If this problem were restricted to only isolated cases, the fervent arguments between Mr. Kimura and other readers would never have been worth the attention they are now receiving.

Although most contributors are fully aware of this negative attitude Japanese take toward language learning, they still seem to be unwilling or unable to *start* their teaching with this reality in mind and design their lessons accordingly. If the student is not able to form or express his opinions on a "common" topic, it is the teacher who should revise his teaching methods or materials in such a way that the learner can have enough time to think it over and enough materials to work on.

In order to achieve the ultimate goal of mutual understanding through the use of language, Occidentals seem to employ the speak-as-much-as-possible strategy, while Japanese tend to use quite the opposite approach. Learning to speak English, therefore, demands on the part of Japanese, fundamental changes in their attitudes toward the functions and roles of language and consequently in their learning habits.

If the foreign teacher treats the Japanese student as though he were one of his own kind, in every aspect, and sticks to the teaching methods he used in other countries, he is bound to be left with impressions such as "Japanese students in general show a deplorable reluctance to discuss any matter of consequence," as Mr. Grant apparently is.

I believe that one of the important qualities for being a good TEFL (teaching English as a foreign language) teacher is an ability to analyze the student's linguistic and psychological problems related to language learning and an ability to devise some way to solve them. In this respect, a trained teacher is at least much better equipped with the knowledge necessary for this task.

Mr. Canales said that "even Shakespeare would be a failure as an English teacher in Japan due to the poor attitude of the students." Of course, Shakespeare would be a failure if he lacked sufficient knowledge of how to teach English as a foreign language and were unable to deal successfully with any problems arising from the student.

This clearly indicates that a native speaker of English, however excellent his English may be, cannot immediately be said to be a good TEFL teacher—even Shakespeare. Another job a TEFL teacher has, besides teaching English and analyzing the student's problems, is to help the student form good learning habits.

All these tasks are formidably difficult even for trained teachers, and probably too much for untrained teachers.

HISAO NISHIJIMA
Kobe, April 5

I was quite as upset at Ms. Hiruma's letter as she was "disgusted" by Mr. Canales'. The belief that "you foreigners" are insensitive, while "we Japanese" have a "mentality of not hurting the other person's feelings face to face" which she holds is, of course, nothing new. Well-known Japanese academics such as Yuji Aida and Takeo Doi, among others, hold the same condescending view toward Westerners.

Yet, offering one's own opinion, or even arguing with someone, need not be proof of insensitivity. Rather, if Mr. Canales or, say, any American were to expect you to play his game and argue good-naturedly, your not doing so would show your insensitivity to his wishes.

It is also sheer nonsense to claim that one must be already fluent to engage in lively discussions. I once taught English to a large group of middle-level executives whose English was mediocre to say the least, but our conversations were much more stimulating than in the case of a number of equally or more fluent students I have had in Japan. Mr. Canales' observation that conversation is a two-way street was right on target. Like quarreling, it does take two sides to converse.

Now, in respect to Mr. Miyazawa's letter about pronunciation problems. He states that "Mr. Saito confirmed a well-known fact, referring to the difference in physical constitution between Occidentals and Japanese, that we cannot perfectly imitate the speech of native English speakers." Since second-generation Japanese Americans have no such difficulties, this difference is obviously an acquired one. Once one has pigeon-holed the entire world of sound into some 50-odd phonemes as young Japanese are taught to do, not only English pronunciation but even the imitation of various sounds of nature is restricted.

Be that as it may, accent itself is certainly nothing to worry about. The problem, if there be one, is needless concern about accent either way. It is as silly to work at developing a Japanese style of English to better assert one's "Japaneseness" as it is to go to the other extreme of striving vainly for the perfect accent.

It is interesting that women, who tend to be less hungup on their Japaneseness and asserting themselves, tend to be better at language acquisition than their male counterparts. Could it be that the biggest obstacle to English learning (following the education system itself) is that Japanese, while admittedly not eager to assert themselves aloud, actually house extraordinarily large egos which make it difficult to let go and absorb a foreign language on its own terms?

ROBIN GILL
Tokyo, April 15

*   *   *

After reading Shintaro Saito's letter (March 24) and then reading Takahito Miyazawa's supporting letter (April 4), I felt I had to write lest anyone should have taken them seriously.

The idea that native speakers have exclusive rights to native accents is completely fallacious. As an English teacher in Japan, I have enough difficulty as things are trying to improve the pronunciation of students' English without "Readers in Council" contributors offering excuses such as physical constitution. There are too many Mongoloid native English speakers for Mr. Saito's ideas to be valid.

While a student making a minor grammatical error in English is usually corrected by his Japanese teacher, one who pronounces a word with a foreign accent is not; teachers have to let the mistake pass, since they are often unable to pronounce the word correctly themselves. By the time most students get to us it is too late: they already have their non-native accents. If languages were taught with meaningful goals in mind, and if the teaching of them were begun early enough by people with native accents, then there is no reason why even Orientals should not acquire native accents.

Admittedly, under the present system, not everyone can learn to speak with a native accent, but to give in before you start, as Messrs. Saito and Miyazawa suggest, is not a healthy attitude in language learning.

M. WYATT
Nagoya, April 18

*   *   *

"Technically unqualified teachers of English conversation are incompetent; students of English conversation are shiftless drones." It is amusing how the debate over these ridiculous generalizations eventually led to the letter of Katsuko Hiruma (April 4).

It should stand to reason that certainly both stereotypes exist. In my experience, both boorish teachers and cloddish pupils seem to infect the field minimally; boors (with or without qualifications) and clods infect *any* field. Of course, any generalizations based on this maxim are treated as frivolous by the thinking reader. One would have expected, therefore, that the well-traveled, fluent Ms. Hiruma would not have felt it necessary to resort to pathetic racist comments.

We have all heard before the quaint assertion that Nihongo's qualitative "uniqueness" makes the learning of another language difficult. It is a surprise, however, to read the accusation that foreigners, as a species, tactlessly force opinions, dominate students, and remain unable to fathom the Japanese mind.

By "foreigner," is Ms. Hiruma referring to the blonde and blue-eyed, helplessly silly gaijins like us in Japan, or has travel abroad allowed her to expand the term to its dictionary sense, meaning the utter whole of the non-Japanese segment of the human race?

Unfortunately, some people *do* embrace stereotypes. I feel embarrassed for my Japanese friends who may be mistakenly included in the stereotype that Ms. Hiruma so eagerly embodies.

ADAIR MEEHAN
Susono, Shizuoka, April 18

*   *   *

I have read other readers' opinions and comments with great interest concerning the teaching and learning of English in Japan. All the letters, I am sure, have been written with a sense of conviction and are meant to address various problems thought to exist. At times I have found myself nodding in agreement or chuckling a bit about certain points.

However, I found myself irate with what I feel is racist commentary by Takahito Miyazawa. The first point about pronunciation is somewhat naive, I think. Does Mr. Miyazawa really think the slight differences in the human anatomy reach as far as pronunication? Why, then, do some of my Japanese friends who have grown up in Great Britain or the United States, speak with "perfect" accents? By "perfect" I mean that were we only to listen to the pronunciation of one of these persons, we would determine his or her articulation to be that of a native speaker of English.

His comment is, at best, misguided. But the item which really hit me was Mr. Miyazawa's fear of "losing a 'Japanese' personality" if English is studied at too young an age. Further, he implies that students in the fourth grade have not sufficiently learned their own Japanese language, culture, and traditions well enough to separate them and keep them distinct from the English language and Western customs and cultures.

Such a limited and narrow view smacks of racism. It seems unnecessarily protectionist, almost culturally paranoiac. It also reinforces something I have suspected from time to time with some of my students in the past three and a half years in Japan—namely, that some Japanese put up psychological blocks to foreign language learning because they feel it is dangerous to their very "Japaneseness." It does not take an educator with any number of degrees to determine that resistance to learning will impede the gaining and retention of knowledge itself.

I do not, for a moment, feel that language and culture are inseparable. Nor do I wish to tell Japanese people when their children should begin to study English.

What I do wish to say is that communication between human beings is essential and that efforts to bridge cultural and linguistic gaps created by differences are a recognition of that necessity. I applaud Mr. Miyazawa's noble belief that the most important thing in studying English "is an honest aspiration to communicate" with people from other lands with different cultural and linguistic heritages and to "make friends with them by understanding their cultures."

However, I must vigorously protest his racist comments which imply that our bodies are so different as to prevent perfect pronunciation in languages which are foreign to us and our parents.

R. J. FENSTERMAKER
Tokyo, April 18

*   *   *

Much has been discussed in this column about teaching English here as a foreign language. As a teacher of English at a senior high school, I would like to say something about this subject.

First, three English lessons per week at junior high schools is by no means enough for the students to acquire basic knowledge of and skills in using English. A language is something to be mastered by constant practice. In the prewar days, middle school boys and girls got one or more lessons in English every day. Today, I fear, students forget more than they learn. In studying English, more lessons will result in better proficiency on the part of students.

Second, English conversation should be encouraged more because it is natural for hearing and speaking to go before the other two skills in using a language—reading and writing. The fact, however, is that grammar and translation play the most important role in English classes because English is taught as one of the key subjects for entrance exams.

Students read aloud individually or in chorus in English classes, but there seems to be little time for them to talk to their teachers in English about topics of deep interest to them. This makes English a difficult or boring subject. Asked, "Why do you learn English?" almost every student answers, "I want to make myself understood in English."

Third, few government-approved textbooks of English conversation have been used at senior high schools because oral tests are not given in entrance exams though colloquial English has been increasingly employed in written exams. In this way, everything seems to be centered around passing admission tests. Colleges and universities should examine applicants orally as much as possible. More conversation books should be used in teaching English to at least those who go into business after graduation.

Last, every junior high student has the right to learn English. I think English should be a required subject, not an elective. English is the global language of today and nobody knows whether a junior high student has linguistic abilities until he or she comes to grips with English.

TAKAMASA ARAI
Tomioka, Gunma, April 18

*   *   *

Based on my ten years of experience trying to help Japanese students learn English, I would like to add my comments to the controversy raging in this column about teaching / learning English in conversation classes in Japan.

As in most controversies, I think that in this discussion both sides are mostly right but partly mistaken. I think the two different points of view result from the different assumptions of the Japanese students and foreign teachers as to what can or should take place in a language class.

The students, after having twelve years of institutionalized passiveness instilled in them by the Japanese education system, too often come to class with a "teach me" attitude. They do not seem to understand that unlike their other subjects, language is a *skill* which can only be acquired through *active practice.*

Too many foreign teachers, on the other hand, come to class without an adequate understanding of the feelings and communication patterns of their Japanese students, so they do not understand that the problem their students face is not only the problem of learning a new *language* but is also the problem of learning entirely new *behaviors* which may not even exist in their repertoire of Japanese cultural behaviors.

Unfortunately, one of these which the Japanese have never learned is how to carry on a conversation with a stranger *in their own language,* and it is unreasonable for them to expect that they will learn (or that they can be taught) to do this in English when they cannot even do this in Japanese. That is, they must first learn to "communicate with strangers" before they can ever hope to "speak to foreigners" in English.

The fact is that if you want to learn a foreign language, there are only two things that you need a native speaker/informant for. First, you need someone to correct your mistakes, and, second, you need someone to answer your questions. Unfortunately, it is precisely these two things that Japanese students avoid, which is one reason Japanese are such poor foreign-language learners.

Finally, as for the question of whether a degree is necessary to be a good language teacher: certainly a degree is not necessary to teach the typical Japanese conversation class, but a degree is useful for a teacher who must evaluate and design texts and curricula in order to meet the particular needs of the students.

As for myself, if I ever decide to study another foreign language (my fourth), you won't see me in a "foreign language class." The idea that attending a language class with other non-native speakers of the language is both a necessary and sufficient way to learn a foreign language is a myth that is propagated by the language schools, and accepted by both teachers and students alike. I know that there are other more efficient ways to learn to use a foreign language, and I would take advantage of them.

RICHARD SHOWSTACK
Tokyo, April 19

[Mr. Horst Ullmann of Tokyo, who contributed a letter on April 19, could not be contacted to request permission to reprint. A summary of his 420-word letter follows.]

Mr. Ullmann, having viewed the World War II television mini-series "The Winds of War," recalls his Prussian grandfather, whose firm belief in German racial superiority had led the grandfather to support Hitler and serve in the German army. The grandfather asserted that Poles "were biologically incapable of speaking proper German," and that the Americans who occupied post-war Germany were not "cultural equals" with Germans. Although teaching Latin to children was acceptable, the grandfather viewed fluency in foreign languages "as the mark of waiters and unpatriotic intellectuals."

His grandfather's concern with linguistic purity, Ullmann feels, masked a deeper concern for racial purity. The grandfather's arguments, however, "would hardly compare with the deft manipulation of the language question here in Japan. Unlike their older German colleagues, the *daisenseis* of language and ethnicity here are most careful to avoid the slightest appearance of arrogant superiority. On the contrary, they season their pseudo-scientific soup with tears of humility and regret for the sad (but unique) linguistic fate of *'wareware Nipponjin.'* "

Among the arguments of Japanese scholars, Ullmann calls attention to Mr. T. Miyazawa's assertion of "the 'well-known fact' that Japanese are incapable of acquiring perfect English pronunication due to 'the differences in physical constitution between Occidentals and Japanese.' " Ullmann particularly questions Miyazawa's belief that "Japan's most internationally effective English speakers are those who have a true 'Japanese personality,' one which has not been adversely affected by exposure to English at a tender age." This argument makes Ullmann feel, sadly, that his grandfather's racism and Miyazawa's call for "ideal English learners, patriots cum *kokusaijin*," share disturbing resemblances.

*　　　*　　　*

Teaching English to the Japanese—in 1859

While reading about Japan in old American magazines, I came upon a letter concerning the efforts of an early American visitor to Japan who started an impromptu English school in Nagasaki. Considering the delays in communication in those days, the letter may have been written more than a year before it was reprinted in The Living Age *for September 3, 1859. Bravo to both teacher and students!*

Teaching English to the Japanese

An *attache* to the U.S. ship Powhattan (probably the chaplain) communicates to the New York *Journal of Commerce* a very interesting account of his labors in imparting a knowledge of the English language to a number of Japanese interpreters. The task was undertaken at Nagasaki, at the request of the Japanese Governor. A room was provided on shore, and our countryman had the honor of opening the first English school in Japan. In honor of his Alma Mater, he called it *Dartmouth College, Jr.* The pupils were nine young men, from eighteen to twenty-five years of age, all of manly form, but not tall, and excepting two, rather slender. Belonging to the higher class of Japanese society, they were dressed in handsome style for the country, wearing the loose under-garments of the East, with a silk or silk and cotton gown over the whole. Their stockings were of cloth; their shoes were of braided grass, covered with blue and finely colored, and were always left at the door. Their hair was shaved from the front part of the head, and the rest formed into a queue on the top, projecting forward and resembling a little pistol. Like all Japanese, they wore no hats, however hot the sun.

The young interpreters were remarkable for uniform politeness to their teacher and to one another. On entering the room they made a profound obeisance, afterwards offering their hands to the teacher, in European fashion. When one of their own number came in late, they all rose, and advancing to meet him, made the same profound obeisance, almost bringing their heads to the floor. During the whole two months' continuance of the school, not an angry or unpleasant word was uttered between themselves. Their faces beamed with good humor, and jokes were frequently interchanged. Whenever any one made a palpable blunder, he was the first to break out into a loud laugh. One, however, seldom smiled; he was the deepest thinker. Such a new world burst upon him — subjects so novel, so profound, and so interesting, that he always seemed serious, and lost in the reflections awakened.

The young men had previously obtained a knowledge of the alphabet from the Dutch, and the first labor, therefore, was in teaching the *sounds* of the letters. This was a task of no trifling magnitude, and hours were spent from day to day in the effort, the pupils' organs of speech having probably become too rigid and fixed by use and time to give the nice modulations necessary. At length, however, the sounds of the letters were all mastered except for the single letter L, which defied all efforts. For two long months this task was repeated day after day, and at last abandoned in utter despair, the young men often bursting out in a loud laugh at their own grimaces, and distorted countenances and unearthly sounds, as they attempted to pronounce this letter, but more frequently mortified, and ready to burst into tears. Some, however, at length came pretty near to the true sounds, while others could do nothing with it. The Japanese have not the sound of that letter, and uniformly pronounce L like R. From the alphabet they proceeded to monosyllables, and from monosyllables to polysyllables, and at last to easy lessons in reading. Next came the formidable difficulty of imparting ideas to words, which to the pupils had no meaning; but through the agency of a wretchedly composed book in Dutch and English, and a few Dutch and English and Japanese and Dutch dictionaries, and by frequent resort to the language of signs, this obstacle was overcome passably well. By the latter mode, complications were solved that would have defied the most astute diplomatist; and when, by motions of the body, swinging of the limbs, or "making faces," the meaning was caught at last, it came with a ring of merry voices. English grammar was conquered without difficulty, with the exception of the verb, which is so different from the Japanese verb in its conjugations, moods, tenses, &c., that it gave them much trouble, but they satisfactorily mastered it before the school closed.

The next study was arithmetic, which was no study at all, for they seemed to understand it by intuition. Like the Chinese, the Japanese use a calculating machine, with which they solve questions with astonishing rapidity and accuracy. They took to the Arabic figures and system of computation very readily, and "walked through" the arithmetic like old experts. They had never seen slate or pencil, and when they were given to each of them, and they saw the economy, as well as the convenience, above the calculating machine, and hair pencils, ink and paper, they were as happy as though they had received a fortune. They were greatly interested in geography, and eagerly scanned the excellent maps spread before them. The magnitude of the United States surprised them, while they laughed in scorn at the insignificance of Holland, which the Dutch had taught them was the greatest country in Europe. When they compared Japan with the United States, a feeling of mortification and despondency at once manifested itself on their countenances, so great was the disproportion. It was a touching expression of patriotism and human nature. Such is a history of the first English school opened in Japan. May those that are quite sure to follow, be as prosperous and useful.

DATE DUE

JUL 2 1987			
July 2, 67			
6-18-89			
7-24-89			
JUN 1 5 1990			
NOV 0 8 1990			
2-28-92			
MAY 17 1995			
SEP 0 9 1996			
OCT 1 5 2012			
GAYLORD			PRINTED IN U.S.A.

PE1068.J3 G84 1986   c.1
                  100106 000
A Guide to teaching Englishan

8 9310 00069446 1
GOSHEN COLLEGE-GOOD LIBRARY